# HUDSON AND MARIA

## JOHN POLLOCK

Christian Focus Publications

*In memory of*

A. J. Broomhall and Leslie T. Lyall

*Missionaries and writers in the Hudson Tayler mould*

© John Charles Pollock, 1962, 1996
First published by Hodder and Stoughton,
February, 1962. 2nd impression, 1962.
First paperback edition, 1965, Hodder and Stoughton
Second paperback edition, 1983, Kingsway.
This edition in 1996 by Christian Focus Publications,
Geanies House, Fearn, Ross-shire, IV20 1TW, Great Britain.

Cover design by Donna Macleod

A Chinese language edition of *Hudson and Maria* is available from
Campus Evangelical Fellowship, P.O. Box 13-144, Taipei 10098,
Taiwan R.O.C.

*By the same author*
The Cambridge Seven
Billy Graham
George Whitefield and the Great Awakening
Wilberforce
The Siberian Seven
The Apostle: A Life of Paul
The Master: A Life of Jesus
Amazing Grace: John Newton's Story
John Wesley
Fear No Foe: A Brother's Story
Gordon: The Man Behind the Legend
Way to Glory: The Life of Havelock of Lucknow

# CONTENTS

PREFACE TO NEW EDITION ............................................. 5
PROLOGUE ..................................................................... 5

## Part One
## THE FORGE OF FAITH

1: BOY WITH A DREAM ..................................................... 10
2: SHANGHAI SURPRISE ................................................... 20
3: FORBIDDEN GROUND ................................................... 31
4: 'IN THE MIDDLE OF THE HONOURABLE BACK' ... 40
5: THE HOUSE ON THE ISLAND ....................................... 49
6: INTERLUDE WITH A SCOT ........................................... 55
7: ROBBERY – AND AFTER ............................................... 62
8: THE GIRL WITH A SQUINT ........................................... 74
9: RUSSELL GOES SHOOTING ......................................... 89
10: THE VISION FADES ..................................................... 97

## Part Two
## A TREMENDOUS RISK

11: LIGHT PURSE IN A BACK STREET ......................... 104
12: BRIGHTON BEACH ................................................... 113
13: 'THIS DEFENCELESS LITTLE BAND' ................... 126

## Part Three
## THE INDESTRUCTIBLE

14: ORDEAL BY WATER ................................................... 144
15: LAUGHTER IN SHANGHAI ....................................... 153
16: THE BATTLE OF THE CHOPSTICKS ....................... 160
17: THE CRISIS BREAKS ................................................. 169
18: RIOT ............................................................................ 173
19: THE BRINK OF WAR ................................................. 184
20: MIDNIGHT .................................................................. 192
21: GLORIOUS MORNING ............................................... 199

# Preface to New Edition

Hudson Taylor's greatness has become yet more widely recognized. Thus, the *Dictionary of National Biography* volume which covered the year of his death in 1905 (published 1912) ignored him; he now has an honoured place in the DNB's *Missing Persons* volume published 1993.

But it is the extraordinary growth of the Christian Church in China which has fully secured his place in history. This book was first published at a time when missionaries had been forced to withdraw, China was a closed land and the persecution of religion was about to enter a most violent phase with the Cultural Revolution. Years later, westerners were again allowed to travel in China. They found that the number of Christians had grown beyond measure despite the persecution, and despite continued discrimination by the Communist state.

More than any other man, under God, Hudson Taylor laid the foundation of this dramatic expansion of Christianity.

John Pollock
Rose Ash
Devonshire
May 1996

Chinese names: for the general reader's convenience, I have retained the familiar 'postal use' and not changed to the recently introduced *pin-yin* system of spelling.

# Prologue

This book is a tale of courage and adventure in old Imperial China, that lost world of pigtails and mandarins and dragon-roofed temples. It is the story of a Yorkshire lad of obscure origin, indifferent education and miserable health who dared the seemingly impossible in the teeth of opposition, western and oriental.

More, it is the epic of the love of Hudson Taylor and Maria Dyer – their discovery of each other when it was almost too late, the astonishing attempt of others to stifle and smash their love; and then the flowering of marriage at its highest and best.

Had the love of Hudson and Maria grown in on itself to become selfish, muting rather than deepening devotion to God, it would not be worth more than passing description; at best it could be an interlude, a handicap to an otherwise commendable record of service. Or if, again, they had been cold-blooded, formal figures, their marriage a mere alliance of like minds; or had the original manuscript letters and journals not survived to reveal Hudson and Maria at last as they really were, this book had been best left unwritten.

James Hudson Taylor founded the China Inland Mission. He founded it in circumstances of extreme difficulty for a purpose which most of his contemporaries considered mad. At the time of his death forty years later, in 1905, his interdenominational Mission numbered eight hundred and twenty-five members and associates, British, American and Continental. Having been the pioneers of the Protestant Church in the interior of China they were now the shock troops, sometimes establishing permanent centres, often leaving other societies to reap the harvest. 'Always on the move,' a Consular official had written, 'the missionaries of this society have travelled throughout the country, taking hardship and privation as the natural incidents of their profession, never attempting to force themselves anywhere, they have made friends everywhere'.

By 1935, shortly before the start of the Sino-Japanese War, the CIM had a roll of 1,368 western missionaries. It withdrew from China, as did all societies, after the triumph of Communism in 1949 forced the Chinese Church to repudiate contacts with the West, and since 1951 (now known as the CIM Overseas Missionary Fellowship) has operated widely in Japan and many countries of south-east Asia among Chinese and non-Chinese.

The China Inland Mission has had an influence far beyond its immediate spheres of operation. This influence has stemmed partly from a high standard of leadership and the qualities demanded of those who serve; partly from its literature; but largely because it has always sought, in financial affairs as much as in activities, to depend on that element of simple faith in God which is foreign to so much of this modern age but is a sure foundation of all lasting Christian endeavour.

These characteristics derive directly from the adventures and principles of Hudson Taylor himself. To most missions a founder is nothing but a name and, perhaps, a bewhiskered photograph on the office wall. The spirit and personality of Taylor permeate the CIM/OMF still. Through all the changes and developments of an up-to-date, go-ahead Mission they have not lost what he gave them.

And Hudson Taylor would never have been what he was, done what he did, without Maria. Thus, although the story which is unfolded here provides an exciting slice of missionary biography, it has a wider, undying appeal as a proof of the wonder and power of Christian love.

Hudson Taylor influenced millions. His fame still commands wide respect in Europe, America and Asia; he is of that select company who belong to all mankind. Notwithstanding, his stature is recognised only by the discerning. This is curious, for the two-volume official *Life* remains a spiritual classic, to be placed on the same shelf as *Pilgrim's Progress*.

*Hudson Taylor*, by Dr and Mrs Howard Taylor, his son and daughter-in-law, has run through many editions, and is still in print on both sides of the Atlantic and in translations. It is very long, over eleven hundred pages in the literary style of the late nineteenth century, but has a timeless, intrinsic quality. In certain respects it is one of the world's decisive books. Yet a sizeable section of the general public has never heard of the man.

The pity of that came home to me when I began to read the original manuscript letters, journals and papers on which the great two volumes and, through them, all the lesser derivative books, are based. By the very real kindness of the China Inland Mission, and particularly of Mr Norman Baker, Editorial Secretary in London, I was given access to all this material, the first writer allowed to use it since the official biographies.

As I deciphered the close-written pages of thin paper which had been filled by Hudson's own hand, freezing or sweating in embattled Shanghai, or in some junk gliding sedately up ancient willow-lined canals, the rather prim, spiritually precocious youth of the *Life* became a warm, affectionate, sensitive personality. The 'revered father-figure' dissolved into a most lovable young man with a strong sense of fun. The drama of his fight to enter forbidden inland China, risking torture and death, sprang to life when separated from gobbets of meditation and reflection.

Dr and Mrs Howard Taylor collaborated in rather an unusual manner. After researching together, Howard drew up a factual 'gist of the narrative'; his wife Geraldine then moulded this into the text that was printed, and the book in its final form is impregnated with her personality. Unfortunately, in addition to expunging or at least severely censoring her father-in-law's sense of humour she suppressed one complete love affair and half of another, and incidents which to her generation might have seemed derogatory or too private. She was guided by advice typically Victorian from Taylor's successor, D E Hoste, which runs against the spirit of modern biography: 'If you begin too much letting the public in behind the scenes you shake confidence'.

At an important phase she was shackled by respect for the

feelings of some who had certainly not spared those of Hudson Taylor: George Moule was alive when the first volume of the *Life* appeared in 1911, and Lewis Nicol was probably still living when the second came out in 1918.

Geraldine Taylor had a Victorian notion of one responsibility of a biographer. The two volumes are notable for copious extracts from Hudson Taylor's letters, set in smaller type between inverted commas. I used to wonder how that young man managed such formal English in his home letters. Now I know. She had pruned and polished him to conform to her own standards of delicacy and elegance. No one would scold her for correcting early spelling and grammar, but she did it right through, sometimes withholding facts.

None of this detracts from her book's weight as a classic. But it does mean that Hudson and Maria come alive in a new way when their adventures together are presented afresh from the original materials.

# Part One

# THE FORGE OF FAITH

## Chapter 1: BOY WITH A DREAM

Meat tea behind a chemist's shop in the Yorkshire mining town of Barnsley, in the mid-eighteen-forties; slabs of beef and baked batter pudding, potatoes and rounds of bread, a pot of tea, and a black kettle steaming on the hob; outside in the swirling coal-laden mist, the sound of clogs on the cobbles.

Twelve-year-old Hudson ate silently admiring as his father, James Taylor, held forth on a favourite topic. Beside Hudson sat his sister Amelia, three years younger; on the other side of the table were flighty little Louisa and a neighbouring youth, Benjamin Broomhall, and at the foot Mrs Taylor. Her eye was on the clock, for the chemist waxed eloquent as usual. 'He was a *great* talker', Benjamin Broomhall records, 'sometimes very random. He was Sir Oracle! Everyone around him took it all as gospel. His knowledge confounded me. He loved to display it, had unbounded confidence in himself. He took enormous pains to memorise.' 'Very interesting and instructive', added Amelia. 'He did not allow the children to talk at meals. We were perhaps too much pressed in this way.'

When James Taylor expatiated as now on his pet theme, Hudson listened enthralled. The chemist, a Methodist local preacher, had been fascinated when young by an account of travels on the coast of China, the shadowy Celestial Empire known to the western world only by the silks and porcelain, jade and tea which trickled out at exorbitant prices. Since then he had absorbed all the few books which existed about this exotic, mysterious 'Cathay'. 'Nearly every person there can read', Sir Oracle declared to the tea table, 'and they all almost venerate a piece of printed paper and will on no account destroy it.' He advocated flooding China with Bibles. He told about the 'extensive ramifications of the Roman Catholic agency', for the Jesuits, once accepted at Peking but since banned, flitted secretly from centre to centre at the risk of their lives, thousands of miles inland. He had read Methodist missionary reports from India and Africa. 'Why don't they send them to China?' he grumbled. 'Why are there only half a dozen Protestants working in all that great land?'

Hudson piped up, 'When I am a man I mean to be a missionary and go to China!' They looked at him with tolerant amusement – sickly little Hudson going to China? The chemist had indeed prayed for this before Hudson's birth, but had long abandoned the hope; it was a mercy that with all his other ills Hudson was not subject to fits like Aunt Sarah.

Amelia says their father made a fine chemist, 'especially good at prescribing for people. He was really half a doctor. People had great faith in his prescriptions'. He had a complex character: genial yet crushing, secretive yet garrulous, pompous and shy. He was generous to the poor and tight-fisted to his own. 'The family were needlessly kept in low waters', wrote Amelia in old age. 'It would have been quite possible to send them to good schools and to have given Hudson medical education; but father felt it to be his duty to accumulate a little capital to leave, and did not see that it would have been for their greater advantage to spend it in the best education.'

Mrs Taylor was loyal, hard-working, delicate, repressed by her dominating, devoted husband. She came from a higher social level, being a daughter of the Reverend Benjamin Hudson, a Methodist minister who transmitted to his grandson Hudson Taylor two qualities: artistic sense, and laughter.

Hudson was small, with sandy-coloured curly hair, grey-blue eyes, straight nose and thick lips. He was intensely affectionate, a characteristic to the end. He had a lively imagination and would sit on Amelia's bed in the frightening dark telling 'wildly exciting and interesting stories' until she fell asleep. His voice became an excellent tenor, and he played the flute at family musical evenings. From his father came strong will, a mind of his own, and mesmeric gifts: at chapel one Sunday he willed a local *grande dame* to turn round three or four times to look at him, but later abandoned the conscious use of this power.

With adolescence Hudson grew restless with the religious atmosphere of home. At fifteen he entered a local bank where, being merry and bright, he was popular, and 'used to wish for money and a fine horse and house, and I longed to go hunting as some did who were about me'. The other clerks brushed his mind free of religion. He scoffed and swore, probably mildly, for he was sensitive and did not relish his mother's resigned glances or Amelia's tears; besides, his father beat him for blasphemy.

The gaslight in the murk of a Yorkshire winter was too much for Hudson's eyes; they were weak for the rest of his life. He left the bank in 1848 to serve the jars and bottles of his father's shop, prescribing for bunions of farmers' wives in to market, mixing powders when the mayor's offspring had colic. Ill health, fast sexual development and gnawing dissatisfaction of soul made him fidgety and unsettled, easily upset and cross.

A year later, in June 1849, his mother was away. One warm afternoon Amelia was out and Hudson had nothing to do on a half-holiday. He looked idly over his father's books and rummaged in a basket of popular 'Gospel tracts'. He picked one out, intending to read the story and skip the moral. He went into the barn behind the house and shop, curled up comfortably and began 'in an utterly unconcerned state of mind, with a distinct intention to put away the tract as soon as it should seem prosy'.

As he read, one sentence gripped him. Suddenly he realised that he approached religion from the wrong angle. He believed Christianity to be a dreary struggle to pay off bad deeds by good. He had long abandoned this struggle. He owed too much. He had gone into spiritual bankruptcy, paying a small dividend to his Divine Creditor in the shape of chapel attendance and of prayers rattled off at night, but with no hope of discharge; like most bankrupts he had sought to have a good time.

One sentence in the tract broke open his mind to a sudden certainty that Christ by His death upon the cross had already discharged this debt of sins. 'And with this dawned the joyful conviction, as light was flashed into my soul by the Holy Spirit, that there was nothing in the world to be done but to fall down on one's knees and accepting this Saviour and His Salvation, to praise Him for evermore.'

No Luther, Bunyan or Wesley had a more complete sense of

the rolling away of his burden, of light dismissing darkness, of rebirth and the close friendship of Christ, than Hudson Taylor on that June afternoon of 1849 at the age of seventeen.

Several days passed before he shyly told Amelia under seal of secrecy. At the return of his mother ten days afterwards he ran to the door 'to tell her I had such glad news to give'. She replied as she hugged him, 'I know, my boy. I have been rejoicing for a fortnight in the glad tidings you have to tell me.' Hudson was amazed. Had Amelia blabbed? His mother denied it. She said that eighty miles away, on the very day of the incident in the barn, she had felt such an overwhelming desire to pray for Hudson that she spent hours on her knees, and had arisen with the unshakeable conviction that her prayers were answered. 'It was perhaps natural', Taylor wrote years later, 'that from the commencement of my Christian life I was led to feel that prayer was in sober matter of fact transacting business with God.'

The summer passed in exhilaration. Hudson revelled in an exquisite happiness compounded of gratitude, love and the excitement of summoning courage to tell his friends what had happened. Reaction set in with winter. Doubts assailed, made worse by Amelia's absence at school and his father's trying temper. Hudson grew prim, and confused boyishness with sin: 'I am apt to be giddy and frothy, and I sometimes yield to my teasing disposition'. When his cousin John mocked prolonged devotions in their shared bedroom, Hudson slacked off, and then was submerged in self-reproach.

D E Hoste once remarked that he was surprised, recalling Luther, that Hudson Taylor had not 'more tornadoes as a lad'. Early in December 1849 he became terrified of total apostasy. 'One night', recorded his mother, 'on going to bed he felt particularly unhappy about it. He knelt down and prayed fervently that God would help him and keep him, and promised to do anything or go anywhere if He would only save him from falling. He made a fresh dedication of himself to God, and such an awful sense of the divine presence came upon him as he could not describe. He felt the offering was accepted; and as distinctly as if a voice had uttered it, "Then go to China", was spoken to his soul. From that hour his mind was made up.'

Barnsley's only book on China belonged to the Congregational minister. Early in 1850 Hudson Taylor went to call.

'Why do you want to read it?' the minister asked as he took the book from his shelves.

The youth, whose boyish face, fair hair and small size made him look even younger than he was, told him.

'And how do you propose to go there?'

Hudson murmured something about the disciples who went without scrip or purse at Our Lord's command and lacked nothing.

The minister laid a fatherly hand on Hudson's shoulder. 'Ah, my boy, as you grow older you will get wiser than that. Such an idea would do very well in the days when Christ Himself was on earth, but not now.'

Britain had held Hong Kong since the end of the shameful Opium War, eight years before, and a foothold in five treaty ports where missionary societies had a few representatives who touched at most a few thousand of the four hundred million subjects of the Dragon Throne. They were strictly confined to the coast, lived hard (or so it was believed) in a trying climate, and were of proved academic or medical abilities. For a chemist's assistant of eighteen without prospect of university education, possessing a physique that barely stood the damps and chills of Yorkshire, all thought of China was ridiculous.

'Poor, neglected China!' wrote Hudson to Amelia, 'scarcely any one cares about it. And that immense country, containing nearly a fourth of the human race, is left in ignorance and darkness.' He gave up his feather-bed, went for long walks on the moors, tried to improve his general education, and made brave, hopeless attempts to teach himself the world's most difficult language.

His heart was full of China – and of a Miss Vaughan. Hudson had fallen in love with a young music-teacher brought home by Amelia for the holidays. He did not declare his love. 'What *can* I do?' he wrote to Amelia on 11th November 1850, 'I know I love her. To go without her would make the world a blank. But I cannot bring her to want'.

In the spring of 1851 he was made dispenser to a jovial doctor in Hull, Richard Hardey, whose brother, an unsuccessful Micawberish stock-broker, had married Mrs Taylor's portrait-painting sister Hannah. The Hardeys formed a vivacious circle in which music, medicine, art, religion and merriment crowded the days, and across the Humber, at Barton, Amelia learned and Miss Vaughan taught. The ferry had a frequent passenger: 'the times when at Barton Miss V used to play the piano and we, side by side, used to sing', Hudson would recall to Amelia. Miss Vaughan and he came to an understanding.

The music-teacher had no intention of going to China; this absurd ambition must wither under the strong sun of her charms. Hudson knew he would swing her round. 'He used to talk so much about China', wrote friends at Barton. 'He was a pale fair-haired slender lad, impulsive and warmhearted.'

In November he moved his lodgings to a noisome dockland called Drainside where he began a rigorous régime of saving and self-denial, spending his spare time as a self-appointed medical missionary to cheerless streets in which low wages, overlarge families and gin produced brutalised husbands and wives, and sickly children. An Irish element fed his sense of the ludicrous, and added spice: sometimes he was 'very roughly treated, while my tracts were torn to pieces'.

Drainside was too much for Miss Vaughan. On 16th December 1851 Hudson wrote to Amelia, 'For some days I was as wretched as heart could wish... until I felt inclined to give it all up'. On Sunday, 'sitting alone in the surgery I began to reflect on the love of God... He thoroughly softened and humbled me. His love melted my icy, frost-bound soul'.

Miss Vaughan's refusal and the austerities of Drainside were not tests enough. Imagining himself deep in the interior, 'far away from all human aid, there to depend upon the living God alone for protection, supplies and help of every kind, I felt that one's spiritual muscles required strengthening... I thought to myself when I get out to China I shall have no claim on anyone for anything; my only claim will be on God. How important, therefore, to learn before leaving England to move man, through God, by prayer alone.'

By somewhat elaborate manoeuvres to simulate circumstances he might find, Hudson learned to live each day without knowing whether he would have money for the next, and once even gave away his last half-crown to save the life of a starving Irishwoman; on that occasion the very next morning's post brought a half-sovereign tucked in a pair of kid gloves from a donor whose identity he never traced.

Hudson Taylor wondered how he should reach the almost unknown land of his dreams. He thought of working his way out as a sailor before the mast; his puny frame would have been buried at sea. He wrote to the London Missionary Society. 'A boyish letter no doubt, full of love to the Lord and little else, probably. I'm glad they didn't answer.' The Methodists had no China work; besides, his father had recently collided with the Barnsley Methodist leaders and joined the new reformed group, while Hudson anchored temporarily among the Plymouth Brethren.

Then, like a comet with a tarnished tail, Karl Gutzlaff flashed over Europe.

Gutzlaff the Pomeranian was half-pirate, half-zealot, bubbling with zeal to spread Christianity in China by the shadiest means. Wanting to flood the coast with admirable tracts, he took a post in a vessel on the illicit opium trade, thereby blessing China with one hand, cursing with the other. A fluent Chinese speaker and writer, he served as magistrate with the British occupation forces in the Opium War and organised their spies, and after the war was Chinese Secretary to the Government of Hong Kong. There he used his salary to organise a magnificent scheme whereby colporteurs should spread throughout the provinces preaching Christianity and selling Bibles; in contrast to most of the few missionaries in the Far East, he believed that China must be converted through the Chinese, that any Europeans should adapt themselves in dress and behaviour; he even urged that they should take Chinese nationality.

It is probable that before he left Hong Kong late in 1849 Gutzlaff already mistrusted his colporteurs' wonderful reports, but he was too proud to admit it, too committed to his pose as a genius and an authority on the Celestial Empire. Throughout 1850 he was hurrying through Europe, hypnotising audiences to contribute generously to his plan for each western country to adopt a Chinese province and finance its conversion. Widespread response was followed by angry reaction on the discovery that Gutzlaff had been hopelessly hoodwinked. The glowing stories had been concocted in Canton. The 2,871 converts, from Mongolia to Tibet, had been genii from opium pipes. Gutzlaff died, broken yet praying for China, in Hong Kong in August 1851 at the age of forty-eight.

Like a puddle on the sand when the tide ebbs, the Gutzlaff craze left a new, small, insignificant organisation called the Chinese Evangelization Society. Its founders were mostly businessmen of Brethren persuasion, though ardent for interdenominational, international effort. They were intensely sincere and impractical. They had scanty funds, one missionary, who later was dismissed for dabbling in the coolie traffic, and a journal, *The Gleaner*, entrancing to read. Hudson Taylor, poring over its pages, had neither means nor inclination to sift the wheat from the chaff.

In the autumn of 1852 he came to London under the auspices of this Chinese Evangelization Society, who arranged to pay for his training as a doctor at the London Hospital in the East End. The CES early showed the culpable lack of business sense which in the end destroyed it, and Hudson shrewdly declined to commit himself too deeply. It paid his fees, but for board and lodging he let the secretary think his father paid, and allowed his father to suppose the Society paid, while he, as a further forge of faith, lived after the example of his hero George Müller, who kept hundreds of orphans at Bristol, and supported missionaries abroad, without possessing a penny of his own or ever appealing for funds except in solitary prayer.

Hudson existed on a loaf of bread and a pound of apples a day, and walked four miles between Soho and the London Hospital on Mile End Waste, past eating-houses redolent of roast beef and onions, and with gingerbread sellers and muffin men actively tempting him in the crowded lanes. This exquisite torture braced him. Indeed, he feared lest too much cheerfulness was unChristian. 'How difficult it often is', he wrote to Amelia, 'to avoid being light and trifling when you feel well and in good spirits.'

The endurance test summarily stopped after six weeks when Hudson caught 'malignant fever' while dissecting a disgustingly septic corpse. The doctor said he might survive if he had not been 'going in for beer and that sort of thing', and ordered chops and port wine. Hudson went home to Yorkshire for convalescence and returned in the new year of 1853 with parental funds which he could not misapply to concoct further tests of faith.

Hudson could not bear the thought of China without someone to love and be loved. He persuaded his old flame, Miss Vaughan, to forget her objections and they became engaged again, a fact discreetly ignored by his biographers. He refused to admit her unsuitability in outlook, constitution or training, but in a few weeks he was wailing to Amelia, 'I knew I loved her and she says she loved me. But I know she does not love me as she did... I fear it will have to be broken off. Do pray for me and write soon.'

The matter was settled in April 1853 by her father, the Reverend Mr Vaughan, who said that nothing would give him greater pleasure than Hudson as a son-in-law in England, but, Mrs Taylor reported to Amelia, 'he *never will consent to her going abroad*. Hudson thinks Mr V ought not *now* to oppose their going abroad... but as his mind is made up, and Hudson cannot remain in England, they *mutually* agreed to break off the engagement. Poor lad I feel *very sorry* for him! It will be a painful stroke, but I believe it will be well in the end.'

In the early summer of 1853 astonishing news reached Europe. An obscure Hakka from South China, called Hung, had been hailed as Emperor. He claimed to be a Christian, and named his fast-increasing empire the Heavenly Kingdom of Great Peace, '*T'ai-*

*ping T'ien-Kuo'*. After nearly two years' revolt the Chinese southern capital, Nanking, had fallen in March 1853. The Heavenly
King's armies were marching on Peking. The alien Manchu dynasty
tottered. The Dragon Throne might soon be held by a Christian.

In May the Governor of Hong Kong, British Plenipotentiary in
China, had sailed up the Yangtze in HMS *Hermes* to visit Nanking, now the Taiping capital, and despite the difficulty caused by
the Heavenly King's assumption, in the classic Chinese tradition, that
the English brought the Queen's allegiance as a tributary sovereign, the expedition confirmed that the Taiping leaders professed
to be fellow-Christians. The Plenipotentiary suspected a ruse to obtain western arms. Others were impressed by the Taipings' de-
struction of idols and prohibition of opium, their printing and distribution of Gutzlaff Bibles, their teaching of the Ten Commandments
and the Lord's Prayer. The rebels were extremely muddled in
ideas, and the slaughter of Imperialists after the fall of Nanking
had been frightful, but the rebel Emperor, it was known, had been
in contact with a western missionary only, for a short time six
years before, after conversion by means of visions, and the reading of tracts given him by a Christian Chinese in Canton.

HMS *Hermes* brought back Taiping literature, which convinced
the Bishop of Victoria, Hong Kong, that the defects of the movement were 'the natural shortcomings of men without instructions
and guides, having their minds distracted amid the arduous toils of
campaign'. The Heavenly King addressed his one missionary acquaintance, an independent Baptist from Tennessee, Issachar
Roberts (who could not recollect him), 'to request you, my elder
brother, if you are not disposed to abandon me, to come and bring
with you many brethren... so shall be obtained the true doctrine'.

Enormous enthusiasm was aroused in Europe by the prospect
of Taiping victory and the opening of the interior to missionaries.
The British and Foreign Bible Society decided to print no less than
a million Chinese New Testaments.

And the Chinese Evangelization Society, its coffers filling, urged
young Taylor to leave as their representative at once, medical
course unfinished, and reach the Taipings at Nanking as soon as

he had learned the language, or before. He agreed.

For more than three years Hudson had lived in hope of sailing to China. When the time came, home was never sweeter, or parting more grievous. 'I almost feared', commented a friend, 'he would break down under it, he seemed to be so full of affection and love to all with whom he had to do.'

Hudson Taylor left Liverpool on September 19th 1853, aged twenty-one years and four months, the only passenger in the sailing vessel *Dumfries*.

They were nearly wrecked on North Wales rocks in the September gales. They sailed round the Cape and through the East Indies, were becalmed and drifted almost on to New Guinea. Twenty-three weeks from Liverpool to Shanghai: 'a tedious voyage', Taylor wrote, 'which the crew kindly laid to my account as they did every storm or calm or headwind or current, saying that ministers and missionaries generally caused a vessel to be lost. Still we got here safely. On her way home she was wrecked on the Pescadores but all the crew were fortunately saved.'

## Chapter 2: SHANGHAI SURPRISE

As the sampan drew away from the fogbound *Dumfries* the impassive boatmen under the brown fan-wise sail, whose pigtails were curled up in buns, studied the young man in the stern. Sandy hair indicated red-haired barbarian, the spectacles over his grey-blue eyes suggested a teacher; but his legs were encased in the narrow trousers of a coolie.

March 1st 1854. Hudson Taylor sat excited and impatient the fifteen miles up Woosung creek to Shanghai, that tiny lodgement of the West on the vast, mysterious Empire tight closed to foreigners. The cold fog lifted slightly when the boat approached the Bund, and revealed the houses and splendid gardens of the International Settlement, and behind them the slightly larger shapes of two churches, English, and American Episcopal. Around stood a forest of masts.

Hudson Taylor wiped tears of gratitude from his eyes. Scarcely restraining himself from kneeling like William the Conqueror to kiss the shore, he landed in a daze and walked the few yards to the British Consulate.

A bored official received him. Not even surprise at the arrival of an Englishman, unexpected, alone, and starry-eyed, could disperse the languor of late afternoon. Taylor asked brightly for letters. The official yawned. 'The post room shut an hour ago,' he drawled. 'Come tomorrow.' Taylor, dashed, drew out three notes of introduction.

'Tozer?' said the official. 'He's dead. Fever. We buried him a month ago. Shuck? Been back in America two years.' Taylor enquired desperately for the London Missionary Society. The man called a Chinese, gave a few instructions in Mandarin, and turned away.

The Chinese clerk wore a loose jacket and full breeches and had a magnificent black pigtail which fell from his otherwise shaved head down to the back of his knees. He bowed deeply to Taylor, led him to the jetty and engaged coolies. The string of coolies in aladdin hats shuffled off, swinging his bags on long bamboos across their naked shoulders, and Taylor's spirits revived at their peculiar jog-trot and comical sighs and groans. They went up Nanking Road towards the north of the Settlement, where Chinese houses and booths clustered together in a populous, noisy, sharp-smelling, colourful medley, and little boys, their bottoms bare to the March winds, called out cheerfully 'Yang juei-tzu!', 'Foreign devil!'

At the turning into Shantung Road on the edge of the Settlement, a loud explosion made Taylor jump. He ducked at a thunder-roll of guns and a crackle of muskets, and felt thoroughly unnerved by the time he reached the gate of the London Mission house.

A servant came into the courtyard, smiling. Other Chinese faces appeared instantly at doors, round corners, out of windows. 'Medhurst?' asked Taylor hopefully, trying to make it sound Chinese. The man shook his shaved head and pointed into the distance. Taylor felt unutterably lonely. Where was Medhurst?

The servant began to speak in Shanghai dialect, to Taylor a cacophony of meaningless discords. Everyone began to talk at once, louder and louder as they tried to make him understand. But 'the Chinese could not speak one word of English, I not one of Chinese'. Hudson Taylor was beginning to despair when he saw a European approach.

Joseph Edkins of the London Missionary Society, aged thirty-one and already seven years in China, was surprised; the Chinese Evangelization Society had not bothered to send warning. He paid off the coolies, took Taylor inside for a cup of tea, and said that Dr Medhurst in fact was at the Consulate because his house was too near the firing line. Civil war raged outside the International Settlement.

Dr Walter Medhurst, author of fifty-nine works in Chinese, six in Malay and twenty-seven in English, was caustic about the un-expected youth from an upstart society. Dr Lockhart, the elderly medical missionary, gave him a room, and a Scotsman of the Church Missionary Society living in the London compound asked him to dinner; John Burdon was only eight years older than Taylor, whose dissenter prejudice against the Church of England did not survive spontaneous friendship with this future bishop.

Two days after arriving Taylor wrote home. 'My health is won-derfully improved and I am quite a different being from what I was, so strong and well... All the missionaries are kind, very, and Dr Lockhart has taken me to reside with him at present; houses are not to be got for love or money... No one can live in the city for they are fighting continually almost. I see the walls from my room window half a mile off, and can see the firing at night. They are fighting now, and while I write the house shakes again with the noise of the reports... I am so cold I can neither think nor write.'

Lockhart, Edkins and Burdon were not sure what to make of the newcomer. He was cheerful, boyish and small, almost a mas-cot. He had good manners, but would say things impulsively in his Yorkshire accent and send them into fits of laughter. His freshness and enthusiasm, his passion for the 'poor, perishing Chinese' took them back to the glorious days of their own missionary calls. He was a dreamer, and at this stage they thought it kinder not to disabuse his mind of grandiose hopes.

Experience contradicted Taylor's expectation. It was all so comfortable. From 7 am, when a servant woke him with 'hot water to wash, shave, etc, and a splendid cup of warm tea – no small comfort here for it is *very* cold', until evening prayers after a final social cup of tea, life was ordered and affluent, despite the CES's tardiness in transmitting his salary. 'All things considered I doubt there is any place in the world where missionaries are more favoured than in Shanghai', he was to write the next year.

He had imagined himself preaching to pigtailed Chinese, whom he expected to possess slit-eyes at forty-five degrees and skin yellow as a European's with jaundice. Instead, he was caged indoors most of his working hours by the need to learn the language. 'It bothers your brother tremendously', he wrote to fourteen-year-old Louisa. 'My teacher seems to have an oscillating principle somewhere in his neck, for he keeps shaking it while I endeavour to imitate his sounds.'

Taylor had not been prepared for the squalid horrors of civil war on his doorstep. Six months previously a horde of Triads, members of a widespread secret society, had seized the Chinese city near the French and International Settlements. They still held it, invested spasmodically by Imperial troops. The Taiping rebel emperor refused to accept the Shanghai Triads as allies because they had neither discipline nor Christianity; Europeans did not realise this, and incipient sympathy for the Taipings was weakened by a winter of desultory fighting.

Taylor once went with Dr Medhurst to the rebel headquarters, 'a most picturesque place', where splendidly dressed Triads carried assorted arms, and Europeans of doubtful origin strutted around as advisers. On a Sunday night, he watched from the Mission verandah 'the fiercest battle I have yet witnessed. The noise, shouting and yelling, beating of gongs, blowing conch shells and the reports of guns, musketry and rockets – was greater than usual; the flashing of the guns showed plainly, and the rockets (with fire arrows) looked very beautiful in the dark. How long it lasted I do not know for feeling cold I returned to bed and in spite of the noise fell asleep.'

The rubble and the broken signboards with their strips of Chi-

nese characters swinging daft in the breeze, the homeless, the
wounded, the prisoners beseeching honourable foreigners to save
them as they were dragged to decapitation, 'the very thought of it
makes your blood run cold'. Taylor as a medical student was used
to gore and disease, but the cheapness of life sickened him: 'The
other day I was looking at the ruins of a temple near the city, and
down by the riverside I saw a man's stocking. This caused me to
go up and look and behold! the headless corpse of a man, with
two stones thrown on him, by way of burial, and one of his legs
nearly gone – devoured I suppose by the bank dogs who literally
live among the tombs.'

He was disappointed in his high hopes of the Taipings. Naturally he swallowed local opinion. 'If the rebels *do* embrace Christianity nominally, it will be on the part of the leaders entirely, from
political motives... Of the spirit of Christianity they know little and
manifest none.' He had no means yet of assessing the justice of
this verdict, but he was not impressed by the Reverend Issachar
Roberts, the Heavenly King's erstwhile teacher, a boastful, empty-
headed man who now would have reached Nanking had he obeyed
conscience rather than the American Commissioner's ban on his
journey. 'I have seen Mr Roberts; he seems to imagine that he will
be received by the rebels as an apostle, tell them how, and what to
do, baptise them all over again, and go on swimmingly; in all
which I fear he will find himself mistaken and disappointed. In the
present state of affairs it is necessary to be very cautious both in
what one says and does, and not to take for gospel every word
which the Chinese may tell us, or rumour.'

Capping all these surprises was Hudson's puzzlement over himself. Subconsciously he had presumed that the start of his missionary career would work a sea change on character and feelings;
he would become a St Paul in the twinkling of an eye by the act of
landing in China.

Instead, unsuspected scum in his nature rose to the top. He was
forlorn, miserable, homesick. His eyes were inflamed, he had head-
aches and was cold. His consciousness of the presence of God was
weaker than it had been at Hull, 'the brightest part of my Christian

career'. He sought causes. Perhaps he ought not to be in Shanghai at all; ought to be setting out inland, trusting in a Pentecostal gift of tongues. In old age he told D E Hoste that during this time he was in a 'state of fright about getting out of God's will'.

Hours of his leisure were consumed in writing long letters home. 'Oh I wish I could tell you how much I love you all. The love I have in my composition is nearly all pent up, and so it lets me feel its force. I never knew how much I loved you all before'. Letters took at least three and a half months even by the 'overland route' through the Mediterranean and the isthmus of Suez and cost 2s.8d a half-ounce. 'Do write, please', he appealed to Amelia, 'and I will pay the postage, only let me hear from you. I have quite plenty to do, without having no home letters in addition. You have plenty of friends and correspondents – how many have I? I am here a stranger, ignorant of the spoken tongue – am dependent on persons who never either *saw* or *heard* of me till I landed, for a home and shelter. They *are* kind, and I feel it, but that does not alter my position nor feelings. However *the Lord* is with me.'

When a home mail actually brought letters from Barnsley he would slink to his room and indulge in an orgy of lachrymose tenderness, taking out his concertina to play and sing with a wealth of expression a wistful hymn such as 'I am but a stranger here, heaven is my home', to the tune of *Robin Adair*.

1854-55 was a year of uncertainty and restriction. Taylor found his feet slowly.

From the start he was impelled by an urge to get close to the Chinese. As the military situation allowed he explored the nearby countryside, pursuing his hobbies of insect- and plant-collecting.[1] His walks were spoiled only by sight of an occasional head hanging by a pigtail to a wall. The people were friendly because used to foreigners, and too courteous to reveal their contempt, and he

---

[1]He had also a hobby unusual for the eighteen-fifties: photography. He did not attempt to photograph any Chinese, but had the pictures survived which his cumbrous camera took of buildings in the Settlement, 'my photographic failures' would have been among the earliest records of Shanghai.

tried newly acquired phrases in the customary exchange of question and compliment. He compared the Chinese favourably with Yorkshire yokels. 'The people are far more polite than our own peasantry and do not run bawling about when they see a stranger. However if their masters do not, the dogs which swarm in every part do...' Hudson kept them off with a stone. 'There is no need to throw it – only carry one and they won't come too near.'

Other missionaries took him on preaching tours, and the Imperial fleet once nearly opened fire on their boats at night in Woosung creek. At the sound of alarm-gongs on the junks the three westerners started bawling hymns in English to identify themselves. The 'people on the Imperial ship began to shout, and our boatmen began the same trade and I began to laugh, for the whole affair was so *irresistibly* ludicrous, if it had cost me my life I could not have refrained'.

In late summer, having heard in a roundabout way that his Chinese Evangelization Society had dispatched on the voyage to Shanghai a Scottish doctor and family without sending Taylor warning, he took the madly brave step of seeking a house in the besieged native city. Footslogging through the torrid August days because he could not afford a sedan chair, his white jacket and trousers, black cravat and shoes soaked in perspiration, he found at last a filthy, verminous compound of rickety timber near the noisy bustle of the North Gate through the great crenellated wall. Crammed in a cage close by, prisoners wallowing in their own excrement cried for food.

The only missionary actually resident in the native city, he flung himself into work so far as his grasp of the Shanghai colloquial permitted, aided by a fine Christian who had 'a very long tail reaching almost to the ground. He has never had it cut since he was born, and it is beautiful black hair, as all Chinamen have.'

When Taylor's parents complained of bad grammar he replied, 'I generally write my letters when I am half asleep for the very good reason that I have no other time in which I can do so, and you will admit that is neither conducive to elegance in style nor proficiency in arrangement. What with school, patients, preparing and dispensing medicines, Chinese services, and domestic affairs there is not too much time left for study, and the necessary reading for any peculiar cases medical or surgical that occur in my practice. To these add a fearful amount of statistics the Society require, keeping accounts, writing journal and devotional exercises and where in the name of goodness is time to come from for composing leters?... I have no time for photographic operations now.'

Life in the city sharpened Taylor's zeal. He knew little yet of the finer points of Buddhism, of the sayings of Confucius, or the Tao Te Ching, but he had the evidence of his eyes and ears. He saw the 'murdered body of a poor new-born female infant lying exposed in the city drain'; watched women hobbling by on tiny feet or heard 'the screams of a poor girl having her feet bound to make them small'; took a side street to avoid an execution or scene of torture; noticed the money and energy expended on ancestor worship. 'Oh for more eloquence to plead the cause of China – for a pencil dipped in fire to paint the conditions of this people!' 'Oh that you were all here', he apostrophised his sister, 'there is plenty of work, and if you did not all learn to *talk*, and soon too, I should put you down for greater ninnies than I think you are.'

Taylor's brave experiment foundered on physical collapse and the mischances of war.

He had tried to live solely on Chinese food, plying unsteady chopsticks on bowls of rice garnished with scraps of pork or vegetable. Soon he was dragging around, or nursing indoors, a reluctant body in distress of stomach and bowels, hating himself for the bad temper it generated beneath a cheerful exterior. His house came under fire from the besiegers, and rebels in the city mistrusted him as a European; life was no longer safe. 'I have been so harassed and unsettled lately. No one who has not felt can tell the effect of such an incessant strain on mind and body, it makes one feel so nervous and irritable, that we indeed need all your prayers and all our own to enable us to manifest a proper spirit on many occasions which when well and strong would be no trial at all.' Amelia was the recipient of a full-toned dirge: 'My laughing humours as you call them do not often make their appearance now.' If she only knew, he moaned, how lonely it was to be confined to the house by ill-health 'and neither hear one word of English, nor see one English face, you would not wonder at me'.

After an awful night of battle and fire struggling against 'the feeling of utter isolation and helplessness... I never passed such a trying time in my life', he evacuated early in November to the International Settlement. His city house was burned to the ground soon afterward.

Hudson Taylor was astounded by the sharp contrast between his dream in England of what a missionary community would be like, and the facts. 'In Shanghai we have many missionaries, but why some of them come I don't know, unless it was they thought they could get a living easier that way than any other.'

He had expected a band of men and women living in fervent charity among themselves, each helping the other to unearth treasures from the Bible to enrich the surrounding Chinese. He was disillusioned. Some of his criticisms may have been a little unfair, his strongly puritan upbringing made him positively, if privately, priggish on occasions; allowing for the intolerance of youth his secret castigations in home letters were tragically accurate.

He rated most of them self-indulgent and idle. 'The style in which many missionaries live is, I think, scarcely the thing, but however all are not alike. The Church missionaries are as far as I have seen them by far the most pious and consistent... I think the Church of England missionary and chaplain are very excellent and devoted men.'

He was appalled at the idleness of many missionaries, and their 'criticising, backbiting and sarcastic remarks'. The sarcasm was rather catching. 'On one occasion a gentleman was proceeding to tell me of a missionary of *another* society and I could bear no more and I could not help saying I know what sort of a man he is – no education – very affected and presuming and a poor preacher

– since then I have not heard quite as much. I long to go into the country and leave it all.'

When Taylor in England had tried to train himself to 'live by faith' he had envisaged a situation where mountains, a hostile population or uncertain communications might cut his channel of supplies. He had not expected grinding poverty in the shadow of the great British banking houses in Shanghai, induced by no other cause than the failure of the Chinese Evangelization Society to honour its obligations. He had always known his salary would be lower than that received by members of more established missions, but he had expected it regularly, to the full amount. Instead, 'all of my clothes are so shabby I am ashamed to go out on week days or Sundays – from hat to shoes and umbrella – my top coat alone accepted'.

The arrival of the Parkers in November made the financial position intolerable. Dr Parker was astonished that the Society's promised letter of credit was not in his post. Taylor was astonished that the Parkers had been allowed to arrive in winter clothed for the tropics. Shanghai society was astonished that Taylor, apparently, had made shockingly poor preparation.

When Taylor opened the latest *Gleaner* and read lofty strictures on the unspirituality of members of other missions, his indignation with the Secretaries boiled over. 'With all their faults you should not voluntarily irritate those who are more *thoughtful* for the *shelter* and *support* of your missionaries than the Society which sends THEM out seems to be... It is not only morally wrong and highly disrespectful as well as thoughtless in the extreme to act as your committee had done to Dr Parker and family; but men who find they can quadruple their salary by professional practice, or double it by taking a clerk's berth, will not be likely if they arrive totally unprovided for to continue in the service of the Society...'

In late middle age Hudson Taylor once confessed that 'my greatest temptation is to lose my temper over the slackness and inefficiency so disappointing in those on whom I depended. It is no use to lose my temper – only kindness – but O, it is such a

trial.' At twenty-two his letters to the Secretaries were somewhat
sprinkled with Shanghai sarcasm. 'I don't fancy all my letters of
late have been sugar cane to them', he wrote to his parents.

Deeper than any other troubles in this first year lay Hudson's
loneliness, which continually obtrudes into his letters. One week,
he wrote, he had a violet and two forget-me-nots in his room. 'I
look on them', he told Amelia, 'with the greatest affection and
have even given them names; one I call Amelia, and another Louisa
– what I have called a third is no matter of yours. Did you ever
hear of anything so foolish or suspect me of such absurdities? But
you know we must have something to love.' Once when there
were no letters in a home mail during the hot weather, he nearly
swooned. He relapsed into self-pity. 'Is it kind so to disappoint me
when five minutes writing would tell me you are well? But it always has been so with me. Whatever I set my heart on, I lose. I
thought Miss V would prove an exception but it was not so.'

He pined for a wife. 'I am glad to hear any news of Miss
Vaughan you may have. She may get a richer and a handsomer
husband but I question whether she will get one more devoted
than I should have been. But I see she is not fit for a missionary's
wife. It is very improbable that I shall ever meet with one here.'

He knew a possible girl in Hull, Elizabeth Sissons. She 'used to
say she loved me, when at Mrs Hodson's I used to visit as Miss
V's intended and then I liked her very much'. Elizabeth had con-
soled Hudson, when Miss Vaughan broke off the engagement,
with a present of sketches, and he had given her a brooch on
leaving England. After some months in China he wrote to her
asking for a lock of her hair. His mother approved the proposed
match. In January 1855 he received the lock of hair.

## Chapter 3: FORBIDDEN GROUND

In the early months of 1855 Taylor made preaching tours, a week or more with another missionary or alone, on the teeming alluvial plain beyond the range of foreign influence. It gave him a taste of what to expect when the local civil war should end and he would be free to go inland, defying the treaty which forbade the movement of the red-haired barbarians.

He saw walled cities with narrow streets of gaily painted signboards and jostling chattering crowds; temples whose curved roofs supported curling, fierce-headed dragons; farms and little villages where each house had paper guards to ward off predatory evil spirits, and a mirror over the door for them to catch sight of their horrid faces and flee. He passed along canals beside fields of stubble or brown soil waiting for the next rice crop, a checker-board pattern broken by grave mounds; he was rowed into inlets and bays to tie up at night among watermen who spent their entire lives in their junks. In early morning he watched cormorant fishers release trained birds to dive, a ring round the cormorant's neck to prevent it from swallowing sizeable fish, the small fry being its reward. Other fishermen were their own divers, walking on shore or river bottom to emerge gasping with a fish in each hand.

Taylor and Edkins were chased and mobbed at one town by citizens who reacted to western clothes much as Victorian English rustics would have behaved on meeting two unsightly Chinese in loose jackets and nether garments, the front of their heads shaved, long pigtails down their backs. Elsewhere, after being heard with rapt attention by worshippers and priests in a temple, they were confronted by an imposing cavalcade. 'First came two men with gongs, then men followed with immense red cloth caps, bearing flags etc, then came a man with a kind of large umbrella and he was followed by a large sedan chair carried by four bearers.' The mandarin alighted, portly yet good-looking, a mild-mannered gentleman resplendent in embroidered silk and satin robes and long tapering fingernails, his rank marked by the colour of the jewelled button in his brimless hat. With exquisite courtesy he questioned the missionaries, and with Confucian grace assured them their books were very good but that the honourable wayfarers must go no farther. He gave them one of his staff as escort or spy, and retired amid prolonged exchange of compliments. Both sides were blissfully unaware that each in the eyes of the other was an ignorant barbarian.

In February 1855 the Imperial armies with unneutral French support stormed and sacked the starving native city of Shanghai, making the streets hideous with human suffering. Taylor felt 'unutterable disgust and aversion to that government which perpetrates such disgusting and barbarous atrocities'.

At the return of local peace he contemplated permanent residence in some city of the interior, or else finding his way the two hundred miles to the Taiping capital, Nanking. Either course would forfeit consular protection. Before making a final decision he went up the Yangtze for three weeks in April with John Burdon, a trip that nearly cost them their lives.

In the wide Yangtze estuary, on a large long island called Tsungming with a population of a million to whom no Protestant missionary had ever gone, they and their books were received by the Mandarin with typical courtesy. They intended exploring the coast of the island, but while they slept that night the boatmen, craving opium, decided that the foreign devils would be happier on the mainland, the northern shore of the Yangtze.

Accepting the inevitable, they made day trips by Chinese wheelbarrow, a springless unoiled contraption pushed by a coolie to shake bones and set teeth on edge. They preached, gave away literature, and dispensed medical help with an abandon which would have shocked their grandsons taught by a century of experience that free distribution of medicine except in special circumstances is a sure way of collecting 'rice Christians'.

Thoroughly enjoying themselves in this willow-pattern countryside where peach trees blossomed, the two young men decided to take a day off to recover 'our husky voices' by climbing one of a range of hummocky sacred hills on a perfect spring morning heavy with the scent of bean flowers. 'As we approached the hills the scene became beautiful beyond description. Of the five hills in sight the middle one was highest and it was crowned by a fine pagoda, evidently newly repaired and painted. At the foot and side of this hill was a Buddhist temple and monastery so extensive that at a little distance we took it for a village.'

They climbed steep steps between rocks gay with wild flowers, shaded by trees which rejoiced Taylor's naturalist eye: 'The deep gloomy cypress, the light graceful willow, mingled with orange, tallow and other trees... Anything more beautiful I never saw'. They entered the gates of the temple beneath protective dragons. A major festival had drawn a crowd of every degree. In the splendour of ceremonies no one noticed the black-coated foreigners. Majestic landowners in green and blue and gold jackets and robes, circular hats, jade ear-pendants worth a fortune in Europe; coolies and peasants in blue cotton, merchants, soldiers, all gazed at richly vested priests prostrating themselves before an immense dispassionate Buddha in posture of meditation, to the boom of deep-toned gongs. With Chinese incongruity bustling workmen gilded and lacquered nearby.

The whole courtyard was a blaze of colour. 'Nothing was omitted and no expense spared that the eye might be gratified and the beholder captivated. And there is no doubt', Taylor noted, 'that to the thousands who visited it the rites practised therein were most imposing. The beauty indeed *was* extreme, all that nature and art could do seemed brought to bear, and it was calculated for the moment to cause us to forget that this was the temple of Satan. But the poor deluded people, bowing to their idols, burning incense and throwing their cash into paper baskets in front of each idol or set of idols, rendered it impossible.'

Taylor and Burdon climbed onwards past platform after incense-filled platform, to the sound of Chinese music and the gabble of worshippers, until they reached the pagoda, one of those storied pavilions found throughout China on high places of countryside and city, their original purpose as watchtowers having changed into a superstitious role of protectors from evil spirits. At the top the two gasped at the view.

Below lay a panorama in brilliant sunshine. Through Taylor's telescope they could pick out every detail. 'The country, covered with wheat, barley, peas, beans etc, laid out like a garden', was of the loveliest owing to recent rains. The streams, winding between the fields, intersected it in every direction, bordered with numerous graceful willows. Farm houses with their fruit trees and neat willow fences, cemeteries here and there, cypress-shaded, and numerous villages and hamlets dotted the foreground. Beyond these lay the magnificent Yangtze, fifteen to twenty miles broad, its smooth waters speckled with white, red or black sails. Over the river on the sacred hills of the southern shore, sunlight touched the gold of temples. Distance blended all that was harsh or cruel or ugly into a tapestry of loveliness.

Here was China as it had been for thousands of years, as it lay for thousands of miles, home of four hundred million. Untouched inland China beckoned. Taylor responded in an unforgettable moment of resolve.

They descended. In one of the temple courts a priest invited Taylor to adore the Buddha. He could contain himself no longer. Climbing the worship stool he poured out an impassioned address in his stumbling Mandarin to an attentive crowd, and Burdon followed with another in Shanghai dialect. They walked on downward, husky as they had come.

Next day they attacked Tungchow, a city of evil repute.

The Chinese teachers who sought to dissuade them were ordered to retire in haste to Shanghai if their masters failed to return by nightfall. The servant with the book bags sat fearfully in his wheelbarrow for the first two or three miles of splashing and bumping through mud and potholes, and then begged to be allowed to escape certain death. They took the books themselves. A 'respectable man came up, and earnestly warned us against proceeding, saying that if we did we should find to our sorrow what the Tungchow militia were like'. The missionaries kept up their courage by exchanging verses of Scripture or of hymns.

At a minor place halfway along the seven miles to Tungchow,

Taylor preached to a small crowd. He glowed when a listener volunteered in the local dialect to newcomers 'that God loved them, that they were sinners but that Jesus died instead of them, and paid the penalty of their guilt'. 'That one moment repaid me for all the trials we had passed through.'

At the western suburb they told the barrowmen to wait, lifted off the book bags, and took comfort in extempore prayer shaped around the petition of persecuted early Christians in the Acts of the Apostles: 'And now, Lord, behold their threatenings: and grant unto thy servants that with all boldness they may speak thy word.'

The future bishop, being a muscular man, may have had the larger endowment of natural courage; both knew that in a Chinese prison their chance of survival until extracted by the Consul was slight.

After pleasurably unexciting progress except for rude shouts about 'black devil's children', and scowls from militiamen, Taylor ventured an over-optimistic remark. Moments later he was a few paces ahead, his eye on the nearing west gate. At the sound of a scuffle he turned. A tall, powerful, half-drunk militiaman had seized Burdon, who was trying to shake him off, 'and in almost no time we were surrounded by a dozen or more of these brutal wretches and were being hurried on to the city at a fearful pace'.

'My bag now began to feel very heavy and I could not change hands to relieve myself. I was soon in a most profuse perspiration and scarcely able to keep up with them.' Above the din the Englishmen shouted that they must be taken to the chief magistrate. The roughs replied with insults and menaces: they knew where to take them. The powerful soldier, tiring of Burdon, caught Taylor and pummelled him as if he were a puppy, the more because he was too light to resist properly. 'This man all but knocked me down repeatedly, seized me by the hair, got hold of me by the collar so as almost to choke me, and grasped my arms and shoulders.'

Taylor and Burdon were buoyed by exhilaration and peace, like St Stephen at martyrdom, and when thrown together exhorted one another cheerfully, but Taylor called it afterwards 'the most severe trial of faith I have yet undergone, knowing the atrocities perpetrated by the Chinese on the unfortunate rebels who fall into their hands'. The mob did not take these two as foreigners; Taipings also grew their hair without pigtail in defiance of the Manchu ordinance. Taylor had no terror of death, but he had seen 'that persons beheaded, without distinction of age or sex – men, women and children – before execution are stripped of every article of clothing, and naked as they were born are exhibited to public gaze both before and after death'. For a young man of his background to be stripped and exposed publicly was a horrible prospect. He fully expected this might happen, before his head be thrust sharply forward on the ground and the sword fall. He knew his captors, from sheer bestiality, were perfectly capable of castrating him first.

Freeing one hand he thrust it in his pocket for the large red paper bearing his name, a Chinese visiting card, and demanded it should be sent to the chief magistrate. That paper saved their lives. If the roughs had never seen a foreigner they realised now at least that their captives were gentlemen, whose murder would bring trouble. They set off for the magistrate.

'Oh the long weary streets we were dragged through! I thought they would never end; and seldom have I felt more thankful than when we stopped at a place where we were told a Mandarin resided. Quite exhausted, bathed in perspiration and with my tongue cleaving to the roof of my mouth, I leaned against the wall, and saw that Mr Burdon was in much the same state.' Taylor's sense of humour came to their rescue. Burdon told a friend, 'I was feeling particularly sore and injured and all I got from him was a suppressed smile, and "this will form fine material for our diaries".'

Taylor asked one of their captors for chairs. Refused. For tea (there always would be a pot boiling nearby). Refused. 'Round the doorway a large crowd had gathered, and Mr Burdon, collecting his remaining strength, preached Jesus Christ to them.'

The militiamen ran out of the Mandarin's office saying the case was referred higher to the Intendant or Tao-tai. The prisoners declined to move until sedan chairs were brought; since decorum must reign in a *yamen*, they had their way. Bystanders remarked that they did not look like bad men, 'while others seemed to pity us'.

The chair journey was tedious, if less noisy. They entered great gates, saw other gates ahead and for an instant believed they were to be thrown into prison. At last they stood in the presence of the Tao-tai, subordinate only to the Governor of the Province. Their escorts made kowtow. The subjects of Queen Victoria stood stolid.

The magnificent personage had been Tao-tai at Shanghai; he knew foreigners – and gunboats. He treated the missionaries with grave respect, listened to an account of their doings, received their books, plied them with rice cakes and tea in exquisite little cups without handles: milkless, sugarless green tea (Taylor preferred cream and sugar), as much as they wished.

He gave leave for a brief tour of the city and distribution of books, and allotted an escort. The escort whipped a way through the crowds by laying about with their pigtails. Taylor forgot his bruises in laughter.


Ten days after his return with Burdon to Shanghai Taylor set off again, alone except for Chinese, to reach the Taipings.

Their territory lay only a few hundred miles away, and they were at their zenith. Shanghai opinion was still sceptical, on various grounds: Taiping adherence to the Chinese tradition that the Emperor has a harem; the mingling of Christian belief with oriental political methods; their secretiveness, and their conviction that the westerners, though co-religionists, were uncivilised because coming from beyond the Middle Kingdom: these factors, together with the ardent attempts of Imperialists to prejudice western officials against the rebels, and the officials' own reluctance to visit Nanking lest trade with Imperial China should suffer, all contributed to lower Taiping stock in the International Settlement.

It had been reported, wrongly, that the Taipings did not now want foreign missionaries. Hudson Taylor believed the report, and that 'there seems to be every reason to fear that there is more evil mixed up with them than we hoped'. This no longer deterred him, because he had put his finger on the point that mattered: 'But the

*Word of God* is there; if it is freely distributed, is read and understood by the people, it *must* bring forth some fruit'. They needed a teacher, and a channel of communication with western Christians.

Partly to explore possible openings for residence, partly to throw Imperialists off the scent, Taylor proceeded up the Yangtze by leisurely stages. From his boat he visited fifty-eight villages, towns and walled cities, only seven of which had ever seen a Protestant missionary. He preached, removed tumours, distributed books. He endured wind and storm and heat. The noisy curiosity of the people at this strangely clothed creature often made his heart thump and his stomach wildly flutter as he forced himself forward. 'I have felt a degree of nervousness since I was so roughly treated at Tungchow that before I had not experienced, and this feeling is not lessened by my being alone.'

The people would run from him, or show an inclination to throw mud and stones. Medicine box and medical skill proved generally stronger than fears or animosity, but inquisitiveness never ceased. It was provoking, especially to a quick-tempered man who knew that one trace of annoyance could undo all his efforts. It could be amusing too. 'When I took out my watch to look at the time, one grown-up person exclaimed that never before had he seen such spectacles. Another telling him he was an ignoramus, very gravely informed the company that it was nothing less than a telescope I had in my pocket, and that western men were celebrated for making them.'

In the journal kept for transmission to the Society in London, Taylor emphasised the immensity of the task: 'Just to visit them, give them portions of Scripture and tracts, and then, after preaching to them pass on, seems almost like doing nothing for them. And yet unless this course is adopted, how can the Word ever be put into the hands of the people? ...But we see no fruit at present, and it needs strong faith to keep one's spirit from sinking.'

He drew nearer to Taiping territory until, a few days after his twenty-third birthday, he was less than seventy miles away.

Then silence. In after years Taylor never revealed what occurred. In his *A Retrospect* he states merely that he sought to reach Nanking and found it 'impossible to do so'. In old age when he was travelling this route by steamer with his son and daughter-in-law, they found him strangely moved. 'I wish I could tell you about it,' he said, gazing at the southern shore. 'It was over there. But I cannot remember just the spot.'

In 1855 the rebel Emperor and his princes were anxious to be taught the truth they dimly grasped. When missionaries reached Nanking five years later the leaders were too embedded in peculiar heresies to be open to correction; western antagonism and their own follies were already tipping them down the slope which led to defeat and extinction. Furthermore, at the time of Taylor's attempt, the West had not decided whether to support or to hinder. Accurate information from an Englishman in the confidence of the Taipings might have prevented the grievous mistake of the British at the outbreak of the Second Chinese War in 1857, when the Government refused the rebel offer to combine forces, and defeated the alien Manchu dynasty only to prop it up again. Had not the British been so misguided, the rebel Emperor would have come to the Dragon Throne.

The consequences? The Chinese government would have turned Christian officially, and in China the religion of the throne became the religion of the people. The Christianizing of a whole Empire would produce problems intricate as those in the West after Emperor Constantine's conversion, yet none insurmountable, and missionaries, western and national, would have moved freely.

Under a Taiping dynasty China might have absorbed the techniques of the West, willingly fusing them into her ancient civilisation, with railways opening the country, mines being sunk, mills and factories being established years before in fact they were. Instead, she was to be shaken rudely from the sleep of ages, coming to terms with modern times fifty years too late, sullenly, with that deep-rooted hatred of foreigners which would bear bitter fruit in the mid-twentieth century. The Confucian system was no longer capable of directing China's destinies. It could have been replaced

by Christianity to the gain of Asia and the world, not by commu-
nism a hundred years later to the world's loss and danger, had the
Taiping movement received proper recognition and aid from the
West, and triumphed.

Hudson Taylor was of the stuff that could have won the confidence of the Taipings. His lower middle-class upbringing and lack
of university education rendered him less liable than some to despise the Chinese as of a lower culture, or to identify Christianity
with its western forms. It was this identification that raised a barrier between worthy missionaries and Chinese proud of their ancient civilisation, who regarded western consciousness of superiority as another symptom of the boorishness of Outer Barbarians.

Taylor had no sentimental view: 'the Chinese are such a slip-
pery people. You cannot depend upon a word they say... They
will cheat you and lie to any extent but they will not rob you', he
wrote to a friend that summer; but he had unfailing confidence in
the power of God to recreate character. Most missionaries loved
the Chinese; few Protestants were prepared to sink their European
selves in identification with the people. Taylor was prepared, even
if a diet of rice and Chinese food offended his digestion.

He was virtually independent of ties, whether family or mission, which later held other men back from effectual service in
rebel Nanking. He was young, but no younger than George
Whitefield when he was the foremost evangelist of England and
America. He was untried, but the gifts of leadership he displayed
later show that opportunity would have bred wisdom.

## Chapter 4: 'IN THE MIDDLE OF THE HONOURABLE BACK'

Maria Dyer was an orphan. She had been born in 1837 at Penang
in Malaya, where her father, the Reverend Samuel Dyer, of Trin-
ity College, Cambridge, and the London Missionary Society, was
one of the earliest western evangelists to the Chinese. An able,
cultured man who had preferred missionary labours to the hon-
ours and affluence of a legal career, he had won renown among
the Chinese of the Straits. After the annexation he hurried alone to

Hong Kong, his eye on the mainland. He died prematurely at Macao in 1843.

His widow was left in Penang with three small children, Burella (Ellie), Samuel and Maria. She promptly got married again to a missionary called Bausum, and died in 1847, when Maria was ten. The orphans were sent to a married uncle in England, William Tarn, a gentleman of means, a staunch supporter of missions.

The sisters, after education in the North of England, stayed on as teachers until Burella was offered a post at a school in Ningpo, the next treaty port south of Shanghai. Maria went too. The Dyer girls had been bred to be missionaries, they were self-supporting and had always stayed together. And therefore, at eighteen, and for no other reason than that she followed her sister, Maria sailed for China.

Maria was tall, dark-haired, dark-eyed, vivacious and warm. She had a squint. It did not make her less attractive. She was demure, the dutiful younger sister, and no one suspected the strong currents within.

On board ship she underwent a quiet but overwhelming spiritual experience which transformed her from a professional missionary obediently fulfilling her parents' dying wishes, into a disciple whose dominant motive was an intense and growing love for Christ; and, having scarcely known a father, she poured all the brimmed-up devotion that would have been his into the service of God. She saw her activities as a child's response of love.

At Ningpo she subjected herself to the founder and principal of the school, Miss Aldersey, endeared herself to the Chinese children, applied her remarkably quick intelligence to gaining a skilful grasp of the language, and, with all this, was a favourite with the young gentlemen of the European community. Neither Burella nor Miss Aldersey detected her fundamental loneliness.

Maria Dyer was of a different social background from Hudson Taylor. She was closely protected from undesirable suitors. And she lived in a different treaty port.

But that very summer of 1855, at the end of a tour southwards from Shanghai with John Burdon and Dr Parker, Taylor came to

Ningpo. A CMS clergyman and his wife, the Cobbolds, finding him run down by the heat, carried him off to the beauty of the hills and tea gardens. He contrasted the squabblings of Shanghai with 'peace and unity' among the fourteen men and women of different persuasions at Ningpo. He could not tell he was to be the centre of storms which would rock this peace and unity.

He did not even notice Maria.

He would not have been interested. Hudson Taylor had already dispatched a formal offer of marriage to Elizabeth Sissons.

He had painted Elizabeth a distinctly rosy picture of China. Marriage to her would fetter him to Shanghai although instinct prompted uncompromising devotion to the call of the interior, notwithstanding treaty limitations, rigorous travelling and danger; he knew that the Sissons and the interior were mutually exclusive. But his loneliness convinced him that the paradox would somehow resolve.

He puzzled how to marry when dependent on the Chinese Evangelization Society, whose well-meaning secretaries were 'so unbusinesslike, so easily gulled, so positive in their opinions, and show so little confidence in us'. It was true that he had occasional, unpredictable alternative sources of supply: the English chaplain, Hobson, had pressed an unsolicited donation in token of admiration for Taylor's devotion as a missionary. The British and Foreign Bible Society volunteered the bulk of his travelling expenses on up-country tours and the whole of his colportage stock, because he distributed the most Testaments. And a Mr Berger in England, a London manufacturer lately retired to a fine house in Sussex, whom Taylor scarcely remembered, suddenly sent him a substantial cheque. But 'I do not know whether I should be justified in making a matrimonial alliance in my present position'.

Parker decided his future lay in Ningpo. The community wanted a doctor and he could use the income to make a mission hospital, no longer dependent on the CES. Taylor yearned for a regular post, but not in Ningpo. Back at Shanghai he wrote to his parents, 'I am as unsettled as I was on the first day I landed in China'.

On one journey Taylor returned to his boat hungry after a day's preaching and doctoring, for a meal of ducks' eggs and rice fried in oil. His black trousers and jacket were dusty, his leather boots, source of constant surprise to the local inhabitants, showed how far he had walked.

Teacher and assistants crowded round as he attacked his bowl, 'having acquired an honourable sufficiency in the use of chopsticks, to the infinite delight of my companions the Chinamen, who recommended me to get my head shaved tomorrow and change my dress, until one suggested that I could not change my eyes and nose'.

A few tours later he came to an unvisited town. He wore as usual a double-breasted frock-coat exactly like that of every other respectable European professional man, at home or abroad, complete with the slits, pleats and buttons back and front which Saville Row had imposed upon the world. After innumerable patient replies to satisfy the crowd's curiosity about the function, form and origin of each, he started preaching.

One man close beside him stood transfixed, rapt. He was that dream of an open-air speaker, the patently smitten soul to whom questions may be put, the whole audience profiting from hearing him drawn step by step towards personal conviction of the truth. At length Taylor addressed him personally.

'Yes, yes,' replied the man. 'What you say is doubtless very true. But, honourable Foreign Teacher, may I ask you one question?'

Taylor purred. Matters moved fast. He listened carefully.

'I have been pondering all the while you have been preaching. But the subject is no clearer to my mind. The honourable garment you are wearing, Foreign Teacher, has upon one edge of it a number of circular objects that might do duty as buttons, and on the opposite edge, certain slits in the material probably intended for buttonholes?'

'Yes, that is so,' agreed Taylor, deflated. The crowd were all attention, text and sermon forgotten.

'The purpose of that strange device I can understand,' continued the man fervently. 'It must be to attach the honourable gar-

ment in cold or windy weather. But, Foreign Teacher, this is what
I cannot understand: What can be the meaning of those buttons *in
the middle of the honourable back*?'

'Why, yes,' chorused the crowd, 'in the middle of the back!'
Hudson had not the slightest idea.

'*In the middle of the honourable back.*' The words echoed to
his footsteps as he walked. They jumped at him as he took off the
offending garments and saw those three useless buttons. They
summed up the waste and annoyance of western dress in an oriental setting and reminded him of that conversation over the ducks'
eggs and rice.

Another incident clinched his growing realisation that if he
wanted to evangelise beyond the ports he must cease to appear a
Foreign Teacher. Towards the end of July he was summoned before the British Consul, having been cited by the Chinese authorities. The Consul 'said very little, not more than he was obliged to
do, but told me if I continued to violate the treaty his position
admitted no respecting of persons, he must punish me as he would
do a merchant'.

Taylor knew that if he transformed himself into a Chinese,
pigtail and all, he might pass unnoticed. Almost on leaving the
Consul he ordered a teacher's satin robes and shoes.

He argued to himself that he had a legal right to travel the
interior because foreign Roman Catholic priests did so with the
tacit consent of the French Consul, even flying the French flag
over their stations, and by the 'most-favoured nation' clause of
the treaty the British had a claim to any concession obtained by
another signatory government. Not that consular approval eased
the lot of the Roman Catholics. Ten years later Taylor described
them with a turn of phrase almost Churchillian: 'Entering by stealth,
living in concealment, pursuing their labours under the greatest
disadvantages, ever and anon meeting with imprisonment,
sufferings, tortures and death itself, they have presented a remarkable instance of fidelity to their calling'. He did not see why
Protestants should be found wanting.

Native dress involved a black pigtail. Taylor's sandy hair was most unChinese, and he prepared to concoct a dye. He took a large bottle of ammonia, and as it was half-used and the day was very hot, loosened the stopper gingerly. It blew out. He clamped his hand over the mouth despite the pain, and tried to pick up the stopper to save the expensive liquid.

Ammonia spurted out with such force that 'the stream flew into my eyes, up my nose, between my lips, among my hair and on to my clothes. The contest was useless. I had to run.'

Blinded, in agony, gasping, he lurched across the courtyard and through the kitchen, tearing off his spectacles. 'I felt as if on fire. Though I staggered about I fortunately got in, and outside the door was a large water-jar full of water. I ducked head and shoulders and arms into it and it saved me.' The butt had just received the weekly refill – a day earlier the level would have been too low to wash off the alkali, and he would have suffocated.

He croaked in English 'Call Doctor Parker at once!' Then recovered his wits and said it in Chinese. At the servant's shout Parker ran out. He poured castor oil into Taylor's eyes and over his face, gave him laudanum to deaden the pain, placed his feet in hot water to draw blood from the head and put him to bed 'wrapped up like Christmas', ice on head, bandages on eyes.

Taylor was out of pain before nightfall. As he lay on his bed he reflected on no less than five providences: he had been wearing spectacles of double thickness or might have been blinded; he had succeeded in staggering to the kitchen instead of collapsing; the water-butt was full; Parker, so often out, was at home; and finally, they had ice enough for the three days he needed to offset the burns. Within a week he had recovered save for a redness around the eyes and a sneezy feeling in the nose.


At 11 pm on 23rd August 1855, the night before setting out to escort Parker most of the way overland to Ningpo (Parker's family went by sea), Taylor 'resigned my locks to the barber, dyed my hair, and in the morning had some false hair plaited in with my

own, and a quantity of silk cord according to the Chinese custom'. He now had an entirely bald pate except for a long tail
hanging from the occiput. The curly-haired fair young man had
disappeared. Even eyebrows were black.

The process had been painful. 'A very sore thing to get one's
head shaved for the first time, when the skin is so irritable as the
prickly heat makes it. And I can assure you', he wrote to Amelia,
'that the subsequent application of hair-dye for five or six hours
after does not do much to soothe the irritation. But when you
come to the combing out of the hair' (he had allowed it to grow
down his neck to form the basis of the tail) 'you arrive at the
climax, and [I] think, if as some say it is the pains of labour that
make the mother's affection greater than the father's, I shall look
at my tail, when finished, with no small amount of pride and attachment.'

Hudson submitted to the customary massage 'lest sometimes I
should get into a mess by my ignorance of it, so I bore with a most
awful tickling as long as I could, and then the basting commenced,
and my back was sore in some places ere it was over'. He grew
used to the daily beating on which the Chinese set much store for
health, but never enjoyed it.

After the shave and massage, dressing. First, white unyielding
calico stockings and flat-soled black satin shoes with turned-up
toes; he had worn them in the house for the past three weeks but
found them most uncomfortable. He was not surprised that Chinese servants in European houses generally adopted foreign shoes
and stockings. 'Next come the breeks – but oh, what breeks. Mine
are two feet too wide round the waist, which is rectified by a fold
in front, and are kept up by a girdle.' The legs billowed out fore
and aft, immense knee-length pantaloons tucking into the stockings; Parker declared they would hold a fortnight's provisions. A
short wide-sleeved washable jacket replaced the western shirt,
and the whole was covered by a heavy silk gown with long full
sleeves.

Unfortunately in summer no gentleman wore a hat on ordinary
occasions unless he was a Mohammedan, 'which is a great nui-

sance, for the sun is awfully hot'. Taylor protected his newly shorn, sore head with a native paper umbrella.

They left for the south. The effect was immediate. Hudson told his father: 'You would not know me were you to meet me in the street with other Chinese and in a Chinese city I am not suspected of being a foreigner, though there is something in my appearance that makes some look hard at me when I pass'. Most people thought he was a teacher in the foreign doctor's employ until the two talked to each other in English. Taylor had Chinese spectacles of thick rose crystal which camouflaged his eyes; this and the variety of facial types and dialects to be found in China aided him.

When he parted from Parker, Taylor knew without doubt that a great barrier was down. The inquisitive crowds evaporated. On beginning to preach he was generally recognised as an Outer Barbarian but more readily accepted as an honoured guest, not an uncouth intruder.

A further benefit became obvious once he was used to the clothes: their suitability for the climate. Compared with nineteenth-century western fashions, Chinese dress was cool in summer, warm in winter. Never again did Taylor suffer agonies of cold, or in a hot July be obliged to write of white shirt, trousers and stockings 'and of course black shoes and black cravat' all wet through after half an hour's sit, with a piece of paper beneath his hand to catch the sweat, while 'if I were to walk out for half a mile (with my thick white pith hat on and an umbrella as well) I should probably get a sunstroke'.

He came back to Shanghai. Rumours of his conversion to Chinese dress had preceded him. If barriers were down in the country they were flung high in the International Settlement. Merchants laughed in his face. Gossip buzzed, women were horrified, dandy young clerks curled their lips, the coarser looked at the billowing nether garment and cracked obscene jokes, the old hands over their brandy called it a disgrace: the fellow had demeaned himself in front of the natives and harmed British prestige.

The missionary community were annoyed with him. That hurt. His best friends were puzzled and disturbed that a man could be such a crack-pot. 'Disguise, although so universally and success-fully employed by the Romanists, must be regarded as objection-able.' Thus wrote Sir Walter Medhurst, son of the formidable doctor and himself a great Consul. He added, from his lordly view-point, 'It is calculated to lower the individual in the opinion of the natives'. It was certainly calculated to lower him in the opinion of his compatriots. They could not forgive the implied surrender of the superiority of western ways. Even his parents, when they heard, were shocked.

The laughter, still more the disgust of fellow missionaries, ran-kled. Yet they paled beside a new-found inner glory. The Slough of Despond had been left far behind, he climbed the Delectable Mountains. He had Miss Sissons' acceptance, qualified by her father's desire that she should wait; she did not know her lover had transmuted himself into a Chinaman. He had found a surpris-ingly clean little place in the Chinese city. His servant, Kuei Hua, showed such genuine spiritual concern, by startling improvement in character as by affirmation, that he became the first convert Taylor baptised.

All these encouragements were countered by the loneliness of the grave step taken, by life's enormous uncertainties. Yet there was inner glory. Taylor wrote home, in one of those long letters full of spiritual insight if without felicity of phrase, 'The future is a ravelled maze and my path hath ever been made plain one step at a time. I must wait on God and trust in him, and all will be well. I think I do love *Him* more than ever, and long to serve Him as He directs, more than ever. I have had some wonderful seasons of refreshing of late, and how unworthy of them I have been!'

## Chapter 5: THE HOUSE ON THE ISLAND

On 18th October 1855, Taylor left Shanghai with the intention of 'trying to sit down somewhere in the Chinese costume'. Away from a treaty port he planned to open a dispensary where he could live, treat patients, preach, and engage in the man-to-man talks which were his special delight. 'Don't speak of this till we see what comes of it', he warned his parents.

A last-moment hunch sent him to Tsungming, the large island in the Yangtze mouth visited with Burdon in April. He slipped away by water, not carrying much money or medical supplies, half-expecting the trip to be no more than another reconnaissance. He took Kuei Hua and an older catechumen called Ts'ien. After a journey of a day and a half they tied up at a little fishing port and the following morning walked two or three miles inland to a town of nearly twenty thousand, Sin-K'ai-ho. Almost before he knew, Taylor's party had a home.

'I wish you could pop in and see how snug I am in the midst of these people, as easily as you can go over to Dodsworth, to which this town bears a good deal of resemblance, though it is much larger of course.' When the Barnsley tea-table heard that, Mrs Taylor murmured: 'When and where will the dear lad find a resting place?'

He thought he had found one. The townsfolk, rich and poor, saw nothing to fear in this man, dressed like any wellbred teacher, who had such unusual medical skill and potions. They brought their aches and pains, and opened their ears to his sayings, while Taylor, aided by his cats, was still clearing the newly-rented place of filth and vermin. The love and enthusiasm in his nature bubbled over in the delight of receiving and serving these Chinese with their curious habits and ingrained ideas on everything under the sun.

He soon discovered that the dropping of the barrier between himself and the people exposed him to the full force of their heathendom. Because he dressed normally and did not commit too many solecisms, they treated him as they would their neighbours. When he snatched a few moments to write home he would hear them, as they sat about in his house, chat casually about the sale of a girl or the body of another, discuss the rival merits of necro-mancers, estimate the grandeur of a local funeral with its burning of paper houses and money tokens for the deceased's use in the next world. When he preached he could not miss the glazed look in the eyes of the man who had finished his evening opium pipe, or the peevishness of one waiting to smoke.

'There is *nothing romantic* about the Chinese', he wrote early that week, and asserted that love for Christ and for 'precious souls' was the only conceivable motive for sticking it. Otherwise, 'the continuous and apparently fruitless labour of day after day setting forth Christ, will become irksome'.

Only when he went outside at night and looked up and away from the flickering lamps and shadows to the waxing moon could he feel purified and free. This brought out his sentimental streak. 'It is a favourite thought of mine that the beautiful moon which now shines on me, will soon shine on the abodes of those I love. I almost look at it as a messenger and say "go shine on those loved ones".' Whether Amelia or Miss Sissons was the recipient of that piece of tenderness is not evident.

A week. A weekend of malaria, soon over. Two weeks. Supplies ran low and hopes high, for several townsfolk, including the blacksmith, were expressing interest. Taylor toured the country-side, dreaming of establishing little churches here and there until he had built a circuit in the manner of John Wesley.

On Monday November 5th he left Ts'ien and Kuei Hua in charge and returned in fine fettle to Shanghai to restock the medi-cine chest, collect letters and fit himself with quilted winter clothes and a gown lined by lambskin.

Two doctors and four druggists of Sin-K'ai-ho sipped tea beneath blue porcelain medicine jars in the Hall of Tranquillity, the shop of the druggist up the narrow street from the Foreign Doctor's house. Impervious to the dissonance of gossips and shoppers and street vendors outside they had met to confer on a serious hindrance to trade. The urgency of the matter brought them to the point after only two hours of preliminaries.

One doctor reported that several bad legs, steady source of income, had been cured in a few days. A druggist complained of the collapse of the market in itching plasters – customers said quite rudely that itch powders provided free by the foreigner had cleared the trouble. The other doctor bemoaned the loss of ague patients, who were adding insult to injury by publicly denouncing the medical fraternity as incompetent.

The meeting relapsed into silent smoking except for a word from one, a nod from another, a grunt from a third, until imperceptibly came the obvious conclusion that squeeze be sent to the magistrate to eject the foreigner. Twelve dollars were raised in equal shares.

The *yamen* runners took the twelve dollar squeeze. No direct words were spoken, but a long session in the outer court of the *yamen* left no doubt of what was required. The runners, however, saw no purpose in conveying to the mandarin the respects of the druggists in the form of *ten* dollars; they could extract squeeze from all concerned. The treaty-breaking Foreign Doctor would pay well for their silence, his landlord would pay to escape punishment for aiding a foreigner; the druggists were good for another twelve dollars at least.

The runners came to Taylor's house in his absence. They thoroughly frightened Ts'ien and Kuei Hua, but failed to get money. They returned a day or two later bearing a writ sealed with the Mandarin's seal to which they had access by bringing in his clerk. Ts'ien read that the Foreign Doctor was to be arrested and sent to the Tao-tai at Shanghai, who would hand him to the British Consul for examination and punishment. All Chinese concerned were to be brought before the magistrate in Tsungming.

Ts'ien took a boat for Shanghai. He could not find Taylor, and returned, leaving a copy of the writ, which brought his master hurrying back.

Taylor learned of a third call from the *yamen* runners, to a new tune: now they knew the Foreign Doctor's purpose to be wholly benevolent, they would hush up the affair on payment of thirteen dollars' expenses. Taylor 'felt a little anxious for some time not on account of myself but of those who would be implicated on my account if any stir were to arise, and the messengers after coming down to ten dollars and then to three as the price of their silence, finding that I would not give them a cash, farther squeezed the druggists of $13 and came no more. All seemed over.' Taylor held daily dispensary and services, and visited round the district again.

At breakfast nearly a fortnight later, on Monday morning, 26th November, he and his two assistants heard a distant drum. Taylor's heart fluttered. The drumming drew near. He heard the hubbub in the street as vendors pulled back their stalls, night-soil coolies hurriedly emptied a last pail into their containers and made off down an alleyway, mothers hobbled in bound feet to drag children off the road, the crack of whips as the runners cleared a way. The mandarin passed in his chair, oblivious of common mortals crushed back against the walls, his ivory-white hands with long tapering nails holding a perfume ball which he lifted negligently to his nose.

Two runners dropped back to hammer on Taylor's door. They said the magistrate had come to seize pirates at the port and on return would deal with the Foreign Doctor. Ts'ien, Kuei Hua and the landlord, a greybeard of seventy, were to be dragged before him. Unless they gave satisfactory answers they would each be beaten between three hundred and a thousand blows.

Executioners if bribed were adept at inflicting strokes noisy but comparatively painless. No money had passed in this case. The two assistants spent the morning contemplating the full force of a thick bamboo.

'We had worship, and prayed for protection, preached as usual and saw patients, and I determined if any were sent for, to go myself before the mandarin (though that of course would prove fatal to my remaining here) and point out the inconsistency of annoying me while two Catholic priests not only resided in the island, within six miles of me, but had built a Catholic chapel there.'

Late in the day the apprehensive little party heard their turn would come tomorrow.

Taylor kept his people indoors. The next afternoon he was dressing the eye of a woman after operating when he heard the mandarin's procession. The two assistants stiffened. Taylor shivered with excitement and nerves: 'It was well that the operation was over, or I should have found it difficult to complete it'. The noise drew nearer. Taylor tried to concentrate. Sweat beads pimpled his brow. His lively imagination had him writhing under the blows, or tied up so tight that wrists and ankles festered till he died (the fate of *The Times* correspondent a few years later) or even the 'death of a thousand pieces', strapped to a rough cross and sliced up.

The mandarin came in view, looking straight ahead. Taylor drew back slightly and stood rigid. Did the Mandarin's right eyebrow lift a fraction? He was gone. The noise died away.

Two hours' anxiety ended in news that the Mandarin had gone to his capital without stopping. Prayers changed to praise. Taylor began to believe his very presence was unknown to the magistrate; 'most likely the report was a further attempt to extort money by his followers'.

The magistrate's treatment of the problem, as Taylor soon discovered, was typically Chinese. No direct attack – the tortuous was safer. No rumpus, for that might provoke questions from above. Always bland to a foreigner. And, blurring the exact course of events, the factor of bribe.

'Sir – I am directed by Her Majesty's Consul to inform you that information has been lodged at this office by His Excellency the Intendant of Circuit...'

An order to appear in front of the Consul had been sent to Taylor's Shanghai city house. He found it there the evening of Friday 30th November, and realised that the mandarin's complaint had been passed by the Tao-tai to the Consul at least a week before the nerve-chilling procession.

On Saturday morning Taylor went to the Consulate. The Consul looked at the little man in Chinese dress whose dyed hair was beginning to show traces of its native sandiness. The Consul wished this young enthusiast would behave like a self-respecting missionary, stick to a proper mission house in Shanghai and not embarrass British relations. Nevertheless, his voice was not unkind as he reminded him briskly of his former offence, told him to return forthwith to Tsungming, pack his traps and settle his affairs, come back and stay back. In default, a fine of five hundred dollars.

Taylor stated his claim: if French Jesuits, also in Chinese dress, could reside on Tsungming why should not he, under the 'most favoured nation' clause? The Consul took the point but repudiated authority to settle it. His chief, Sir John Bowring, was due in a few days from Hong Kong, and Mr Taylor if he wished could argue before him; meanwhile Mr Taylor must evacuate Tsungming.

The bottom fell out of Taylor's world. 'My dear mother, my heart is sad, sad, sad... I do not know what to do.' Much of Sunday was spent on his knees. He had no means to pay a fine; besides, 'If I disobey I shall bring many Chinese into trouble', yet 'I do not want to be as one of the hirelings who fled when the wolf comes, neither do I lightly wish to run into danger when much may be done in safety. I want to know the Lord's will and have grace to do it, even if it result in expatriation. "Now is my soul troubled, and what shall I say? *Father*, glorify thy name." Pray for me that I may be a Christian, not in word only but in deed and in truth.'

He took boat in the small hours of Monday morning, and the little town on the island witnessed a scene like St Paul's farewell to the elders of Ephesus when they all wept sore, sorrowing most of all that they should see his face no more. With Ts'ien and Kuei Hua he sat once again in the boat, Shanghai bound, turning in his mind the reasonings with which he must persuade Sir John Bowring; the author of the hymn *In the Cross of Christ I glory* had no leanings towards over-zealous missionaries who might prejudice trade and diplomacy.

The forlorn boat-load trailed into Shanghai. Hudson heard that a mail had arrived at the Consulate. He carried a pile of letters back and tore open an envelope in the writing of his girl. She feared she did not love him, he read. Tsungming, Elizabeth. '...And between one thing and another was quite knocked down and had scarcely heart to read my other letters.'

## Chapter 6: INTERLUDE WITH A SCOT

William Burns was a racy Scot in early middle age. His sallow complexion, furrowed brow, and hair tinged with grey had a wild prophetic cast, countered by the smile in his eyes and a humorous curve of mouth.

He had served at Amoy in South China. Returned to Shanghai after an unsuccessful bid to reach the Taipings, he smelt a kindred soul in Hudson Taylor, whom he found at the little city house dolefully preparing his case for Sir John Bowring. Burns puffed it to the winds: Taylor had not been intended to remain on Tsungming, or the Lord of Hosts would have smitten His enemies in the hinder parts. Forget Sir John. Come out with me, Burns said, and we will preach and teach together.

Taylor complied with awe and misgiving. He had heard of William Burns as a fiery revivalist in Scotland many years before: he expected one of the sort who are flaming volcanoes in public and icebergs in personal relationships, but Burns had mellowed with age. Like Taylor he had a keen sense of the ludicrous and, when fit, a trencherman's appetite. As they travelled and worked together during the next seven months, and Burns drew from his store of witty or exciting stories, his full experience and wisdom, Taylor learned more about the principles of mission work than he could ever have gathered by his own observations.

Burns saved Taylor from himself. Rejected by conventional missionaries who identified Christianity with western civilisation, Taylor might have grown into an isolated prig, an individualist adventuring in steadily contracting circles, leaving behind nothing but a few converts and an awkward memory. Burns made him more supple, in adversity less prone to gloom or suppressed rage. Taylor's still impressionable character received from Burns an imprint which never was effaced. 'He is one of those holy men of God one seldom meets with', Taylor eulogised, 'who do possess a single eye to God's glory, and it is no small privilege to labour along with him. He has been wonderfully blessed in England Scotland Canada and Amoy – may he be so here. The secret is easily learned and told, he is a man of prayer – added to which however he possesses an iron frame, and a strong will which would not be easily moved from its purpose.'

The benefit was two-sided. At work together, the Yorkshireman with native dress and hair, the Scot in western clothes covered by a local gown, the peak of his cap cut away to look a little Chinese, the veteran noticed that it was the apprentice who had the quiet crowd and no train of rude boys, and had invitations to gentlemen's homes. Eleven days after first leaving Shanghai with Taylor, Burns 'concluded it was my duty to follow his example', and put on native dress.

In February 1856 the promising partnership seemed about to break.

Coming up from their boats on return from tour, they went to a missionary prayer-meeting at Dr Medhurst's, and heard a sea captain describe the appalling state of distant Swatow. A thousand miles south, almost to the latitude of Hong Kong, Swatow was not a treaty port. On Double Island offshore a western settlement had grown up with the connivance of the Chinese to trade in sugar, opium and coolies – tricked on board by local dealers with tales of fortunes overseas, or kidnapped, to be shipped to virtual slavery in Cuba and South America. The Europeans of Swatow formed an entirely male community openly practising illegal trades. For wild heathen ways, said Captain Bowers, there was little to choose at Swatow between westerners and Chinese, 'and there is no missionary to preach the Gospel'. He would give a free passage to any who would go.

Taylor heard a call. He refused to obey. Leaving Burns could not be right: 'I had never had such a spiritual father'. In tumult of soul he went with Burns one evening to drink tea with an American missionary couple. After the cups had been cleared the young wife sang a long, soulful song, *The Missionary Call*: by other than mid-Victorian standards it was poetically and musically threadbare. 'I had never heard it before,' wrote Taylor in his *A Retrospect*, 'and it greatly affected me. My heart was almost broken before it was finished, and I said to the Lord, in the words that had been sung, "*And I will go! I may no longer doubt to give up friends...*".'

He asked Burns to come home to the house by the South Gate. Closing the door he burst into tears and told of this new call, of his rebellious refusal, capitulation, and desperate sorrow at parting. Before he had finished he was conscious of a look of astonished merriment. Burns confessed he had determined to divulge that very night his regretful decision to leave Taylor. He had heard the Swatow call.

Taylor's first memory of Swatow was an enormous Chinese meal.

They arrived in Captain Bowers' ship on March 12th off Double Island, where the European ships lay in a profusion of furled sails, tar, and sailors sweating, for Swatow is on the edge of the tropics. Having no desire to identify themselves with wicked merchants they took a boat the few miles up to the port, which stood on a promontory. Off the sea front anchored five or six hundred junks: tall, pooped and dragon-headed junks from Canton, lower and graceful vessels from Siam and Indo-China, rough semi-pirates from Formosa, and in the medley of tongues and races jostling on the quays, deep-brown Malays from the far South, Brunei, Sarawak, Java. The town pulsated with action, symbolised by the army of coolies reclaiming land for more shops, warehouses and opium dens.

Captain Bowers' Cantonese supercargo invited the missionaries to join the party he was throwing for local cronies in his favourite eating-house. Taylor wrote: 'Beginning with birds' nests and sharks' fins there must have been forty courses and I never enjoyed a dinner more in my life. But it was well I had learned the use of the chop sticks before or I should not have got much. Each dish came in a sort of tureen of pewter, the cover was taken off and everyone dipped his chop sticks into the dish and took out what he desired, put it into a kind of spoon and ate it coming again or not as he felt inclined. Wine was served in small cups not quite as high as your thimble but broader and containing a small teaspoonful.'

The rest of that day and all the next, returning to the ship at night, they trudged the streets searching for quarters. At last a

Cantonese gentleman, delighted when Burns addressed him in his own dialect, produced an important relative who, with a great show of generosity, secured them a single room over an incense shop, directly under the tiles, without ceiling; the rent, by Shanghai prices, was exorbitant.

They divided the room by sheets and a few boards into three – two bedrooms and a strip of living room. Beds were deal boards, and they rigged a table by placing a box lid across two piles of books. They bought a couple of stools and a bamboo easy chair. Overlooked, and open to the shop below, the rooms attracted scores of eyes reporting every coming and going, every demeanour and action. Nights were often hideous. 'Only 2 nights ago for nearly 2 hours', Hudson told Amelia on March 30th, 'my ear was racked by the most heart-rending screams from two female voices, and on enquiring was told that they were "most likely newly-bought women who being unwilling to become prostitutes would be beaten or otherwise tortured till they submitted".'

'The people are very passionate and unruly.' Taylor had expected southerners to be 'not very lamblike in their dispositions', and a short experience convinced him. Swatow men 'are the least inviting of the Chinese I have yet seen; they seem naturally ill disposed, quarrel among themselves and have no idea of making themselves agreeable to anyone else. They are thorough idolaters, and most superstitious, poor and wretched.' Taller, coarser in build, with high cheek-bones and harsh voices, with 'great force of character and a good deal of push', the people of Swatow in Kwantung were Fukienese by origin. Their dialect was unintelligible to everyone else.

Taylor did not acquire a new dialect easily; for the first two months he battled to understand and be understood. He hated fumbling and groping in an effort to expand the message of his tracts, or to understand and answer questions, hated the restriction imposed by ears and tongue upon heart. 'I do love the Chinese now. It is no sentimentalism – and I know how low they are as a mass, how hardened and prejudiced they are – and no wonder – and I love and pity them. O to be a blessing to them.'

In this moral cesspit where 'men are sunk so low in sin as to have lost the sense of shame... Their rulers and mandarins are as bad as themselves, and instead of governing are governed by money and opium', Taylor felt agitated by the influence of western merchants, all 'Christians' to the Chinese. 'If it be *possible* to be worse than the people, the sailors, captains and traders who reside on and off Double Island are so.' An exception was a doctor called De la Porte, a Christian man who told Taylor that at Swatow, 'it is pleasanter to be among the Chinese than the English'.

Such were the Europeans whom the Chinese presumed typical of their race. Up and down the coast the import of opium and export of coolies, the arrogance, cheating and whoring were far louder advertisements of the character of a Christian nation than the devotion of a handful of missionaries. There were grains of gold in this dross. Taylor, visiting merchant ships on a Sunday, was received sometimes with tears by officers and men: 'many who have a desire to be Christians suffer from contact with evil and want of the means of grace'. When Burns eventually was arrested inland, the urgent pleas of the wicked traders saved him from a horrible death.

The first weeks at Swatow were too wet for exploration of the hinterland. Afterwards the countryside appeared 'exquisitely beautiful'. Picturesque hills of granite enclosed fertile little valleys of rice terraces and sugar cane, banyan trees with great branches and creepers drooping to the ground, aloes and cactus, palms, and bananas which grew barren at Shanghai but here were heavy with fruit. On the hill tops 'we have fir trees which remind one of home'.

Where every prospect pleased, man was vile. 'Dog!' 'Foreign Devil!' echoed in Taylor's ears, though sometimes he met kindness and playfully would be dubbed 'white mouse' or 'young shoot of ginger', because his skin was pale and strong streaks of fair hair showed through the black dye which he had decided not to renew, as too smacking of deceit.

He tried to rent a tiny cottage at a village called To-pu. He went back the next day to take possession. 'One of the first things I saw there was the body of a newly-born infant in the canal. A number of people were bathing within a few yards, and took no notice of it; so little emotion does infanticide cause here.' Next he noticed his intended landlord running up to shoo him away: 'Go back at once! My neighbours will not allow me to let you the house.' He evangelised all day in the village, his servant trembling with anxiety. The people were amazed at Taylor's apparent lack of worry, whether as to shelter or the danger of arrest. They did not know that within him itched the memory of a local man who had been strung up by the Mandarin and all the little bones in his ankles broken with a hammer, one by one. After dark, a Hakka barber offered foreigner and servant a sleeping-place, where Taylor suffered an acute attack of diarrhoea.

Tropical summer heated Swatow. Burns was used to it. Even Chinese dress could not save Taylor from exhaustion, prickly heat and unending perspiration as he sat cabined under the unlined tiles which fizzed if touched. The stench of the night-soil pails seeped through their heavy lids. In May he went off his food: 'the rice got so dry and tasteless I could not get on with it; so now I take tea, eggs and toast to breakfast, and have the rice in the evening only, when it is cool from the sea breeze which comes up'.

June brought the heaviest wet season that local ancients could recall, and made the rooftop room at dusk a menagerie. Fortunately Taylor had not forgotten how to laugh. He would, he told his youngest sister Louisa, answer her last note 'if the mosquitoes, cockroaches (two inches long and flying about in all directions), centipedes, lizards, crickets, flies and all the rest of the tormenters will allow me... Sometimes I stop in the middle of a sentence, kill 3 or 4 fleas and 1 or 2 cockroaches, and then go on again. The other night I felt something very strange in my trousers and looking to see found a centipede two or three inches long'. It bit him on the abdomen. Hudson roared and danced in agony. He dabbed on the swelling some stuff from the medicine chest given by his father, with immediate relief, by which time the Chinese household had hurried in loudly clucking in sympathy. Someone brought a hen, 'what was to be done with it I don't know, but I sent them away telling them of the virtue of my medicine at which they looked reverently enough'.

Dr De la Porte, who later joined Burns as a missionary, subsequently told a public meeting about the twenty-four-year-old Taylor in those months at Swatow. 'I have seen that man come home at the close of the day footsore and weary, his face covered with blisters from the heat of the sun, and throw himself down to rest in a state of utter exhaustion, only to rise again in a few hours to the toil and hardship of another day. It was very evident that he enjoyed the highest respect from the Chinese and was doing a great amount of good among them. His influence was like that of a fragrant flower, diffusing the sweetness of true Christianity around him.'

But Swatow was a by-path, a cul-de-sac. Two inner conflicts had to be resolved.

At Elizabeth's rebuffs, when he was thrown out of Tsungming in December, he had written her a long reply 'to plead my cause and that of the heathen'. The affair dragged on, increasingly one-sided. 'I don't know what I shall do', he wrote to his mother from Swatow on May 30th, 'if I get an unfavourable letter this mail. I sometimes feel as if it would be *more* than I could bear and would quite break me down. But I know it is wrong to give way to such feelings, that does not make it easier to avoid them.'

In another letter home he put his finger on the whole trouble: 'there is something in my nature that seems as if it must have love and sympathy'. Hudson's career had shown his compulsion for love. His muddled attempts to end loneliness had led him to make offers which, if accepted, would have snuffed out the flame of his pioneering zeal. His existence cried aloud to be organised, to be understood; his natural impatience made him flounder about trying to construct a partnership which could come only as a gift.

The other conflict concerned that thorn in his flesh, the Chinese Evangelization Society. Shortly before Taylor came south their latest false move, in all godly, gullible innocence, 'placed me in a nice fix', from which he was rescued only by the kindness of the Shanghai agents 'who have seen something of the porridge they make of business'. Soon after arrival at Swatow he learned that the CES had nothing to send him; he was saved by timely generosity from Mr Berger.

By midsummer 1856, both situations were fast becoming impossible. He agonised over what he should do. Round and round chased desires, fears, puzzlings. Return to England, finish the medical course and qualify? He could not bear to leave the Chinese. Cut away from the Society? His resignation might ruin it. Get married? He could not afford it; Elizabeth would not have him. Go home and plead with her? He could not desert his post.

'The good Lord has hitherto led me blindfold as it were – shown me step by step and not one in advance. His way of getting me out of difficulties has ever proved far better than any I could devise.'

## Chapter 7: ROBBERY – AND AFTER

Burns and Taylor could not secure a preaching hall in Swatow but believed an informal medical mission would provide an opening – a cured Mandarin had told them as much. Taylor found the southern heat trying, and since two Chinese Christian assistants from Amoy had appeared, and a Captain Brown offered a free passage up the coast, he came north in July 1856 to fetch his medicines.

The voyage made him a new man – until he saw the charred ruins of the London Mission godown. Most of his precious instruments and all medical stores in ashes, thirty thousand of the Mission's New Testaments too, but Taylor's personal loss vexed and dismayed him, and shook his confidence in an omnipotent, beneficent God. 'My disappointment and trial were very great.'

Parker might sell surplus replacements at a favourable price. Taylor set off for Ningpo by the canals in the last days of July, a leisurely journey which renewed his spirit; part holiday, part evangelistic tour, delightful because places that had refused his previous ministrations welcomed him. 'I am very well, as well as ever I was in my life, I think, and find my boat as cool and airy as any place can be in hot weather, and in the evenings I get a bathe, swimming about with my swimming belt on and enjoy it famously.'

His stock of tracts ran out after a fortnight, at a town called Shihmenwan, where the level of the Grand Canal precluded further travelling by boat; in the drought the peasants had siphoned water on to their fields. A day's road journey, sixteen miles, would bring him to Haining on Hangchow Bay, where he could take a junk for Ningpo.

The march went wrong from the start. Before sunrise on August 4th Taylor hobbled away by himself in his cramping, blistering Chinese shoes, leaving his new servant, Yoh-hsi, to bring on the coolies. At the first halt, Shihmen, after a tedious wait in a teashop, he saw them straggle in. Their exhaustion was induced by opium. Yoh-hsi wanted to stop at the place all day to visit friends. Taylor refused and walked on. The coolies threw down the loads before reaching the South Gate to the open countryside. Yoh-hsi promised to engage substitutes.

Unwisely Taylor again went ahead. At the next stage, Changwan, he waited. Hour after hour, sipping endless cups of tea, while vendors shouted their wares outside, countrymen trudged past loaded from market and mules kicked and coolies swore. 'I felt somewhat annoyed and but that my feet were blistered and the afternoon very hot, I should have gone back to meet them and urge them on. At last I concluded that my servant must have gone to his friend's, and would not appear until evening. But evening came and still there was no sign of them.'

He made enquiries. He secured reasonably convincing evidence that his party had passed through towards the sea and he had missed them. Darkness and fatigue precluded hurrying after them that night. He must find a bed, and no one would lodge a foreigner. He tried the far end of the town where news of his arrival might not have penetrated, where the darkness would disguise his features and he would not be denounced and arrested.

At a miserable low-class inn he asked what food they offered and was told cold rice, and snakes fried in lamp oil. He did not want awkwardness; he ordered this horrible collation. The rice

was burnt, and his stomach rebelled before he had emptied half
the bowl.

'I suppose I can spend the night here?'

The landlord said yes, and produced a large register, mumbling
about unsettled times, authorities' regulations. 'May I ask your
respected name?'

'My unworthy family name is Tai.'

'And your honourable second name?'

'My humble name is Ia-koh' (the nearest resemblance to James:
Hudson was untranslatable).

'Ia-koh? What an extraordinary name! I never heard it before.
How do you write it?'

Taylor explained the characters and added with a poker face,
'It is a common name in the district I come from.'

The landlord asked questions of his route, and then, 'What
may be your honourable trade?'

'I do not trade. I exhort people to repentance, and heal the
sick, without a charge.'

'Oh, write down "doctor".' He closed the book, to Taylor's
relief. The landlord's wife spoke up: she had a daughter with leprosy. 'If you will cure her, you shall have your supper and bed for
nothing!' The total cost was less than the equivalent of a penny-
halfpenny.

In declining to attempt an instant cure for leprosy he let slip
that he was a foreigner. The landlord said in alarm, 'If you must
stop here, don't tell me you are a foreigner, lest I get into trouble.
I shall put down in the book, "From Shanghai, going to Ningpo".'

That night Taylor slept in a fetid, airless, ground-floor dormi-
tory, eleven 'beds' of planks laid across stools on the bare earth.
Half were already occupied, and the rest filled before midnight, by
snoring Chinese; a close-packed, odiferous nest of homeless coolies, mean wayfarers, and the heavy smell of opium. Hudson could
not undress for fear of theft. He arranged his paper umbrella as
pillow. Despite the close air he soon felt cold. 'The boards were
very hard and the mosquitoes very troublesome, added to which
my pillow was too low and the stiff paper was sharp. To obviate

that, I took one of my shoes off and put it on the umbrella for a pillow, and found it an improvement.'

He rose next morning feeling sick. Nausea worsened during a tedious wait for breakfast. Next he had to haggle wearily because his one coin, a comparatively high-value dollar, had a chip and they would not give full change. He lost nearly twenty-five per cent, carrying away nine hundred little copper 'cash' tied up in a handkerchief. After further fruitless enquiries Taylor set out for Haining, no more than eight miles, but most of it under a pitiless sun, after a bad night's rest, without proper food.

'I got there walking and resting, wearied and footsore, and carrying such a heavy load of cash, it took most of the day.' His spirit sagged. When a sharp shower delayed him at the halfway tea-shop, it was only by forced effort he managed 'to speak a little to the people about the truths of the Gospel'.

He dragged himself into the northern suburb of Haining, was questioned closely by *yamen* runners, tried to follow up a rumour that his bamboo box and bed had been seen. Long after dark, worn out, he engaged a man to search while he bought food in a cook-shop. 'The rice I could not eat so got some rice gruel and managed a bowl of that.' A crowd gathered to watch this unusual foreigner who was actually dressed like a civilised man. Dead tired, Taylor preached.

When the searcher returned empty, they combed the streets for a bed. Two taverns refused because a *yamen* runner shadowed them. A third took him, and Taylor paid off his guide. The 'police' arrived and once more Taylor found himself in the street.

A young man shamed the landlord for his heartless behaviour, and said, 'If we cannot get better lodgings for you, you shall sleep at my house'. Taylor did not notice his shifty eye. They went to a tavern which agreed to give a bed. They brought tea, and he threw off his gown, grateful for shelter at last.

Even as he drank, a face, eerie in the miserable candlelight, peered round the open door. A cry, and a clatter of wooden shoes and bare feet; before Taylor was aware, a crowd had collected to stare and comment. The landlord hurried forward and begged him to withdraw: 'Go and sit in a tea-shop until all is quiet'. The young man led him to a tea-shop where they waited until midnight. Once more he followed the fellow, whose candle-lantern could not give adequate warning of the stones and jagged breaks of the darkened streets, and who, to cap it all, announced that he could not find the tavern. 'He led me about, I feeling every moment I should drop into the earth.' In a distant part of the town, at about one a.m. the man said roughly that the foreign doctor must fend for himself, and disappeared into the night.

A minatory dragon scowled dimly from the curved roof of a temple across the road. Taylor staggered towards it and sank down on the steps beneath. 'It was very cold and damp but I could go no further. I put my money under my head for a pillow, and for a time could not sleep for exhaustion. I was just dozing when I was suddenly awakened by a person by me feeling about, and wanting evidently to take my little all – when I spoke he made off. I saw my money would not do there, so put it in my sleeve and pocket (the latter could not hold more than a third of it) and made a pillow of a stone coping, and should have soon been asleep had not the rascal made his appearance again.'

Hudson lay still, nerves taut, heart thumping. The man groped gently. Hudson silently 'sought protection from Him who alone was my stay'.

'What are you doing?' Hudson spoke almost in a whisper.

The man moved back and sat at Taylor's feet. 'Finding some-where to sleep, like you,' he answered.

'Please go to the other side. There is plenty of room. You will get more fresh air than by stopping close to me.'

A second beggar crept near. Hudson sat up with his back against the wall.

'You had better lie down and sleep,' the beggars fawned, 'or you will be unable to walk tomorrow. Do not be afraid. We shall not leave you. We will see no one hurts you.'

'Listen to me. I do not want your protection. I am not a Chi-nese. I do not rely on stupid idols. I worship God. He is my Father. I trust in Him. I know well what you are and what you want, and I'll keep my eye on you, and I won't sleep.'

One of them went away and returned with a third. Hudson could hear their heavy breathing, see and smell them in the dark. He used to say of this period that he 'fully expected to be murdered in the interior'. Death was very near now: a quick leap by the three, a dagger thrust, and no questions would be asked. For an eternity they played cat and mouse grimly in the bitter cold. If Hudson's head nodded, one would rise softly. Hudson would speak and they sit back. He was not a naturally brave man; this situation required conscious, deliberate facing if his nerve was not to snap. 'As the night slowly passed on, I felt very weary; and to keep myself awake, as well as to cheer my mind I sang several hymns, repeated aloud some portions of Scripture, and engaged in prayer in English, to the great annoyance of my companions, who seemed as if they would have given anything to get me to desist.'

This nice piece of poetic justice won the battle. They left him shortly before dawn and he fell asleep.

He was shaken awake at sunrise by the deceitful young man. 'He was very rude, and insisted on my getting up and paying him for his trouble, and even went so far as to try to accomplish by force what he wanted.' It was too much. The jaded, exhausted Hudson Taylor lost his temper. 'I seized his arm with such a grasp as he little expected I was capable of, and dared him to lay a finger upon me again or to annoy me further.' He did not. Hudson lay still, and angry, until he heard the gun that signalled the opening of the gates, when he rose, and the man begged money to buy opium. After argument Hudson consented to give 'him the price of two candles that he said he had burnt while with me'.

Two or three hours later he no longer doubted his servant had stolen the baggage and deserted. Gone was the travelling bed; that could be replaced. Gone were all Hudson's spare clothes, his two watches, the surgical instruments which had survived the fire, his concertina, Amelia's photograph, two hymn books ('very sorry for the loss') and a Bible given by his mother ten years ago. It would appear that the box also contained money.

Betrayed, indigent, perplexed and hurt, Taylor realised that he

must abandon hope of Ningpo and find his way back to Shanghai.
He had reached the end of his tether. Anyone who told him the
worst was over would have had his head snapped off.

'It was very hot, and my feet were so sore, each foot having
several large blisters, and I was quite weak and weary to begin
with.' The eight miles to Changwan 'seemed very long and took
me a long time to walk, and when I got there I was ready to faint.
I bought some cakes and two eggs and went into a small tea-shop
at the very extremity of the long town, got some hot water, washed
myself and bathed my inflamed feet, had the eggs boiled and made
a very nice meal, the only comfortable one I had had since Sunday', over forty-eight hours.

He slept till four and took the road much refreshed. Tension
began to ease. Before he had done a mile Hudson Taylor's anger
and pain dissolved in a realisation that he had denied his Lord. He
had not prayed for guidance or provision before that awful night
in the open on the temple steps. His loss of temper with the lying
young man was thoroughly unChrist-like. 'I felt condemned, too,
that I should have been so anxious for my few things, while the
many precious souls around me had caused so little emotion. I
came as a sinner and pleaded the blood of Jesus, realising that I
was accepted in Him, pardoned, cleansed, sanctified – and oh
the love of Jesus, how great I felt it to be!'

He thought of the Son of Man who had nowhere to lay His
head; Hudson now knew something of that. He thought of Him at
Jacob's well, weary, hungry and thirsty, yet doing His Father's
will; at Calvary, 'and I felt more than ever I had done before the
greatness of that love which induced Him to leave His home in
glory and suffer thus for me. I contrasted it with the littleness of
my love and was melted in tears'.

Floodwaters of emotion surged in. He bathed in the love of
Jesus. Four miles flitted by as he sought forgiveness, confessing
that he had resented disasters, had expected God to order affairs
at dictation; he begged grace to recognise all circumstances 'as
necessarily the kindest, wisest, best because either ordered or permitted by Him'. Prayer poured out, for himself, his friends, his

colleague, his wicked servant, 'and before I was aware of it I had with a light heart reached my destination... Took a cup of tea, asked about my lost luggage, and spoke of the love of God'.

'At home', he wrote a few weeks later, 'you can never know what it is to be alone – absolutely alone, amidst thousands, as you can in a Chinese city, without one friend, one companion, everyone looking on you with curiosity, with contempt, with suspicion or with dislike. Thus to learn what it is to be despised and rejected of men – of those you wish to benefit, your motives not understood but suspected – thus to learn what it is to have nowhere to lay your head, and then to have the love of Jesus applied to your heart by the Holy Spirit – His holy, self-denying love, which led Him to suffer this and more than this – for *me*; *this is precious, this* is *worth* coming for.'

He was now where he had last spoken with his servant and paid off the opium sots, and into the shop where he was buying native cakes walked one of them. Taylor made him find the servant's friend, whose guarded replies confirmed robbery.

This could not shake Taylor's serenity. A man on a grounded boat outside the city wall offered him space to sleep, 'another token of His ceaseless love and care... The night was again very cold and the mosquitoes troublesome. Still, I got a little rest, and at sunrise was up and continued my journey. I felt very ill at first and had a sore throat, but reflected on the wonderful goodness of God in enabling me to bear the heat by day and the cold by night so long. I felt also that quite a load was now taken off my mind. I had committed myself and my affairs to the Lord, and knew that if it was for my good and for His glory my things would be restored; if not, all would be for the best.'

At the Grand Canal he found no boat going towards Shanghai. 'I scarcely knew what to do! Though my money might do without delays it could not do with them.'

He saw a letter-boat turn into the canal at a junction a few hundred yards up. He chased it as fast as sore feet allowed, a whole mile. The men refused him. Hudson fainted.

He came round with voices in his ears, Shanghai dialect from a trading boat high and dry on the far bank. They sent their skiff to fetch him, gave him tea, bathed his feet, let him rest, and, in marked contrast to behaviour met in previous days, the captain even stood surety when the only available boat proved too expensive for Taylor to pay before Shanghai: a fast, slim, letter-boat express with a crew of two propelling oars with their feet and paddles with their hands, relieved at stages to maintain speed day and night, while Hudson lay exhausted, relaxed and content.

Taylor had lost £40 worth, almost his total assets. He refused the offer of Shanghai missionaries who, kinder perhaps than he had credited, wished to raise a subscription; they had little enough themselves. Something came from the sale of scanty furniture left in the South Gate house. Then the home mail was reported. Taylor hurried to the Consulate. Among envelopes in his mother's precise longhand, Amelia's spindly writing and a few others, was a firm businessman's script which he recognised as Berger's. He tore it open. And was much impressed, but not, since the ecstasy on the road, astonished, to find a cheque, posted months before, for exactly £40, 'a token of love and respect'. In that mail came also an overdue sum of compensation from the shipping company for loss of a box on the voyage out.

Taylor decided not to prosecute the defaulting servant, who when arrested would probably never come to trial but disappear into prison until gaolers had squeezed him dry, or he died. He had wrestled with this man's soul. To cast him into prison was 'not a Christian course'.

He wrote him a straight letter, saying that because of Christ's command 'to return good for evil... [I] would not injure an hair of his head. I told him he was the great loser not I; that I freely forgave him, and exhorted him to flee from the wrath to come'. Taylor did appeal for the return of English books useless to a Chinese. The servant did not profit from this Christianly action. But the letter to England describing it had a decisive effect on Taylor's own life.

He went down to Ningpo safely, enjoyed a rest, rejected the temptation to stay indefinitely among delightful missionaries and friendly Chinese. 'My present position calls me to a more arduous post, to pioneer work, and in my dear devoted brother Mr Burns I have an inestimable companion whom I shall rejoice to meet again.'

He never saw him again. Delay after delay hindered departure from Shanghai, until, about to embark on October 9th, he received a message from Burns, under arrest, and being sent to Canton, urging him to abandon the voyage; alone at Swatow he would be ineffectual and in danger. Indeed, had they known it, the attack on the *Arrow* which caused war between China and England had occurred the day before. Burns eventually established a permanent mission at Swatow, worked later in Peking, and died in Manchuria in 1868.

Taylor had brought with him from Ningpo a new colleague of the CES, John Jones, whose small son had needed medical treatment in Shanghai. Jones had fallen ill on the trip and Taylor therefore escorted him back, unaware of what awaited in Ningpo.

The robbery which thus led Taylor to Ningpo had a further influence.

The principle linked above any with the name of Hudson Taylor is that of 'Living by Faith', the attitude illustrated by his famous remarks: 'Depend upon it, God's work done in God's way will never lack supplies', and 'You must not look to the Mission but to God'. Because of Taylor's youthful experiments in England it is sometimes believed he went to China wedded already to this principle. Nothing could be further from the facts. Certainly in the storm off the Welsh coast which nearly wrecked the *Dumfries* he suffered scruples about putting on a life-jacket as showing lack of faith in God's power to intervene, but he soon laughed at such extravagance. 'I believe I can trust the Lord in some respects as much or more than ever I could, but I am a good deal modified in some of my views and do not think it right to neglect proper precautions.'

He came out to China like any other missionary. 'They promised me a fixed salary before I left England, a sum was named for my private use; if it proved insufficient they promised an increase. They gave me power to draw money, but for two years my almost monthly repeated question as to the amount of private salary has been disregarded and only noticed once, and that as a complaint that I seemed to be thinking too much about money. Since September '54 I have received nothing from then till this mail, £25.' That was written from Ningpo in December 1856. (A further £25 was said to have gone to Swatow and astray; the agreed sum had been £70 a quarter.) He would have been destitute had not his expenses fallen sharply when he adopted Chinese dress and learned to live on a level of bare subsistence; and had not Berger sent continual unsolicited gifts.

The CES was in debt. Taylor believed no Christian, certainly no Christian mission, should live and work on borrowed money. 'To me it seemed that the teaching of God's Word was unmistakably clear: "Owe no man any thing." To borrow money implied, to my mind, a contradiction of Scripture – a confession that God had withheld some good thing, and a determination to get for ourselves what He had not given.' Although deep in debt the CES sent the Joneses, with four small children, to China. And sent them so ill-provided that to get to Ningpo they had to depend on missionaries at Shanghai, which rocked at the scandal.

During the winter of 1856-57 Taylor knew he must resign. He worried over the future. 'I often wish now I was connected with some older organised body than the CES. I doubt whether it will continue much longer.' 'Is it right for me to allow my best years to pass over without some attempt to improve my position which might leave me at any moment penniless on a foreign shore, without means to go home and without any trade or profession to turn to? ...neither a minister nor a doctor, to what society can I look in case of my own failing me? ...I almost suspect I shall have to come home to qualify.' As late as March 1857 he had thoughts of applying to another society.

The arrival of Berger's £40 by the next mail after the robbery, however, had planted a seed in his mind which slowly germinated.

In March or April 1857 Taylor received another windfall – from George Müller, his hero of the Bristol orphanage who 'lived by faith'. Müller had seen a copy of the letter about the robbery and the refusal to prosecute. Always on the alert for suitable recipients for the money which came to him in answer to prayer, he sent out £40 to cover the loss, and told Taylor he would pray for him in future.

Müller's gift, what he knew of Müller's outlook and experiences, brought to bud the germinating thought. Müller had given spontaneously because he had learned facts which prompted action by a man of faith and prayer. Taylor believed that the prompting, of Berger before and Müller after the robbery, was not human but divine. He was beginning to understand that God promises to be a Heavenly Father, who 'knoweth that ye have need', that a Father in Heaven can be relied upon for necessities as surely and as simply as a father on earth.

Taylor resigned from the CES. He did so in fear and trembling. 'I was not at all sure', he wrote years later in his fragment of autobiography, *A Retrospect*, 'what God would have me to do, or whether He would so meet my need as to enable me to continue working as before'. Berger could not necessarily be relied upon, for Taylor did not feel he should reveal his financial position to man. He wanted 'to give up all my time to the service of evangelisation' and could live on a pittance; if God did not supply his gifts, he was ready to undertake 'whatever work might by necessary to supply myself', using all spare time for 'more distinctly missionary efforts'.

In 1857 Hudson Taylor, turning twenty-five, had no grandiose view that this was the way to run a mission; nor did he think that other missionaries should abandon regular salaries. It was a decision purely personal and individual, though in fact Parker and Jones followed his lead. The break with the CES was without bitterness. The missionaries continued to send reports for *The Gleaner* and did not refuse money from the Society, which by failure to fulfil obligations could be considered in debt to the three men – not that they pressed for payment. The derelict Society died in about a year, its misdemeanours redeemed by Pearse, the Secretary, long afterwards going himself to China.

'My soul has been much blessed in connection with the step', Taylor wrote on 3rd July 1857, 'and I am very thankful that I have been led to take it. My position was anomalous. If asked if I had a fixed salary or not, I could neither say yes nor no, without qualification or more explanation than I could in propriety make.'

It was courageous: all the more so because he had fallen head over heels in love – and not with the Sissons.

## Chapter 8: THE GIRL WITH A SQUINT

Ningpo, within six miles of ivy-clad walls dominated by an ancient pagoda, stood at a fork twelve miles from the sea, the normal position of Chinese coastal cities, secure from pirates and foreign foes. Its network of streets better built than many, Ningpo had also an International Settlement and a hinterland of deep green woods, placid lakes, canals, sheltered villages, rising to the tea gardens of the Western Hills, bright in spring with azaleas, wisteria, hawthorn and lilac. Its people, tall and strong, spoke a dialect akin to Mandarin and were noted for both literary and commercial prowess.

The missionary community were not slothful in business, were fervent in spirit and, on the surface, kindly affectioned one to another with brotherly love. The Church Missionary Society, the American Presbyterians and the American Baptists owned spacious compounds, scattered schools and chapels. Dr Parker had bought for his projected hospital a strategic site on the river bank between city and settlement, a contrast to his present home lapped on three sides by paddy fields, overlooking a dreary cemetery. The Joneses rented a semi-native house.

Into this hive of faith and good works, with its nicely ordered gradings of seniority, of experience, of social background, had stepped little Hudson Taylor, with his Chinese clothes and now distinctly piebald pigtail. He joined the Joneses in mission work, but by this time had a reputation for meandering around China without denomination or settled purpose. 'A mystic absorbed in religious dreams, waiting to have his work revealed' was the memory of W A P Martin, afterwards one of the greatest American missionary educationalists. 'Not idle, but aimless. When he had money he spent it on charity to needy Chinese, and then was reduced to sore straits himself. When the vocation found him it made him a new man, with iron will and untiring energy.'

Parker used an old hall for services and school, a broad room spanned by heavy beams supported by a central row of timber pillars, black and worn with age. He gave Taylor the attic above. As in Swatow, this bare home possessed no ceiling. The tiles were proof against rain but not against snow flurries. A canal on one side, its little bridges edged by potted shrubs, and low roofs on the other made 'a quaint view but smelly and dirty... relentless smells and noises of street in front and canal behind and the boys' school below'. 'I am very comfortable here. And having gone to the expense and trouble of papering my room look, as well as feel, quite snug and tidy. And to add to my comforts, Mrs Cobbold is going to lend me her concertina!!!' For scanty leisure as for work, Taylor became part of the menage of John Jones and his wife, capable, merry, of good background. 'I find more real companions and sympathy in the Jones' than I have done since I left home, only excepting Mr Burns.'

Once a week they all dined at the school run by the *grande dame* of Ningpo. Miss Mary Ann Aldersey was a tiny little Englishwoman, nearly sixty, who when no longer young had betaken herself, with immense verve, and private means, to Java; after the opening of treaty ports she became the first woman missionary to China. 'She was a remarkable and somewhat eccentric character', Hudson Taylor recalled towards the end of his life. 'She was a very earnest missionary but so peculiar as to somewhat alarm the Chinese.' She walked the walls at five a.m. precisely, rain or fine, summer light or winter dark, and she climbed the pagoda in hot weather to sniff sea breezes; the Chinese thought her a witch. She exerted upon them an enormous influence for good.

She had a decided sense of the proper, and she ruled her two young helpers. Burella and Maria Dyer had been committed to Miss Aldersey's protection, though the legal guardian remained Uncle William Tarn in England. As if to make a pack of Happy Families, Samuel Dyer's widow (née Maria Tarn) having married Mr Bausum and then died, Mr Bausum had married Miss Poppy, a young missionary in Borneo, and then died; and Mrs Bausum (née Poppy) arrived in Ningpo a few weeks after Hudson Taylor in the autumn of 1856, to take over the school on Miss Aldersey's imminent retirement.

This was the household, *grande dame*, young ladies, Mrs Bausum, at which Hudson dined.

A marrying spirit was abroad. To top it, John Burdon from Shanghai had got engaged to Burella. Maria, whom Hudson casually described in a home letter as 'despite the slightest cast of the eye, a good looking girl', who was reputed to be devoted to her calling and the second-best Chinese speaker in the community, had already refused young Robert Hart of the Consular service, afterwards the great Sir Robert of the Chinese Customs. She had laughed away a Shanghai missionary, but he was rumoured to be renewing the attempt.

Hudson complained to Amelia, who was about to marry Benjamin Broomhall, 'Everybody seems to be successful in these matters including you, while I alone have to wait in doubt. I hope this mail when it comes in may bring me a letter from dear Elizabeth... but I am thinking that if there were no Elizabeth, bachelors have the best of it after all but with Liz there can be no two opinions, *she* is *such* a treasure.'

Elizabeth Sissons had refused him twice. He would not take no for an answer.

Maria Dyer, she of the squint, wrote to her student brother Samuel in London concerning these autumn days: 'I met a gentleman and, I cannot say I loved him at once, but I felt interested in him and could not forget him. I saw him from time to time and still this interest continued. I had no good reason to think it was reciprocated, he was very unobtrusive and never made any advances.' She said she was led to take the matter at once to God.

On Christmas Day 1856 the Reverend Frederick Gough of the CMS and his wife gave a party to all the English missionaries, sitting down fifteen. 'We had a famous dinner – beef and plum pudding', wrote Taylor, 'and in the afternoon the Misses Dyer enlivened us playing some duets on Mr Gough's pianoforte, a very superior one, so with the party and my mail I had quite a treat.' He thought Gough 'one of those to whom is to love and be loved', and liked Mrs Gough because she reminded him of Elizabeth.

The day after Christmas he confessed in his home mail that despite Elizabeth's decided refusal, hope lingered. 'At times I have felt so discouraged at this and some other things that I have felt quite dispirited and even thought of giving up the missionary work, for her father said if I were living in England he would have no objection.' The excuse for return would be to complete his medical studies. He regretted profoundly his lack of a diploma. 'I ought to have had one at all costs.' But when he thought now of return to England, a blight crept over his prayers.

Hudson consulted Mrs Jones, who did not know of the Sissons's existence. Mrs Jones snapped her fingers at desertion, said he needed a wife, offered to use her influence with Maria Dyer, 'of whom', noted Hudson, 'I know nothing really', except for her squint, her fluency in Chinese and her zeal. 'This is all very well, I say, but' – how could he afford a wife of her social standing when he could not afford to live European style as a bachelor? Mrs Jones answered with a slice of Hudson's own doctrine, 'The Lord supplies your need now, and if your need gets greater, so will the supplies'. Taylor agreed, but it was of no use. Mentally and spiritually he was on a switchback; 'these outward affairs disturb my peace of mind and lessen my usefulness'.

In fact, he deceived Mrs Jones. He told naught of strange feelings unlike any evoked by Miss Vaughan or Miss Sissons. 'Ere I was aware of it', he recalled a few months later, 'my acquaintance with Miss M Dyer ripened into an attachment, which, as soon as I perceived, far from encouraging though unable to repress it, I strove to confine the knowledge of it to my own bosom.' Miss Aldersey penetrated his defences at once.

Maria, meanwhile, in the first days of January, had a tender talk with Mrs Bausum. 'I told her she would perhaps think me very foolish but explained to her my feelings towards Mr Taylor. She said she had not seen anything which would lead her to think that he was interested in me, and remarked that it was a dreadful thing to love without the love being returned.'

The Anglo-Chinese War took a hand. Threats, plots, rumours induced the Consul to order women and children to evacuate Ningpo for Shanghai. Miss Aldersey cried fiddle-de-dee and contented herself with keeping handy two coolies and an empty coffin in which she could be smuggled to the hills. The Misses Dyer elected to stay, all the Joneses to go. Hudson Taylor, as an unattached and not particularly necessary male, was persuaded, against his inclinations, to travel as one of the escort. On January 26th Maria waved farewell to the steamer *Japan*.

Maria: 'Before he left I had some little reason, perhaps, to think that he might be interested in me but I thought I had better not be too sanguine. I still continued to make the subject a matter of prayer.'

Hudson: '[My] state of feeling was one of great anxiety and pain ... Still I did not move in the matter, and in the latter part of January went up to Shanghai, making it a matter of prayer as before.'

Hudson was riding two mares. All January and February 1857 he considered himself bound to Elizabeth if she accepted his open offer, but she would not write. On March 1st he told his mother: 'The sooner this is settled the better... Propriety and self-respect preclude my continuing a correspondence I have already protracted too long'. This tune sounded different from that of seven months before, when he had written, 'We are both young and I can afford to *wait* another year but I cannot afford to lose her'.

He had sent home regular bulletins about Elizabeth. Of Maria, not a word. Desires lay too deep for exposure. Privately he thought her 'a dear sweet creature, has all the good points of Miss S and many more too. She is a precious treasure, one of sterling worth and possessed with an untiring zeal for the good of this poor people. She is a *lady* too...' As for the 'decided cast in one of her eyes, very noticeable', it was now not a defect but doubly dear, 'for I felt it gave me some chance of winning her'. To his wonder, his gratitude, his agony of anticipation and fear of failure, every quality looked for in a missionary wife had been found in the most adorable girl in the world.

Not until mid-April did Hudson receive from Elizabeth Sissons a reply which enabled him honourably to close the correspondence. 'I have quite dismissed the matter as a settled question. I am thankful it has been ordered as it has.'

Indeed so, for he had jumped the gun. On March 23rd he had written a letter to Maria enclosed in a cover note to Frederick Gough.

Gough's reply, dated Ningpo, April 10th, after remarking that the letter had been 'more than a fortnight in reaching me!' assured Taylor that 'Except for myself and my dear wife who executed your commission the next morning, your matter will be breathed to no one here. You have *our* sympathy and our frequent prayers. I know, dear brother, something of all the experience you speak of: the Lord Jesus made such a season to myself the occasion of much *personal manifestation of Himself.*'

At Ningpo on the morning of April 8th, Maria, fresh 'from a short pleasure excursion into the country' (danger had temporarily receded) taught in the tree-lined American Presbyterian compound where Mrs Bausum had removed the school. Miss Aldersey had retired to live with the ruling couple of the CMS, the Russells. She was not of the Church of England, but Mrs Russell had been her ward.

A servant slipped into the classroom. Maria came out to see what Mrs Gough wished. 'She put into my hands two letters which she said had come the day before, one directed to myself and the other, in which it had been enclosed to Mr Gough. She said that those letters were all that she and Mr Gough knew about the matter, that they had prayed for us both and she begged me not to send a refusal until I had prayed over the matter. I guessed from what she said what the purport of them was.'

Maria slipped the letters into her satchel and returned to the class. She did not know Hudson's handwriting and feared they were from the suitor she had laughed at. She had 'to go on with my school engagements as if nothing had happened or was going to happen. When school was over I retired to my room. Before opening the letters I prayed over them. I had a sort of hope that they might be from Mr Taylor but I could not think that they were – that was not likely.'

The word 'Swatow' in the cover letter to Gough gave a clue. She looked at the signature and her heart leaped. 'I then opened my own letter and read of his attachment to me, and how he believed God had given him that love for me which he felt. I could hardly understand that it was a reality. It seemed that my prayers were indeed answered (and who can say that they were not?), he asked me to consent to an engagement to him. He begged me not to send him a hasty refusal which he intimated would cause him the intensest anguish, and concluded by expressing the hope that ere long all his doubts and fears would be removed and his fondest hopes realised. He signed himself my most sincerely and affectionately, James Hudson Taylor.'

She completed that day in a golden dream. Next morning she told Burella, and called on Miss Aldersey.

'I have received a letter from Mr Taylor.'

'I presume you would not think of accepting him?'

Maria, dashed, respectfully asked to be excused yielding at once to her advice, 'as the matter seemed to me to be so much of divine direction'.

'Mr Taylor? That young, poor, unconnected Nobody! How dare he presume to think of such a thing?'

'But – '

'But he is not a *gentleman*. He is without education, without position.'

'But – '

'He is a ranter. He is a canting Plymouth Brother. He does not keep the Sabbath' (an odd idea of Miss Aldersey's for he was as much a Sabbatarian as any of the Church missionaries or herself, but happened to call the day 'Sunday' or 'the Lord's Day'). 'He has been connected with a *most* peculiar missionary' (that is, Burns). 'He is short, you are tall. And – and, he wears Chinese clothes!' Her nose wrinkled. 'Sit down at that desk! Daring to ask your hand when you are not of age.'

'Might I write to my uncle?'

'Quite unnecessary, my dear, he would say as I say. Now we will write to Mr Taylor.'

Maria was forced to take paper, forced to pen words which not only were deceitful but blasphemous.

'My dear Sir... I have made the subject of your letter a matter of earnest prayer to God, and have desired I think sincerely only to know *His* will and to act in accordance with it. And though it does indeed give me no pleasure to cause you pain, I must answer your letter as appears to me to be according to God's direction. And it certainly appears to be my duty to decline your proposals. But think not dear sir that I do so carelessly, and without appreciating the kind feelings which you express toward me. And I have too great a respect for those feelings (although my duty requires me entirely to discourage them) to expose you and the subject of your letter to ridicule... I regard you dear sir as a brother in Jesus and hope ever to bear towards you those feelings which disciples are commanded to bear one towards another. But ask me not for more. I request you not to refer to the subject again as I should be obliged to return you the same answer.'

Miss Aldersey, standing over her shoulder, probably remarked as they sprinkled the ink with sand, 'He will never return to Ningpo after *that*'.

'O dear Samuel,' Maria wrote to her student brother in London months afterwards, 'those days were days of trial indeed. It seemed to me God had manifestly answered my prayers and it seemed to be His will that Mr Taylor and I should love each other and yet Miss Aldersey so strongly opposed it – it seemed as if God's will and Miss Aldersey's were opposite...'

She dreamed of her beloved: his love for the Chinese, his devotion to Christ, his merry nature, blue eyes, love of music; she was not sure about the Chinese dress, but what he had adopted must be right. Certainly he was a little gauche but he was genuine. As to his education, 'the mind is the stature of the man, and his intellectual capacities are by no means of an inferior nature... It seems to me that Mr Taylor is just the sort of person as my dear father were he living would approve of for me'.

She tried to believe that Miss Aldersey acted from desire for the best 'and to appreciate her kindness, though it seems very, *very* difficult to do so'.

Even a touching little note from Frederick Gough could not assuage Hudson's sore heart. 'I am tried almost beyond my strength to bear', he wrote on May 15th to Amelia, who could not be told about Maria. Detained in Shanghai by the Jones's desire to wait for a family from England, he threw himself into famine relief, preaching, itinerating. He saw one ray of hope: Maria had refused him 'on the simple ground of *duty*'. And he 'strongly suspected that the hindrance lay with Miss Aldersey'.

At the end of June they all returned to Ningpo, somewhat inappropriately coinciding with a brutal, if deserved, attack on Portuguese semi-pirates who had infuriated the Cantonese colony, had been refused protection at the British Consulate, and had run to the graveyards, to be pulled out and hacked to pieces. The fortuitous arrival of a French warship prevented a general massacre of all foreigners.

Hudson did not go back to the attic but made his home with the Jones. 'Well', runs his letter which eventually revealed the whole story to his mother, 'Miss Aldersey got into a great stew when I came down, went to Mrs Gough's and made her promise not to promote our meetings or help the matter on. Then she came to Mrs Jones... She spoke most indignantly to Mrs Jones about it. How dare he dream of such a thing? "Why of course," replied Mrs Jones, "he could do no other." "He has no society behind him; friends may die." Mrs Jones full of indignation, told her that such attachments were made in heaven and that it was a very serious thing to try and interfere.' However, lest Maria be forbidden her house, or city-visiting in her company, Mrs Jones agreed not to push the affair. She stoutly refused to maintain secrecy and made haste to tell Hudson.

After seeking advice from the Goughs he decided to see Miss Aldersey. Maria says she 'avoided calling at Mrs Jones and he had too much good feeling to intrude himself upon me. So that though we often saw each other, not a word or a look was exchanged between us.'

The interview of July 13th was polite but strained. Miss Aldersey positively declined to move an inch from regarding him as a thoroughly undesirable and impertinent suitor. Hudson learned of Miss Aldersey's deep offence, with good reason in the light of Victorian conventions, that he had not sought her permission before writing. He learned that she had virtually dictated the reply, that Maria had not attained, as he supposed, her majority, having been born at Malacca on 16th January 1837. And, most important, he discovered that Miss Aldersey was not the legal guardian. She had written to Mr Tarn since Mr Taylor's return; Miss Maria Dyer of course had not. Miss Aldersey's objections would be removed only if Mr Tarn gave consent. A most improbable expectation, she ventured to add.

Hudson Taylor digested this information for a week, during which Maria took matters into her own hands and sent off a letter to follow Miss Aldersey's on the long journey to her uncle and aunt in England: 'I do not wish to throw myself away, which Miss Aldersey seems to think I should do by marrying Mr Taylor. Nor would I wish to unite myself to a man such as she *thinks* Mr Taylor to be. But I desire his character and principles to be sifted.' A closing paragraph breathed unaffected piety: 'Though I sometimes feel that the greatest earthly pleasure that I desire is to be allowed to love the individual whom I have mentioned so prominently in my letter, and to hold the closest and sweetest intercourse with him spiritually as well as temporally that two fellow mortals can hold, I desire that he may not hold the first place in my affections. I desire that Jesus may be to me the chiefest among ten thousand, the altogether lovely.' Both Maria and Hudson had been taking refuge in The Song of Songs.

Hudson knew that he must ask Maria's permission before approaching her uncle. On Monday morning, 20th July, in Maria's account, 'Burella and I were going to take a few of the children to Mrs Gough's for a treat. We were all standing by the street door when a note was brought in directed to me and the bearer said that a foreign gentleman was outside. I opened the note and saw it was from Mr Taylor, requesting a few words.' Maria had been suffering her one serious qualm, 'for who was I that I should set myself up against Miss Aldersey and old established Christians?' The note threw her into agitation. 'I allowed Mrs Bausum and Burella to read it and I told Mrs Bausum she should decide as the lady of the house whether Mr Taylor and I should have the interview or not. Burella very strongly opposed it thinking Miss Aldersey would not approve of it. As I had placed it in Mrs Bausum's hands she did not like to allow it, when Burella was so strongly opposed to it. So it was thought best that we should proceed to Mrs Gough's leaving Mr Taylor with Mrs Bausum.' Maria heard his voice. Mrs Bausum asked him upstairs, was very kind, made excuses, dropped hints, so that 'I think he must have left the house that morning with a lighter heart in one respect than he had had for some time'.

Maria prayed secretly that 'if it was God's will, if it was not wrong, we might have an interview'. She was tempted to concoct an encounter, 'but I preferred that it should be of God's overruling and not of my arranging'.

Two afternoons later the Ladies' Prayer Meeting took place that week at the Joneses. Men stayed well away. Hudson and John Jones had heavy work among opium addicts. The weather brewed suffocatingly sultry and sticky, a typhoon in the offing; several ladies absented themselves and the rest might be excused lethargy in their prayers. During tea and gossip afterwards a waterspout swept up the river from the sea and burst over the city. Streets flooded, coolies unable to bring sedan chairs; chaos, delays. The two men were later than usual returning, to find the girls' school servant still outside, from whom they learned that Mrs Bausum and Maria were within, waiting for their chair, but not the opposing Burella.

Maria chatted with Mrs Jones. 'Mr Jones came into the room and called me aside, saying he wished to speak to me a moment. I went with him out of the room when he said, "Mr Taylor begs that you will allow him to have an interview with you". I said, 'It is what I of all things wish and I think it is remarkable that I prayed if it was God's will, we might have an interview. Is it to be private or may another person be in the room?" He said, "It is to be as you wish." I said, "I should like Mrs Bausum to be present." Mrs Bausum was called and we were shown into Mr Jones's study. After a few minutes Mr Taylor came in.'

In the next moments both knew, by look, sense, the feel of a handshake, that love was mutual. 'We remarked' (in Maria's words) 'that if it was God's will the matter would be brought to a favourable issue, and if it was not His will, nobody wished it. It was suggested that we should pray together and we all three knelt down and Mr Taylor engaged in prayer.'

Hudson sent a letter to William Tarn by the more expensive route, overland via Trieste, to beat Miss Aldersey's fortnight's start. No answer could be expected before late November, possibly not until December. Four long months at least. It might be negative.

Mrs Gough advised Maria to tell Burella and Miss Aldersey of the unexpected meeting and that she had written home. 'You know dearest we never really lose by being straightforward.' Maria did so. The volcano erupted.

On the morning of Monday 27th July, the Reverend W A Russell (afterwards first Bishop in North China), a founder and now leader of the Church Mission, called on Hudson Taylor. Russell was an Irishman who expected to be obeyed. He carried a letter for Taylor from Miss Aldersey. A formal and a furious letter in the third person: 'By attempting to see Maria he had been determining if possible to take advantage of her youth to induce her to trample on the prohibition which had been laid upon her by... one who well knew what would have been the parents' view on the subject. That interview prevented', she continued, dropping the third person, 'you subsequently had recourse to an expedient which I can regard in no other light than *disgraceful*. In the absence of myself and of the elder sister you have availed yourself of a meeting convened exclusively for religious exercises among the ladies of the missionary circle, to obtrude upon Miss Maria Dyer the forbidden subject. While I am astonished at the offensive indecorum of this last step (with all other like acts) makes my path of duty more clear... If you persist in continuing your addresses, not awaiting the permission of Miss Dyer's aunt I shall be constrained to take steps of a more formidable character...'

There was much more, in such unkind terms that Mrs Jones when shown it became quite ill. Russell demanded, in Miss Aldersey's name, an Explanation; and in the approved manner told Hudson he 'ought to be horse-whipped'. (Miss Aldersey to Maria, in a cruel, undated note: 'Not only Mr Russell but all the missionary brethren to whom he has spoken in this grievous affair are exceedingly indignant at the conduct of Mr Taylor and are pretty well agreed in the opinion expressed to Mr Taylor by the mild and temperate Mr Russell that a man acting as Mr Taylor "ought to be horsewhipped")'.

When he had finished reading, Hudson defended his character, motives and actions to Russell. He kept his temper. 'I did not tell him that I had learned of the agony Miss Maria Dyer had suffered when Miss Aldersey had *compelled* her to reject my proposals. No! there are some things which it makes one indignant to *think* of and much more is it unsafe to *speak* of them.' Russell said he could 'in no way recognise him as a Christian. He was no gentleman either'. Mrs Russell had orders to cut him dead. As Hudson complained to his mother, 'Why? Because I don't think a maiden lady qualified to judge in love affairs.'

One remark of Russell's explained much of the opposition though scarcely condoning the cruelty: 'If you go home to England and take a medical degree, or be ordained, we should all take you by the hand'. John Burdon, as her future brother-in-law and Taylor's friend, told Maria that a few months before in Shanghai Taylor 'was most exercised on the point whether it was not his duty to go home and remove his anomalous position either by taking his diploma as a medical man or receiving ordination... He felt keenly then that as he said *he was nothing* and I strongly advised him, as well as others who highly valued him as a missionary brother, to go home for a short time. *Now*, I think his affection for you is another call to him to pursue this course and if he is unwilling for your sake to do it, I would think him unworthy of your heart and hand. Both of you are young yet, and neither would be losers but, believe me, a great gainer by this deferring of the matter for two or three years... I do not say give him up. I do not dwell on the little peculiarities or faults that I may have noticed in him.'

Maria's answer showed the spirit of the girl: 'I would wait if he went home in order to increase his usefulness. But is he to leave his work in order to gain a *name* for the sake of marrying me? If he loves me more than Jesus he is not worthy of me – if he were to leave the *Lord's* work for the *world's* honour, I would have nothing further to do with him.' 'She *is* a noble girl,' was Hudson's comment.

Miss Aldersey and her allies were bent on extinguishing Maria's love before Tarn's reply could reach Ningpo. 'Once more I come to you dear Maria as your faithful monitor', runs one of a series of notes from Miss Aldersey, 'warning you against the mad step to which a strange infatuation characterised by and endorsed by religious romance appears to be hastening you'. To Maria's plea that she had prayed about it, and believed marriage to Hudson a call of the Holy Spirit as well as of her own heart, Miss Aldersey had a short answer: 'Why not see the answer to your prayers in the wishes of your friends? Do you expect a voice from heaven?' She threatened to keep her captive under her own eye. Russell would refuse her the sacrament 'until you should give evidence of repentance'. Hudson told his mother on August 8th that 'dear Maria is charged with being a maniac, being fanatical, being indecent, weak-minded, too easily swayed; too obstinate and everything else bad'. She was harried and harassed until faith nearly snapped and sickness weakened her.

Had Maria disliked Miss Aldersey the price might have been

less. She had loved and respected her, and worked hard to heal the breach. Miss Aldersey was implacable. When Maria one Sunday that autumn, leaving church, sought impulsively to kiss her protectress, Miss Aldersey not only humiliated her publicly but forced a written apology. 'O dear Samuel', cried Maria to her distant brother, 'I have suffered persecution for righteousness' sake. And the persecution (if I may call it so) coming from the quarter it does has staggered me, for Miss Aldersey, how should she be in the wrong and I in the right?'

Hudson tried to be fair. 'There is a good deal to be said in excuse for one now about 60, with failing memory, who has always ruled supreme over a large establishment and been spoiled by the deference and flattery shown her. She cannot brook contradiction – was offended by my not first asking *her* leave – and does not believe in prayer, trusting in God, etc, etc, in the way *He* has taught us to do. And as it is only grace that makes us to differ, if indeed better in any point, there is no room for boasting.'

The lovable Frederick Gough, who discerned seeds of greatness in the man whom nearly all European Ningpo dismissed as 'fanatical, undependable, diseased in body and mind, totally worthless', advised his young friends that, 'however painful or trying', their duty lay in not attempting to meet or communicate until Tarn's verdict. If Miss Aldersey took Taylor to law the scandal would 'cause offence and hindrance to the work of *our* Lord here'. Taylor agreed. 'Dear girl it is very trying to be thus separated from her, but so it must be for the time at least.' He threw himself into mission work, famine relief, teaching, answering questions, tract-distributing, doctoring, quite unable to stop during the last and worst of the summer heat of 1857, until in early September he fell seriously ill.

During a month in bed, enforced passivity made him meditate. It was then he adopted as mottoes, painting the equivalent Chinese ideographs on scrolls, two Hebrew place-names which the Old Testament not only records but explains: *Eben-ezer* and *Jehovah-jireh*. These ancient, queer-sounding names were potent to Taylor. He read in the seventh chapter of the First Book of Samuel that after a great victory given in immediate answer to prayer, Samuel raised a memorial stone 'and called the name of it Eben-ezer, saying Hitherto hath the Lord helped us'. Taylor read also in the twenty-second chapter of Genesis that where the Lord had stayed Abraham from sacrificing Isaac and had provided a ram, 'Abraham called the name of that place Jehovah-jireh.'[1]

If cast down, or anxious Taylor looked at his scrolls. 'My faith... often, often failed, and I was so sorry and ashamed of my failure to trust such a Father. But oh! I was learning to know Him... He became so real and intimate.'

## Chapter 9: RUSSELL GOES SHOOTING

An American bachelor missionary early in October 1857 caught smallpox in its most virulent, painful, revolting form. None of his society nor his sister dared nurse him to his inevitable death; they had children. Hudson Taylor, scarcely convalescent, volunteered. A decision not of compassion only but of faith; he had been vaccinated yet recognised this smallpox as highly infectious, the vaccine uncertain, his resistance already lowered through illness. And he knew he would marry Maria.

When the tortured body had been buried Taylor could not emerge from isolation because he must destroy all infected clothes and had no money with which to order new: as Dr Martin said, he was always giving away what he received, and had lately sent £37 to a missionary in distress. At this precise point of need a box of clothes given up as lost arrived from Swatow.

He did not escape infection, which induced a high fever but without a legacy of permanent pox. Miserably ill, he slept fitfully. In the early hours of October 20th, 'at 3 a.m. I heard a noise which awoke me and caused me to get up very much alarmed. You will judge of the state of my nervous system when I tell you I could not bear the sound of my watch lying at the other end of the room and had to have it wrapped up. Well I could not get to sleep again and read a little in my Bible and then laid down with my

[1]The Lord will see, or, provide.

eyes shut but my heart fluttering like a frightened bird and my mind too excited to sleep. All at once I became conscious of the presence of dear Maria. She came in noiselessly as a breath of air and I felt such tranquillity steal over me – I knew she must be there. I felt spellbound for a short time but at length without opening my eyes I put out my hand and she took it so tenderly and with such a soft warm grasp that I could not refrain from a look of gratitude. She motioned me not to speak and put her other hand on my forehead and I felt the headache which was distracting, and the fever, retire before it, and sink as through the pillow. She whispered softly to me not to fear nor be uneasy, she was my Maria and I her dear Hudson...' He slipped from half-awake dream into deepest sleep, to awaken in broad daylight soothed in mind, the fever broken: 'all my fear in the fever had been that our love would be in vain'.

Reverie dissolved at prostrating news: Maria would shortly leave for a month in Shanghai, with Burella after her honeymoon. This scheme appeared a nefarious plot. 'I know,' Hudson wailed, 'they *hope* to keep her longer and that thus the affair may be kept in abeyance or broken off. If I could but have an interview with her – but how I know not – she is wretched like I don't know what. God can give me one however if it is His will.'

He did. When Hudson walked weakly across to Mrs Bausum's cosy brown house in the Presbyterian compound, to pour his troubles into her sympathetic ear, he heard that Maria unexpectedly was there, 'but I must not see her. I begged very hard but in vain for fear of a row and Mrs Bausum went out to tell her not to come. Scarcely had she gone when by another door dear Maria entered and so I got an interview. It has so helped me, you don't know how much better I feel for it'. They could not have been together more than a minute, but she told him never would she leave Ningpo without him.

Throughout the wearisome wait for Tarn's reply the lovers were not engaged: most of their colleagues pretended ignorance that they wanted to be. Officially Maria was on the open market.

A newly-arrived Dutch missionary, friendless, whom Hudson

in his impulsive generosity took to share quarters, confided in him dramatically that, having lately dispatched two proposals of marriage, one to a girl in Holland, the other to Germany, he thought Miss Maria Dyer 'looked nice and that he intended to win her'. Hudson, 'inwardly furious' (so he told his son Howard), remarked mildly that it would be awkward if each accepted: and eventually heard delightedly that all three had refused.

Next came news that 'another gentleman was much smitten and determined paying his addresses to my dear Maria and I knew he was favoured by those who opposed me'. This suitor was a missionary down from Shanghai, called Aitchison, whom Hudson remembered with respect and affection. That Aitchison should be allowed in honest ignorance to foster emotions and hopes which would never fructify struck Hudson as cruel and unfair. He called and attempted to explain. Aitchison 'asked me if we were definitely engaged. I could not say we were but told him I considered we were *conditionally so*'. Aitchison professed to be upset that others had misled him. Suppose, he asked, the guardians refused consent; would Maria be free? Hudson could not answer. Aitchison admitted subsequently that all along he knew the truth; he flew a kite to aid them.

Hudson retired from this interview to nurse a growing determination that uncertainty and dissimulation should cease.

'My dear Miss Maria I understand you are talking of going to Shanghai and we are intending to start on Monday, and may I ask you if you will kindly come over here a little while, as I would like to speak to you of a little matter if quite convenient. Will you not come at once – very affectionately yours, L H Knowlton. PS: If you are engaged will you please mention when you can call as I must be out a part of the day.'

Maria scented breathless significance in this innocent note of Saturday 14th November, from a married American missionary who lived outside the walls, far from prying eyes and gossip, a dear friend in no way involved in the dispute.

Maria called for her sedan chair and quietly disappeared without word to Mrs Bausum. Ellie on her honeymoon need never know.

Mrs Knowlton greeted her with a whisper that Hudson waited in another room. Maria was very frightened, 'for Miss Aldersey is so violent'. She calmed herself, reflecting that uncle's letter must arrive any day, perhaps before the 'Protectress' discovered mutiny. Whatever the letter's tone, her twenty-first birthday lay two months and two days ahead. Hudson had suffered enough – and had been very upset that past week, the Ningpo grapevine told, by a most disgraceful affair between the Jones-Taylor cook and the children's lately baptised nurse which had mocked months of patient shepherding. Ill, defamed, misjudged. And he was her Hudson.

His eye was on the door. It opened – she was in his arms. 'The result was we were engaged whether the guardians answer was favourable or otherwise. She is a dear noble disinterested devoted girl and now I know *all* she has passed through I love her more and admire her more than ever.' Their stories of pressure and persecution tumbled out. They talked and they kissed and they prayed and they planned and they kissed and they laughed and they prayed and they – 'I was not long engaged without trying to make up for the number of kisses I *ought* to have had these last few months.' Six hours together, Hudson discovered to his amazement when they parted.

It was very naughty by contemporary standards. And very, very human. They decided to keep their secret until Ellie and John Burdon left for Shanghai, unless Tarn's letter came. It did not. The Burdons sailed north. On the evening of November 30th, 'with Maria's consent I waited on Miss Aldersey, and informed her of our engagement. She said little – she evidently dared not trust herself'. Next morning Maria received a peremptory summons from her 'guardian' to which was sent a counter note gently denying the accuracy of such status. 'I think Miss Aldersey wanted to get her there and then lock her up or something of that sort, but as a *friend*, if Maria calls on her, she will not go alone.'

Russell returned from the country, heard the news, and immediately called in a cold fury on Taylor to demand apology and reparation for his 'rude and unheard of step... unaccountable conduct' in stealing an interview with Miss Dyer and announcing to Miss Aldersey that he and Miss Dyer were to be considered engaged, 'thus not only manifesting the greatest rudeness and disrespect towards a lady of Miss Aldersey's age and character but even exhibiting a total ignorance of the common amenities and proprieties of life'.

On Taylors' declining to apologise Russell turned his back, cut him, campaigned against him. A missionary community split at the seams because two young things wanted to marry. Neither entered the controversy. They wished only to be left alone. The flames of dispute, of defence and attack, everyone taking sides violently, to the astonishment of the Chinese, reached such heights that Gough, the peacemaker, approached Hudson on December 9th with the suggestion that for unity's sake he make concession. Hudson, having consulted Maria, drew up on the night of the 10th a letter for Gough to publish wherever he wished: 'That *fully* satisfied that our betrothal with all our previous steps in this matter have been right, and consequently desiring that it may be fully understood that this step is in no sense an apology or admission of claims which have been made, I now simply with the desire to promote the unity of the body of Christ, and at the sacrifice of our personal feelings...' He agreed not to see Maria again until Tarn's reply arrived, except in the event of serious illness or political upheaval.

Hudson signed but never sent that letter. On the morning of December 11th a note was thrust in his hands: 'My own dear, I have received a letter from my aunt and she tells me that she and my uncle "certainly have not heard anything to induce them to oppose my wishes". Do come quickly, your *own* loving Maria.'

Mrs Tarn told Maria she must wait until she was of age. 'You understand that we do not oppose... though we do see some objections.' Tarn, assistant secretary of the Religious Tract Society, a cripple who could only sit up on his bed a few minutes at a time, told Hudson in a letter received after Christmas that the testimonials he had secured 'are as favourable as we could wish and such as to lead us entirely to approve of the proposed union'. They

objected, however, to his resignation from the Chinese Evangelization Society: 'In some cases it may be allowable to act on faith,
as Mr Müller of Bristol for his orphan school, but I think in regard
to the support of a wife and family it is not justifiable.' He had,
however, assurance from the secretaries of the CES, and Hudson
must have grinned, 'that they intend to send your supplies as heretofore'. Most of his letter concerned the appointing of trustees for
Maria's small annual inheritance of between £40 and £50 'very
inadequate for the support of a family... It will be for you to arrange how the half-yearly dividends may be remitted to you'.

To Mrs Bausum Tarn wrote bluntly: '...and hearing from several quarters very favourable accounts respecting him we saw nothing in Miss Aldersey's letter to justify in not giving our sanction to
dear Maria's wishes, in fact it in my opinion condemned her whole
manner of proceeding, I have by return of mail told her so and
condemned her want of judgment, your letter has tended to con-
firm this opinion and in all that now concerns Maria we trust you
will act a mother's part... What dear Mrs Bausum can be the
cause of Miss Aldersey's strong objection and prejudice against
Mr Taylor it is so weak to be influenced by his personal appearance...'

Hudson wrote home: 'We hailed the favourable reply with unspeakable delight. Our position was painful because we do not
wish to see divisions among the Lord's people.'[1] He could now
meet Maria freely, nightly; and once again blissfully ignoring prim
Victorian convention, 'they always sat together and held hands no
matter who was in the room', so Mrs Bausum's daughter recalled.

An American, John L Nevius, famous later for his writings on
Chinese demonology, remembered them vividly. In his wife's words:
'When [Taylor] fell in love it was a headlong plunge, and by no
means a slight or evanescent passion. And his fiancée with her
strong, emotional nature was in this respect not unlike him. My
husband was rather a special friend of both, and he sometimes

---

[1]The official biographers do not mention this final row because, decorously, they place the
engagement interview at Mrs Knowlton's *after* the receipt of the Tarns' approval (see Vol
I p 450). There is excuse: Hudson Taylor in oral recollections noted down by his daughter-
in-law seems to have confused the order of events.

indulged his propensities for good-natured teasing at their expense.'
One night they played a game which required hands beneath the
table. Nevius received an unexpected squeeze. Guessing it was a
matter of mistaken identity he returned the squeeze hard until
Maria's flushed cheeks and eyes full of tears warned him the joke
had gone far enough. 'These bright, merry young people... those
were the days when to laugh was easy.'

The growing flotsam of Chinese thrown into Ningpo by the Taiping
advance found Taylor and Jones a sure centre of relief. Other
missions distributed food to the poor from carefully allocated funds.
Taylor and Jones, uninhibited in generosity, were, as another criticised, living from hand to mouth. 'Yes,' rejoined Taylor, 'from
God's hand to my mouth.'

On a day in November, the cupboard almost empty, a mail
arrived a week early. They nearly wept in gratitude, 'as we saw
not only our needs supplied, but the widow and orphan, the blind,
lame and destitute provided for by the' (Taylor concluded
misquotedly and quaintly) 'bounty of Him who feeds the ravens
through the liberality of dear Mr Berger'.

A fortnight before the wedding date the money bag dropped to
a single coin; and no mail due. After a scrappy breakfast they
faced starvation. 'We could only betake ourselves to Him who is a
*real* father, and cannot forget His children's needs... Credit to any
extent we might have had, but that would not have been in accordance with our principles in the matter of debt.' They took a
clock to a Chinese merchant, who promised to buy – if he could
watch it work satisfactorily for a week. They carried their port-
able stove to sell as scrap iron to the foundry across the river, but
the bridge of boats had been swept away and the ferry fare was
double their fortune.

Famished and disconsolate, they searched their house from
top to bottom, unearthed a packet of cocoa and brewed it. They
refused an urgent offer of a loan from one of their servants, telling
him, 'Our Father will not forget us'. 'Though [Jones] spoke with
confidence, our faith was not a little tried as we went into his

study and... cried indeed unto the Lord in our trouble.' They were
yet on their knees when the servant ran in. 'Teacher, Teacher!
Here are letters!' Days before schedule an unexpected mail brought
another gift from Berger.

That night Hudson held Maria's hand specially tight and offered
her freedom: 'I cannot hold you to your promise if you would
rather draw back. You see how difficult our life may be at times..'

'Have you forgotten?' she replied, 'I was left an orphan in a
far-off land. God has been my Father all these years. Do you
think I shall be afraid to trust Him now?'

Russell and Miss Aldersey remained implacable. Russell refused
to consider Hudson other than a cad. On December 27th, without
Maria's knowledge, Hudson wrote very humbly 'entreating for
reconciliation and a restoration of that communion and mutual
love in the Lord Jesus which formerly existed between us'.

Russell, who ought to have been better employed, replied on
December 29th with twelve foolscap pages, concluding with demands that Taylor should appear before all the parties, openly
retract, and agree not to see Miss Dyer for three months, during
which she shall consider herself unbound by the engagement 'which
I and others hold to be null and void in the sight of God'.

Russell snorted at the reply of nine foolscap pages, for Taylor
freely forgave without 'seeking any apology or reparation', and
admitted he should apologise for wrong or injury he had done.
But of such, in this affair, 'I am unconscious'. Six days before the
wedding date Russell suggested arbitration of the dispute by three
missionaries. Taylor declined to accept arbitration on the question
of delaying the marriage, but agreed to be judged 'as to whether I
have given sufficient cause of offence' to justify Russell's continued refusal of fellowship, 'if that is the only way in which the
unhappy differences can be removed'. He doubted this the best
course. Why rehash the affair? He himself had forgiven 'personal
insult and injury': 'if you *think* I have erred, forgive it'.

The Arbitrators sat on January 15th or 16th. With pleasing
sense they rebuked Taylor for meeting Maria at the Knowltons,

'highly injudicious and improper under the circumstances', rebuked Russell for the 'use of expressions which are calculated to
wound the feelings of Mr Taylor'; declined to judge whether the
dispute had adversely affected the Chinese or the spread of the
Gospel, and recommended 'mutual forgiveness and the exercise
of the usual courtesies of Christian Society'.

In response to this call the future bishop declared that as the
proper officiating clergyman of the British community he refused
to marry them. Frederick Gough took his place. The British Consul must be present as registrar to validate the marriage. Hudson
Taylor's oral recollections tell how 'Mr Russell and Miss Aldersey
actually got the Consul to leave Ningpo on a shooting expedition
in the hope that the proceedings would be stopped. Diplomatically
the Consul pleased both sides. He went shooting and he left the
Register signed as present, and his assistant Robert Hart to act for
him. ('I have got my kiss at last!' Hart said after the signing.)
Russell, gun over shoulder, walked out of the marriage, but not,
unfortunately, out of the story.

The Consul returned the fee, on the score that Taylor had
often helped as interpreter. This was as well; feeding the destitute
had left him again so low in funds that he was married in a plain
cotton robe.

January 20th 1858: 'We had a beautiful day for our wedding;
the sun shone brightly and all our friends seemed pleased to see us
happily united. We sat down 18 to breakfast after the wedding. At
the ceremony 24 were present amongst whom were the officers
of the ship of war in port. The American consul, Dr Bradley,
kindly lent me his sedan chair for the occasion; it is the *prettiest* in
Ningpo, in fact the prettiest I have ever seen and it looked prettier
I thought, when *Mrs Taylor* was in it than ever it had done before.'

## Chapter 10: THE VISION FADES
1858, 1859, on into 1860. With John Jones as pastor and Maria
running a little school, Taylor's group at Ningpo trudged doggedly
the undulating road of mission work in a great heathen city in

troubled times, gathering with infinite pain and prayer a little knot of believers.

One endeavour among others older and more established, Taylor's church was not of importance except for the principles hewed out of experience, which were to receive far wider application: the basis of faith, that with no secure financial foundation but Maria's trifling income a mission could be maintained, if without affluence; the decision never to employ paid Chinese church-workers – those that served, served voluntarily from the same motive as missionaries who received no fixed salaries; the tireless emphasis on the supreme importance, in God's sight, of the 'one sheep' to be sought; and the refusal to baptise except on irrefutable evidence of genuine, life-transforming belief, thus restricting numbers but minimising the risk of cluttering the Church with 'rice Christians'; not that disputes or backslidings erupted less than in churches of New Testament times.

Far more significant was the influence of Maria upon her husband. Her religious development had been more orderly; she served to steady Hudson's faith while he deepened hers. She came from a pioneering background and never held him back. For Elizabeth Sissons he had been prepared, in weaker moments, to entrench himself in the semi-comforts of a conventional missionary career and would have been constantly at war with himself. Maria tempered without quenching his zeal, was largely responsible for the common sense and balance characteristic of Taylor at the height of his powers. She made him take holidays. Under the influence of her less mercurial yet gay temperament he shed those moods of melancholy; he could discuss every matter with her and forget to be introspective. He became more assured, grew up; Hudson Taylor at twenty-eight, forthright as at twenty-two or three, no longer was on the defensive, no more a prig.

Her passionate nature fulfilled his warm-blooded yearning to love and be loved. She gave him full response, a fostering and feeding affection so that together they had such a reservoir of love that it splashed over to refresh all, Chinese or European, who came near them.

Though his was the finer intellect, Maria had a more thorough education. She improved his cumbrous style, teaching him to write good English though she never cured him of split infinitives. She brushed up his Greek and his Ningpo colloquial. She must have eliminated all but a trace of his Yorkshire accent, for it was never noticed in later years.

Maria by birth was a 'lady' in an age that set much store by good breeding. Taylor, for all his natural courtesy, had been uncouth. Imperceptibly she polished him; when in future he needed to enter social circles where his father would have been miserably shy and gauche, the son could move with reasonable ease and acceptance.

Undoubtedly the overriding factor in their marriage was an equal uninhibited loyalty to their vocation. But without Maria, Taylor never could have embarked on his life's work.

In February 1859, a bare year after the wedding, Maria, three months pregnant, fell grievously ill. Dr Parker reluctantly left Taylor to watch life ebbing as she lay in their apartment over the preaching hall, the old home refurbished.

At the hour of the usual weekly meeting for all Ningpo missionaries, who had 'most warmly responded' to his urgent request for prayer, Taylor at the bedside thought of an untried remedy. He dared not apply it without consulting Parker at the new hospital two miles off, but should he leave her? 'It was a moment of anguish. The hollow temples, sunken eyes, and pinched features denoted the near approach of death.' He took a last look, and hurried through the streets. 'On my way, while wrestling mightily with God in prayer, the precious words were brought with power to my soul, "Call upon Me in the day of trouble: I will deliver thee, and thou shalt glorify Me". I was at once enabled to plead them in faith, and the result was deep, deep, unspeakable peace and joy. All consciousness of distance was gone. Dr Parker cordially approved of the use of the means suggested, but arriving at home I saw at a glance that the desired change had taken place in the absence of this or any other remedy. The pinched aspect of the countenance had given place to the calmness of tranquil slumber, and not one unfavourable symptom remained to retard recovery.'

On July 31st their first child, Gracie, was born, with the temperature at 103° indoors and anti-foreign feeling blown to such heights that many Europeans left the native city and the Taylors kept an escape rope tied to their window and a boat moored in the canal.

The following month Parker's wife died suddenly. He was obliged to take the children back to Scotland. His hospital with thirty free beds, and thirty paying patients undergoing opium cure, had the respect of foreigners and Chinese at Ningpo, where no other qualified western practitioner resided. Since he financed the medical mission from fees received from Europeans he prepared to close it until he could return. The dispensary he offered to the unqualified Taylor.

Taylor gave no answer for two or three days, 'when I felt constrained to undertake not only the dispensary work, but that of the hospital; relying upon the faithfulness of a prayer-hearing God to furnish the means of support'. Parker left money to cover expenses and Chinese assistants' salaries for the current month, no more. On learning that pay could not be guaranteed, the hospital staff resigned. Taylor 'told the circumstances to the members of the little church, some of whom volunteered to help me, depending, like myself, upon the Lord'. Maria even took over management, Taylor the medical superintendence, even doing amputations: 'in answer to prayer... success was given'. By preaching and personal conversations 'many were convinced of the truth of Christianity'. And supplies rapidly dwindled.

The fate of the hospital bred speculation in market and mission house. Even the Taylors' devoted Christian helpers felt qualms. The cook reached the last sack of rice. He doled out a day's supply. It went. The next. That went. The large bag had nearly emptied.

Taylor knew the stake: his daring to credit divine promises; to build upon divine care, wisdom, control of circumstance, for friends in England could not have heard even of his added responsibility.

The mail arrived. The familiar Berger handwriting lay in front of him. He opened the packet. £50, and a letter which totally vindicated his belief that in assuming control of the hospital he had not acted wilfully. Berger wrote that his father had died, leaving him considerably richer. He did not wish to spend more on himself. He enclosed £50 and asked if there was further need. When Taylor sailed home nine months later 'I was able to leave more funds in hand for the hospital than when I undertook it'.

This was settled work, such as Hudson Taylor needed to complete his training. Exhausting, satisfying. And restricting.

The Treaty of Tientsin, signed in 1858 though not ratified until 1860, gave missionaries the legal right to travel freely throughout the Empire. Premature excitement at possible advance into the interior had evoked in the Taylors no emotion beyond regret that the claims of their little church and the hospital must clinch them to Ningpo.

# Part Two

# 'A TREMENDOUS RISK'

## Chapter 11: LIGHT PURSE IN A BACK STREET

Londoners early astir on a foggy morning of November 1860, hardly believed what they saw: three Chinese in native costume – two men and a woman – walking through Bayswater from the railway station to 63 Westbourne Grove, home of Amelia and Benjamin Broomhall.

The tallest, a fine figure with a magnificent pigtail and pronounced slit-eyes, carried a baby girl of about fifteen months, somewhat incongruously dressed in English nursery clothes. Close behind came a tall young woman. The policeman peering through the fog remarked to the milkman in a loud voice (since Chinamen could not understand English) that they must be husband and wife and that insignificant little fellow behind, their friend: not noticing his most unChinese grey-blue eyes twinkling at the joke.

During the early months of 1860 in Ningpo Taylor's fragile health had collapsed under the strain of the hospital, until by summer he was faced with the alternative of certain death or a long voyage home to England.

Hudson, Maria and Gracie sailed from Shanghai in August on the *Jubilee*, 700 tons, Captain Jones. They were the only passengers except the Captain's wife and a mad woman who 'at first was very wild but now is less annoying'. After a horrible time when the pain in his chest eased only when he suffered incessant diarrhoea, and *vice versa*, Taylor slowly improved, but Maria had an acute attack of gastro-enteritis. They had brought a Chinese convert, Wang Lae-djun, a house painter, whose first step to faith had followed his eavesdropping, when painting a ceiling, a conversation between irritated mandarins' ladies and a basket-maker who politely declined orders to make incense-holders for idol worship, and gave his reasons. Painter Wang had now volunteered to leave wife, family and father to escort the Taylors in their weakness. He 'is invaluable here. In the day he takes charge of baby and this greatly relieves me, in fact without him I do not know what I should do'.

The *Jubilee* became a nightmare. The Taylors had suspected the religious jargon that splashed Captain Jones's lips. At a provisioning stop in the East Indies, Hudson declined for conscience' sake to interpret and bargain for trade on a Sunday. 'This made him furiously angry... Nothing would turn away his anger or allay his spite, and for the next three or four months he did everything in his power to render my life miserable.'

When Maria suffered such terrible sea-sickness in the Indian Ocean that Hudson grew thoroughly alarmed, the Captain 'rudely refused' to allow the cook to serve her soft foods. He refused to allow a spirit lamp in the cabin, or even a candle. Hudson tore up magazines to make spills which he burned one after another under a tin cup to cook a few teaspoonfuls of arrowroot, 'the only means I had of keeping her alive'. In Table Bay, believing that otherwise Maria must die, he 'implored the captain to land us', in vain. 'I was almost in despair and could do nothing but cry to God.' Gradually her strength returned to make her almost well before home.

The Captain was brutal to his wife and to the mad woman who 'was kept chained up, sometimes on deck. He used to beat them both with a dog whip – unmercifully; and his wife was in terror of him and yet she seemed fond of him! His spite continued to the end notwithstanding all my endeavours to conciliate him.'

Amelia dressed Maria in her longest black silk skirt 'not too short for her', until she could get tailor-made jackets which suited her height when worn above a crinoline, now the universal fashion. Hudson felt strange in western clothes. He sprouted nice whiskers and his fair hair regained a boyish fringe. They all went to Barnsley for Christmas, complete with Lae-djun. Everyone fell for Maria, but when an incautious relative suggested to Hudson an operation to cure the squint 'I was very indignant! I loved her and I loved it. I loved her just as she was and everything about her. I would not have had it changed on any account. I would not have changed anything she was or did.'

Hudson and Maria made their home until after the birth of their first boy, Herbert, in April 1861, with the Broomhalls in Bayswater, where Benjamin from Barnsley had a partnership in a draper's shop, a kind-hearted pious man, somewhat unstable in

money matters. Amelia's years were spent rapidly providing him
with his quiverful. Neither took seriously Hudson's and Maria's
hints that China beckoned, but Benjamin lived to do it considerable service from a distance.

Taylor waited impatiently to hurry back to 'those among whom
my heart still remains though my body is not present'. He reckoned the breakdown of health 'a great calamity... nor was sorrow
lessened when medical testimony assured me that return to China,
at least for years to come, was impossible'.

From Ningpo, viewing openings in the surrounding province of
Chekiang, he had written to his parents, 'Do you know any earnest, devoted young men desirous of serving God in China, who
– not wishing for more than their actual support – would be willing
to come out and labour here?' He set his sights on five. And he
believed he could find and use men and women 'from the class
that missionary societies usually think beneath their notice'. In
England he at once sniffed for hopefuls. Two Barnsley men offered tentatively, one of whom, a mechanic called James Meadows, did not withdraw on reflection.

Wider reaction to an unconnected nobody aged twenty-nine
was what might have been expected, 'The Church is asleep; and
armchairs and sofas and English comforts possess more attrac-
tions than perishing souls; besides which [the Chinese] are "half
savages"'. England in the heyday of Lord Palmerston, the late
war with Russia forgotten, trade and prosperity increasing, had
little time for distant lands except as likely markets. Churches were
full, for religion was in vogue and the opening salvoes in the battle
with science had not echoed far beyond Oxford. Any trivial interest that could be spared from insular concerns had been caught by
Africa, for Livingstone, briefly returned from the Dark Continent,
had swept through Great Britain the previous year. 1859 had seen
too the beginnings of a spiritual quickening which, when in full
strength, would be ready for Hudson Taylor; and Taylor for the
Revival. If the times were not ripe, nor was the man.

In disappointment at lethargy and in his search for health
('...quite poorly all this week. Indeed I have spent a good deal of it

in bed... last night my head was all swimming...') Taylor found outside the family one sure sympathiser: William Berger. The Taylors always were welcome at Berger's fine house and property, Sainthill near East Grinstead in Sussex, out towards West Hoathly.

Berger owned Berger's Rice Starch, a brand widely popular. Middle-aged, he had already retired from business, but returned later in order to make more money for missions. 'A tall thin man', a young Scotsman remembered him, 'decisive and sharp in manner. Quick, and a little bit inclined to be severe but very loving; at the bottom of his heart there was intense love. A man of prayer, thoroughly so, a godly prayerful man who really walked with God. His wife was a loving bright energetic little body, but she did everything so quietly that you seldom knew she had done it – so efficient and yet so much out of sight. She was a great woman of prayer.'

Brought up an Anglican, he underwent as a youth a startling experience. In the words of his niece: 'A young lady at an evening party spoke to him about "the joys of religion" (he thought of his sins three days later) and he received Christ straight away and went behind the drawing room door to hide his tears of thankfulness. He and his brothers went to tell their clergyman, Prebendary Griffiths, that they had been converted. He scolded them roundly and sent them away. If it had not been for this he would probably never have left the Church of England. They felt he knew nothing of it. Yet he was *good*.'

Berger joined the Methodists, and later the Brethren, but had no patience with the exclusiveness of some of them. He cared nought about a man's church loyalty. Hudson Taylor had now become what he remained, a Baptist. The criticism that he 'wanders from one denomination to another' lost its force, yet except for one resounding error of judgment, Taylor never obtruded distinctive denominational principles. He would work with anyone whose heart was where he believed it should be. And in Berger he found a second father. Hudson had never been close to James Taylor, despite mutual sympathies and affection, and James's world was narrowing, his shyness more marked, his mind less supple. In the growing intricacies of the next years, it was Berger whom Hudson consulted, Berger who advised, discerned and sometimes restrained.

When Hudson Taylor accepted the impossibility of speedy return to China he decided, on the advice of the London Hospital, to take their Practical Chemistry course, Midwifery, and the Diploma for Membership of the Royal College of Surgeons. 'I feel the price a great one, of giving up to study nine months, instead of being with my friends in various parts of England'. Shortly after Bertie's birth the Taylors moved to a back-street house in the East End, 1 Beaumont Street, close to the hospital.

Their neighbours rough working people in a mean district, their rooms barely furnished because funds were low, the Taylors made themselves cosy and happy with two children, one Chinaman to cook and launder, and Maria's harmonium so that song need never be far away. They had a girl to help with the children, for domestic service was cheap; and since no 'lady', even one as unpretending as Maria was, would have scrubbed the steps in the eighteen-sixties, they probably employed a char.

Attendance at lectures and in hospital taxed Taylor's strength, until on May 10th 1862, he went with Maria to Lincoln's Inn Fields, and found a little restaurant where she waited while he registered for the examination at the Royal College of Surgeons. He returned and they spent two hours there cramming for the papers. He went to the hall leaving her sitting in the restaurant silently praying (the proprietor appears to have been most accommodating). Papers were given out. Taylor could not find one he could answer, every fact and theory had vacated his brain. Head to paper, heart rose soaring heavenward. 'Lord, I am quite willing to fail if Thou dost wish. This is not my concern but Thine.' He looked again; his mind focused, and he wrote a good paper. It was much the same at the *viva voce* four days later 'I feel so nervous and am not very well'. Questions were catchy but he passed. He took his finals in July, his Midwifery in October 1862, to become MRCS, LM.

James Meadows, the Barnsley recruit, stayed with the Taylors the previous autumn for some haphazard training ('and gives us unmixed satisfaction and gets on famously'), before sailing with his young wife at Berger's expense in January 1862 for Ningpo where, at his own nervous request, he was introduced to that somewhat censorious community as of no higher status than 'Scripture Reader'. Meadows left a pen picture of Taylor in his late twenties. 'His strong yet quiet faith in the promises of Scripture, his implicit confidence in God, this it was which compelled submission on my part to whatever he proposed for me.' The Taylors seemed perfectly free from anxiety, and Hudson evoked almost blind loyalty because there was 'none so sympathetic, none so tenderly affectionate, as he, concerning our wants and our work'. Hudson was determined, then and later, that no one responsible to him should ever suffer as he had suffered from the neglect and inefficiency of the CES.

He talked much but used well-chosen words; and 'everyone who knew Mr Taylor must have been struck with the fact that the man walking about his room was a man of prayer. Nothing was too trifling, he used to say, for us to take to a Father'. Victorians, especially chapel-going nonconformists, were prone to long extempore prayers, and from some lips pious words slipped with oleaginous ease, as they had from Captain Jones of the *Jubilee*. With Hudson and Maria, together or singly, aloud or unspoken, brief or unhurried, prayer was the unselfconscious response of children to their Father.

Meadows, from a humble home, was amazed at the austerity of Beaumont Street. The Taylors 'practised self-denial in a natural manner; made no fuss of it, seemed to esteem it a privilege rather than a sacrifice'. They never knew when or from where supplies would come. 'Returned home', runs an entry in Hudson's journal. 'Remarked at tea to my dear wife, how nice it was to be again reminded of Jehovah Jireh by our old Chinese scroll... At 8 pm received a kind note from Mr Berger enclosing £20 for our own use. Praise the Lord!' Twelve days later: 'Received by this morning's post £10 from Mr Müller; another answer to prayer for supplies and faith.' And the summer of 1863: 'About this time we felt we needed a change but funds were low. We made it a matter of prayer, and received from Miss Stacey £5 and from Mr Gough, £5, from father also, 2 guineas'.

Funds at times almost failed. Borrowing would have been easy but a denial of principle. Nor could straits be revealed. On one occasion, 'our money nearly spent', Taylor paid tradesmen and servants on a Monday. No money came, only a party of two women and two children on Tuesday, long-invited guests. Hospitality drained resources until on the Sunday, when Taylor gave his normal church collection, 'in faith and as due to God', he had nothing left but a few pennies, and the provisions already in the house. The next day the sister of one of their guests came up for the day from her Buckinghamshire farm, bringing 'one goose, one pair of ducks, one fowl, etc', The following day, hiding their extremity, the Taylors secured a trifling sum to spend when one of their house-party wanted stamps and bought Taylor's stock. Not until Thursday did the crisis break.

Prolonged embarrassments puzzled Taylor until it occurred to him that if God promises to meet all needs, 'the *trial* of faith is one of the needs which He ministers to and supplies'. The London years brought tests more severe than any that followed in China. In conversation thirty years later Taylor said, 'As a rule prayer is answered and funds come in, but if we are kept waiting the spiritual blessing that is the outcome is far more precious than exemption from the trial'. And in old age he loved to tell one particular story of London.

He returned from a holiday in Barnsley the day before the rent fell due, unlocked the drawer where he had placed a pile of sovereigns in readiness, counted and found he had put aside one too few. He could anticipate the rough-tempered landlord's witheringly brutal sarcasm. The Taylors spent most of the night on their knees. The morning brought no post; the hour for the landlord approached. Taylor screwed himself for the ordeal; he hated scenes, and courage had always to be summoned by effort. The hour passed, the morning, the afternoon, the evening – no landlord.

When the man knocked next day, unwontedly affable, he apologised for failing to call yesterday. Business had detained him – most unusual; could not account for it. 'But I can,' cried Taylor, 'I had a sovereign in the post this morning!'

And no doubt, when the door then closed, he picked up the nearest child for a few glorious moments of play. Hudson Taylor adored children. Gracie and Bertie were followed by Freddie (Howard) in 1862 and Samuel in 1864. As the responsibilities increased, as the vision grew more piercing, the call more insistent, the children kept Hudson's feet on the ground. For them he would throw down his books and romp round the little sitting-room singing at the top of his voice.

Hospital training was work enough for a man in indifferent health. Taylor accepted further responsibility: the revision of the Ningpo New Testament. The present version was admittedly poor, and its use of ideographs put it beyond the understanding of any but the classically educated for ideographs bore no relation to the sound of words in Ningpo colloquial. Taylor wished to use roman letters phonetically, thus placing the New Testament in the reach of millions who could be taught to read quickly. Lae-djun had come to England partly because of the aid he could give.

The British and Foreign Bible Society sponsored the Revision, on an honorary basis, and would print it. The Church Missionary Society released Taylor's old friend, Frederick Gough, skilled in Greek and in Ningpo Chinese, to spend furlough on the Revision; Gough had brought home his sick wife, to see her die a week after landing.

When the medical course ended, Revision became the major feature of Taylor's existence, six, eight, nine or more hours a day. Maria contributed her fluency, and Lae-djun postponed return to China nearly two years. 'Revision 13½ hours', runs the journal entry for April 25th 1863, 'several answers to prayer today. Mr Gough did not commence till 11.30 am and I felt very much tried, but the Lord helped me.' Gough had an oriental conception of time, and being the older man could not be ordered around.

By the agreement with the Bible Society, the Revision must be submitted to Russell, the acknowledged expert in the Ningpo dialect, who came home in the summer of 1863. Russell had not reconciled himself to Taylor.

Early in September the revisers received his first opinions on the draft they had submitted. Taylor reported Russell's conclusions: '1. The Ningpo version sadly faulty, 2. Our revision of it a failure, 3. Could not join us under these circumstances. In the letter he criticises our work as substituting mistranslation for mistranslation, and thinks that we had better stop – the sooner the better.' Russell told the CMS to withdraw their endorsement. He tried to bring the Bible Society to heel. Gough 'received a letter from Mr Russell very angrily speaking of him, of the revision, and of me... Mr Gough who cannot bear up against a rough and personal opposition is, I fear, giving way; so that humanly speaking there is little hope of the continued aid of the CMS or the BFBS.' Both societies, however, unexpectedly took Taylor's part.

By that time, Mrs John Jones had returned to England, her husband having died at sea. It is pleasant to record that in course of time the Taylors' two great friends, Gough and Mrs Jones, sank their sorrows in matrimony.


Revision, with its discipline of attention to the original, its discussion of exact meanings, its comparing of texts, formed a most thorough and systematic Bible study, a vital preparation for the future to a man with the unshakeable conviction that he was handling divine truth. 'I have dealt with the Bible,' he could say, 'as I have dealt with my guide books of science and medicine.' A textbook described facts, and experiments by which they could be proved. 'In the same way it has been my privilege to take the *Word* of *God* and believe it means just what it says, and further to put it to the test of actual trial.'

One experiment described in this divine text-book he determined to carry out at once. '*Pray* ye the Lord of the harvest that he will send forth labourers into the harvest.' Taylor decided that the divine method of raising missionaries did not lie in 'elaborate appeals for help, but, first, *earnest prayer to God to thrust forth labourers*, and, second, the deepening of the spiritual Life of the Church, so that *men should be unable to stay at home'*.

Taylor began the experiment. In 1863 at the age of thirty-one he set himself to pray.

He scarcely expected the answer that came.

## Chapter 12: BRIGHTON BEACH

A large wall-map of China dominated the minute study at Beaumont Street. Ningpo appeared a small dot on the far right-hand side.

For five years Ningpo had swallowed Taylor's energies and ambitions, extinguishing his dream of the evangelisation of an Empire. As he looked at that map Ningpo began to drop back into proportion. 'Daily viewing the whole country on the large map... I was as near to the vast regions of inland China as to the smallest districts in which I had laboured personally.' Not to Ningpo or Chekiang only, nor Shanghai and Kiangsu, nor the five other provinces, all but one being coastal, where served a sprinkle of missionaries which decreased yearly as Americans were drawn home or kept home by the Civil War; but to Kiangsi, Honan, Hunan, province after inland province untouched.

He viewed an Empire, 'its vast extent, its teeming population, its spiritual destitution and overwhelming need' – four hundred million, as the population then was estimated in the West, and all but a few thousand ignorant of the name of Christ. Inland China weighed on him. The weight bore more heavily as 1863 turned to 1864, 'and prayer was often the only resource by which [my] burdened heart could gain any relief'.

Gough sympathised. Taylor urged action. The gentle clergyman took his younger, more impulsive friend on a round of visits to implore secretaries of missionary societies to open inland China. They were turned away with courteous, total refusal. Financial stringency quenched hope of expansion, except that the new treaty port of Hankow, over six hundred miles up the Yangtze, now had, as they knew, a London Mission station. Even if money became available, said the secretaries, the venture would be impracticable.

Conditions were too disturbed. The Taipings lay almost prostrate, their once extensive Heavenly Kingdom at its last gasp. Ningpo had been in their hands for a time, and at Nanking in 1860-61 missionaries at last spent several months with the rebel Emperor's court, but all was over. Twenty million Chinese had died in the Rebellion. Vast tracts of the great Yangtze basin were impoverished, infested with brigands. And the Imperial government considered the clause of the treaty ratified in 1860, which guaranteed freedom of movement to missionaries, as a dead letter. 1864 was the worst conceivable time to extend missionary operations inland, 'even if we had the money or the men'.

Rebuffed by the Church Missionary Society, the Baptist, Methodist, London societies, Taylor could do nothing but pray.

Meanwhile his constant addresses at chapels or prayer-meetings, sometimes reported in the religious press, brought him forward as one speaking simply, urgently, with a grasp of facts, who made no secret of a belief that China missions had a place for working-class people. He entered into correspondence with several, on behalf of Ningpo. In December 1864 a Miss Notman left on the P&O steamship *Ceylon*. She was to serve at Mrs Bausum's school. The Foreign Evangelisation Society paid her fare. The Taylors had selected and provided the rudiments of training.

Seven other men and women, attracted by the magnetism of the man and his call, wanted to prepare for Ningpo. Beaumont Street was too small. The Taylors moved further east to a larger house in Coborn Street. Gough insisted on paying the difference in rent. The Eastern Counties Railway clanked and rattled across one end of Coborn Street, drays and heavy carts rumbled over the cobbles of Bow Road at the other, and a Seamen's Orphan Asylum stood almost opposite, but the house had a tiny garden and the district was more residential. Here in the autumn of 1864 developed an informal school for children.

That winter the Neviuses, over from America, saw how far Taylor had developed: 'The strong, tender, quiet young man, it was marvellous to see how God used him'. And in referring to his later life they illumine obliquely his character as it was in 1864: 'It seemed to us quite as wonderful that such extraordinary power and influence never harmed him. On the contrary he was more humble, less dictatorial, more deferential in the opinions of others in his later years than in his youth.'

The Taylors planned to escort their seven candidates in the spring of 1865 to Ningpo, to immerse themselves once more in the war-ravaged province of Chekiang. On March 6th they suddenly received an offer of two free passages for the imminent maiden voyage of the steamship *Corea*. Whereupon the whole Ningpo projects might have been laughed away by the absurd affair of Richard Truelove.

Truelove came from Staincross, outside Barnsley. He had approached Hudson Taylor, by then a hero to the local Methodist youth, in May 1863, and spent several months of 1864-65 at Coborn Street. At the *Corea* offer Truelove agreed to go; secretly he 'felt much hesitation'. The other free passenger would be Stephen Barchet, a German medical student at the London Hospital, a slight figure, very energetic and able, literate in five languages, and of charming personality.

Taylor brought Barchet to Glasgow where the *Corea* lay ready. This first visit to Scotland gave a foretaste of triumphs to come. 'My darling wifey', Taylor scribbled after the weekend, 'I spoke for China on Friday, Saturday, 4 times on Sunday, this morning, this afternoon; and tonight there are 40 or 50 persons taking tea here to hear of it. *Wrestle* mightily with God for me and for the work. I tremble almost when I think of the consequences of my visit. I believe God is working. There are 6 or 7 persons saying "here am I send me" to God – not to me.' The next morning: 'My own Darling, I never remember such a meeting as last night's. God was with us of a truth. There will be a great work in China in answer to such prayers as were then put forth. Much love from Stephen and self to you and the pets.'

One of those present remembered Taylor at those meetings: 'He was a young looking man even for his age, and he was only 33. Not particularly impressed by his appearance, but very much impressed by the power of every word he spoke. He spoke very quietly, every word was carefully chosen, and told.' Here in the Clyde valley, home-ground of Livingstone, the former mill-hand, Taylor evoked a new hope among the nondescript and nameless that foreign service was not a sole prerogative of the educated, well-born or exceptionally gifted.

Taylor came to earth from these glories, heavily. Richard True-love should arrive from Barnsley at 6 pm on Tuesday. Taylor reached the station a few minutes after the train was in, and no Truelove. Taylor or Barchet met every express until after mid-night, when the dreary station had emptied except for drunks and destitutes. Truelove would have missed the ship had she not run aground. On Wednesday Taylor reported her 'still on the bank, fortunately for us though not for the owners'.

They met every train on Wednesday. On Thursday, Hudson wrote to Maria. 'Poor Truelove must be in sad trouble: of course we are uneasy. We have been to many hotels and temperance coffee houses but in vain. If he only had gumption (as poor Mr Jones used to say) to telegraph to you or father for an address he might have got a reply long ago. I hope he is not sick or short for money... I feel weary today. I long to be once more quickly at your side, and to get on with our work.' On Friday Hudson combed Greenock.

Late that night in London loud knocking penetrated Maria's dreams. She threw up the window to see Richard Truelove below. She dressed hurriedly and let him in. Between mouthfuls of hast-ily prepared supper he said he had gone to Greenock, not alighting at Glasgow or even glancing out of the window. There he heard that a steamship, the *Asia*, had just left for China. He had forgotten the name of his ship and on learning that he could catch the *Asia* at Cardiff he looked up trains and travelled back down England, through Wales to Cardiff. When the *Asia* put in he was told the fare to China would be £60. Must be a mistake. When in distress or doubt, run to Mrs Taylor. He left his trunk at Cardiff and took the train to London. Maria asked him if he was ready to go to Glasgow. 'Poor fellow, dead tired, said he would rather go to bed.'

Maria tucked him up and came downstairs to pray for guidance. In the Post Office directory she found a letter posted at the General Post Office in the City by 7.45 am, would reach the stationmaster at Cardiff that night, to ask him to forward Truelove's box. She spent most of the night making arrangements. As soon as it was light enough for a lone woman's safety from footpads she threw on her wraps and walked down the Bow Road to the Mile End turnpike, where she was 'so extravagant as to take a cab to the Bank'. At the all-night telegraph office she sent a telegram to Hudson – fifteen words reply paid for the princely sum of ninepence, plus sixpence delivery charge for the reply. After posting her letter she walked back through the early market crowds to Fenchurch Street Station but found no local train. 'I had to walk all the way home for I did not want to be extravagant again' – a good three miles of streets, on an empty stomach.

Maria woke Truelove to a hurried breakfast. 'Richard seemed as if he could not realise that he must act immediately.' She hustled him out of the house to Bow Road Station for the roundabout journey to Euston Square; the short stretch of newly opened underground railway could not help them. They were in time for the 10 am express, and had between them just two shillings over his fare; this she gave him, leaving herself penniless. Another telegram to Hudson ('the person was quite civil and took thirteen postage stamps for a shilling'), and Maria walked the whole way back through Pentonville, across the City, out through Stepney to Bow, an effort on cobbles and hard pavements in the midday noise and crowd which would have seemed stiff enough for a man in strong shoes with a good night's sleep behind him. Not surprisingly that evening she felt 'quite used up... my feet are so swollen and tender I can hardly hobble about the house'.

The *Corea* obligingly remained grounded on the bank until Richard embarked. She beat down the Irish Sea and the Chops of the Channel and into the Bay of Biscay. Richard Truelove had a cold, and during those days and nights suffered such seasickness he wished he were dead. In rough weather in the Bay the *Corea* sighted a derelict which the Captain decided to tow back to Plymouth, delaying his onward voyage, to obtain salvage money of thousands of pounds – which handsomely rewarded the owner for the £100 value of the two free passages.

At Plymouth on April 7th Richard Truelove and Barchet came ashore; Richard brought his carpet bag 'thinking that if I did not feel better I should not go on board again. I did not mention this to Mr Barchet.'

On April 9th Taylor in London was alarmed by two telegrams from Barchet: Truelove had disappeared. Taylor caught next morning's express. Barchet and Truelove, who had missed each other by a misunderstanding, played hide-and-seek in Plymouth nearly three days before the wretched Richard was run to earth. On hearing that Taylor had come, 'this made me feel the more agitated'. That night and the following morning Taylor and Marshall, Truelove's London pastor at Bryanston Chapel, talked with him seriously, displaying the consequence of his turning back, but not pressing him to go forward. He decided to withdraw.

Taylor returned to his hotel room almost in tears. His failure to discern Truelove would render his judgment and ability suspect. Few would want to follow a man who chose candidates so badly. He could almost hear mocking laughter. The one hope lay in George Crombie, an Aberdonian now at Coborn Street. Crombie was about to marry a close friend of Maria called Anne Skinner, and they planned to make the voyage out their honeymoon.

Taylor's extremity may be gauged by his willingness to spend £1 8s. 6d. on an express reply-paid telegram to Maria of no less than one hundred and two words and the address. It was subtly phrased. 'Truelove has drawn back Stop The injury to our whole cause the disgrace to our blessed Saviour will be immense Stop If anyone could take Richard's place this would be much lessened Stop I cannot ask Crombie to go without seeing his parents without Anne on the shortest possible notice Stop The sacrifice it would be to him cannot be easily overrated but if he were led to volunteer it would be an odour of a sweet smell to the Lord whose love is untold untenable Stop just let him see this telegram Stop If the Lord leads him to volunteer telegraph to me Hudson.'

Anne said to Crombie: 'Go, George, and let the world see that you love the Lord Jesus more than me.' He was in Plymouth next evening. The owners consented to the transfer. Unexpectedly, Anne was able to follow him out a fortnight later.

Chasing Truelove up and down the British Isles gave Hudson Taylor time for thought. The urge to action generated by the wall-map became fiercer, less controllable. Its fire received fresh fuel by the preparation of Taylor's first publication, *China's Spiritual Need and Claims*.

The pamphlet arose from a request by the Editor of the *Baptist Times*, W. G. Lewis, who was also pastor of the Bayswater Chapel which the Taylors often attended with the Broomhalls, for a series of articles on the Ningpo Mission. After the first had been published Lewis returned the manuscript to suggest that Taylor expand it into an appeal for all inland China. Taylor worked at his pamphlet whenever he could throughout the spring of 1865.

Methodical as a chemist preparing the ingredients of a pre-scription, he amassed information, compiled statistics, drew up diagrams to confront the reader. The cumulative effect of his re-searches appalled him.

The Chinese Empire extended to 44 times that of the United Kingdom of Great Britain and Ireland; 104 times that of England. Its population: 400 million. 'What mind can grasp it?' He imag-ined them walking past him, hour after hour, day after day, month after month, taking, he reckoned, over twenty-three years. And the total number of Protestant converts – say 3,000 – would pass by in as little as an hour and a half. The daily mortality was esti-mated at 33,000, or more than the population of Leeds; in three months deaths outnumbered the population of London. And al-most all died, in St. Paul's phrase, 'having no hope and without God'. Indeed, Taylor loosely summed up his findings by coining a slogan, 'A million a month dying without God', a slogan which hammered on his mind, bore down on his sleep, dominated his prayers.

He found that in the seven provinces with mission stations a

total of 185 million souls were at present 'utterly and completely
beyond the reach of the Gospel'. Eleven provinces inland, total-
ling in population 197½ millions, had not one single missionary.
And beyond those eleven was 'Chinese Tartary', by which he
seems to have meant Mongolia and Turkestan, an enormous re-
gion unknown to Europeans.

Since every missionary society had refused his plea that the
eleven untouched provinces, and 'Tartary', should receive at least
a crust from Christian England, there grew a deep conviction that
a special agency was essential for the evangelisation of inland China.
He told Maria, Gough, the Bergers. They agreed, and sighed with
him at such an airy dream. In Taylor's inmost private mind the
dream took shape until, to his dismay, it became a personal demand upon himself. God's whisper grew louder: 'I intend to evangelise inland China. if you will walk with Me I will do it through
you.'

He was already planning to send four recruits to China during
1865. 'It is much pressed on me to try and get 20 *more* European
missionaries besides these four, so as to send at least two into
each province of China proper in which there *is no* missionary
and two into Chinese Tartary; and to try to send them an equal
number of Chinese helpers, making in all 48 persons.'

Two serious difficulties faced any such scheme. It might interfere with existing missions. Secondly, 'the *money* question was
*the* rub'.

Eleven years later in an address at Westminster Chapel in August 1876 Taylor expounded the problem as he saw it in 1865.

'I was very anxious that we should not appear for one moment
to conflict with the work of any of the older societies; and still
more that it should not divert any help of any kind from channels
already existing, because that would have been no gain to China
or to the cause of God. But that we should have such a method of
working given to us as should draw out fresh labourers who, probably, would not go otherwise; and should open fresh channels of
pecuniary aid which otherwise, perhaps, would not be touched.'

It was an expansion of his earlier revolutionary project of search-

ing for working-class recruits. The LMS in early days had sent out
carpenters and builders as full missionaries, but they went prima-
rily to carpenter and build; an educated minister would be in charge
of spiritual work. Taylor intended such men to be evangelists, not
artisans. He believed that suitable men and women of such sort
would do very well for the type of mission he contemplated: they
were to be a band of evangelists under his direction, not missionaries of the more orthodox sort who required considerable education to administer mission stations. He wanted his evangelists to
go like St Paul on missionary journeys through untouched provinces: staying awhile in a centre, seeing a church grow around the
first converts as St Paul saw one grow at Philippi or Thessalonica
or Corinth, and then moving on, always with native volunteer
Christians as fellow-workers. Mission stations, with their buildings and paid native staff, might be the right way to open Africa,
an uncivilised continent. For an ancient civilisation, whether Roman or Chinese, St Paul's missionary method showed the way. If
China had to wait for college graduates qualified to found, equip
and develop full-scale stations, a century might pass before the
more remote provinces so much as heard the name of Christ.

Taylor would not mind if his people lacked formal education.
And he cared not at all what churches they sprang from if they
shared basic evangelical beliefs. His inland mission would be 'a
voluntary union of members of varying denominations agreeing to
band themselves together' for a specific purpose.

An interdenominational mission, in that age of disunity, was
highly suspect. The only major attempt, apart from two subsidiar-
ies serving all the Church – the British and Foreign Bible Society
and the Religious Tract Society – had been the LMS, founded
jointly by churchmen and dissenters. Very speedily it had become
predominantly Congregationalist.

An undenominational society, mainly working-class in texture,
would attract severe criticism. Even more might the structure of
control. 'There was no possibility for *me* to found a mission on
ordinary lines, for I had no denomination at my back.' A nonen-
tity could not gather an imposing committee. Taylor wanted a

more personal, a family relationship. And the defunct Chinese Evangelisation Society had given him a strong dislike of remote control by committee. Decisions, therefore, would be made on the field, and Headquarters would be in China, not London. Funds would be distributed through himself. Because he believed it to be the only way by which inland China's millions could be reached speedily with the Christian Gospel, young Hudson Taylor proposed to make himself a dictator; indeed, as an American contemporary in China dubbed him, the Ignatius Loyola of Protestant missions.

The problem of financial support rose like an impassable barrier. An appeal for funds would run counter to Taylor's determination not to deflect support from other missions. As an alternative he considered Christ's words to His itinerating seventy disciples, in the tenth chapter of St Matthew: 'Provide neither gold, nor silver, nor brass in your purses... And into whatsoever city or town ye shall enter, enquire who in it is worthy; and there abide till ye go hence.' He realised that this, laid down for a limited circumstance, would lead to disaster if followed in China.

The other alternative would be to apply the method by which he had financed his personal endeavours since resignation from the CES to the finance of a mission: to act in the spirit of Our Lord's words in the sixth chapter of St Matthew: 'Seek ye first the Kingdom of God; and all these things shall be added unto you.' 'Matthew VI was very clear – these things should be *added*; not do without them; not take them from the "Gentiles"; depend on our Father for them all... I felt it best just to leave oneself open to receive such remittance through the post as God might lay on the hearts of His children to send; in this way interfering with no collections made in places of worship, nor with any collections made in other ways.'

That was the theory. To contemplate evangelising a heathen Empire without actually asking a single congregation in the Christian West for a penny, shook even Taylor in the vigour and imagination of thirty-three.

Looking back in 1894, at the age of sixty-two, on nearly thirty years of proving that 'God is sufficient for God's work', the leader of more than six hundred missionaries then active in China said: 'God chose me because I was weak enough. God does not do His great works by large committees. He trains somebody to be quiet enough, and little enough and then He uses *him.'*

That did not seem obvious in the spring of 1865. It looked fantastic.

The adumbrative mission grew sharper. Even its name had been coined in Berger's drawing-room: the China Inland Mission. But Taylor did not dare commit himself to founding it. 'I had a growing conviction that God would have *me* to seek for Him the needed workers, and to go forth with them.' He had no doubt that if he prayed in the all-prevailing name of Christ, he would be given them and their support, 'and that doors would be opened before us in unreached parts of the Empire. But I feared that in the midst of the dangers, difficulties and trials which would necessarily be connected with such a work, some who were comparatively inexperienced Christians might break down, and bitterly reproach me for having encouraged them to undertake an enterprise for which they are not equal.'

It was his old enemy – fear. Fear of being hurt. 'It was... the devil getting one to feel that while prayer and faith could bring one into the fix, one would have to get out of it as best one might.'

The inward struggle became fiercer. By the end of May Hudson Taylor was heading for nervous collapse.

The first week of June the Taylors and the six candidates then with them went to Sainthill. In the June sunshine Hudson boated on the lake with his children, and played in the woods. During the warm nights heavy with the scent of hay he tossed and turned.

He saw an endless procession of the lost. It marched mute and pleading. 'A million a month dying in that land, dying without God. This was burned into my very soul. I scarcely slept night or day for more than an hour. I feared I should lose my reason. Yet I did not give in.' The voice of God: 'I intend to do it through you.' 'No!' The voice of the devil: 'Go on, God will give you helpers.

Take them to China. They will break down. They will reproach you. Can you stand that?' 'No!'

He heard the bloodlust of a Chinese crowd, saw some lad from English forge or office, his arms bound, his clothes torn from his back, the bamboo rods crash down, the horror, misery, reproach in his eyes as he looked in his agony at the man who had deceived him, allowed him to die unassuaged by the love of a God who had deserted. He saw a young woman from some Midland city violently weeping as she laid her baby in a distant Chinese grave. Saw the husband, pinched and drawn with starvation, wring his hands, moaning 'Why did we come? Oh, why did that man deceive us?'

The endless procession again, mute and pleading as they disappear into the darkness. 'These souls, and what eternity must mean for every one of them, and what the Gospel might do, would do, for all who believed, if we would take it to them!' On June 13th the Taylors returned to London. The next week, on Wednesday, June 21st, Taylor was back at the Bergers' regular local prayer-meeting. He prayed openly for the money and the men to evangelise the provinces now without any missionary, 'but had not at that time surrendered myself to be one of them, and their leader'.

The day following he went for two nights to Tottenham, an affluent suburb of North London where a group of his sympathisers lived in fine houses. On Saturday, June 24th, at Coborn Street he learned that Frederick Gough would not be coming for the morning's Revision. 'Proceeded at once, therefore, to East Grinstead and spent some hours in conference with Mr. Berger.' The Bergers' coachman drove him to the station and he travelled south-west to Brighton, where he was to stay the week-end with his old friend, the former secretary of the ill-fated CES, George Pearse of the London Stock Exchange.

Hudson was a harassed, burdened man. Not even Maria fully understood the reason for the unusual lack of laughter or song, the unwonted tightness of lip and thrust of jaw. Even she detected only dimly the frightful struggle of a man who dared not obey God. He had not told her all, nor Berger, nor his Tottenham friends.

At Brighton Station he found that Pearse had sent to meet him a mutual friend who was down from London for a few weeks by the sea, a middle-aged Presbyterian minister called J M Denniston. Denniston had exerted, twenty-six years previously, a formative influence on William Burns. This endeared him, and because Denniston was not involved directly in the issues tearing at will and reason, and was a man easy to confide in, Taylor unexpectedly disgorged his pent-up fears that Saturday evening as the station cab rattled through the streets and slowly up the rise to Pearse's home on the edge of the Downs.

Denniston was to preach for a Baptist friend on the following morning. He resolved secretly to pray that he should deliver an address specially applicable to his younger friend.

Subject and text are lost. Taylor told Mrs. Denniston on her husband's death in 1896 that 'a sermon from him was the turning point in my decision'.

At the moment it seemed to worsen the situation. As the full congregation rose to sing the last hymn, Taylor looked around. Pew upon pew of prosperous, bearded merchants, shopkeepers, visitors; demure wives in bonnets and crinolines, scrubbed children trained to hide their impatience; the atmosphere of smug piety sickened him. He seized his hat and left. 'Unable to bear the sight of a congregation of a thousand or more Christian people rejoicing in their own security, while millions were perishing for lack of knowledge, I wandered out on the sands alone, in great spiritual agony.'

Brighton beach at church time on Sunday morning in 1865 was almost deserted. Taylor walked down across the shingle to the narrow strip of sand left by the receding tide. Decision no longer could be averted. Breaking point had come. He must go forward, or else for ever hold his peace.

He trudged the sands in gloom and fear. As he turned his eye took in the glassy sea. He thought of heaven. 'Well, if God gives us a band of men for inland China, and they go, and all die of starvation even, they will only be taken straight to heaven. And if one heathen soul is saved would it not be worth while?' He walked on, a trifle more cheerful. He stopped, recalling some taking point of Denniston's sermon. 'Why,' he said to himself, 'if we are obeying the Lord, the responsibility rests with *Him,* not with us!'

'*Thou*, Lord! *Thou* shalt have the burden. All the responsibility lies on thee, Lord Jesus! I surrender. The consequences rest with Thee. *Thou* shalt direct, care for, guide me, and those who labour with me. I *will* ask for the workers to come forward.'

He took his Bible from under his arm, a parallel Bible of Hebrew and English, Greek and English, designed to give two chapters for each day of the year. On the fly-leaf he wrote: 'Prayed for twenty-four willing skilful labourers at Brighton, June 25, 1865.'

'All was joy and peace. I felt as if I could fly up the hill to Mr. Pearse's house. And how I did sleep that night! My dear wife thought Brighton had done wonders for me, and so it had.'

## Chapter 13: 'THIS DEFENCELESS LITTLE BAND'

Hudson Taylor's Christian service had never been a selfish scheming to curry divine favour, but a humble and hearty thanks for the experience of redemption by Christ. After Brighton beach this service took on a deeper tone.

Hudson's self-searchings had sent him into agonies but, once again, his acceptance of a command, his recognition of a revelation, had thrust him forward in a burst of light on his path. He knew now that God cared about his fears and had allowed for them in shaping His plan; God understood. The dominant feeling in Hudson's mind, therefore, more than ever before, was that he served in a relationship of love. God had called him and he had yielded himself as an instrument in God's hands: God could do what He liked with him and would be responsible for directing him. But God was his Father. It was a Father who had called him, a Father, who loved him so much that He could not allow him to lack anything.

Through Christ at his side Hudson had immediate access to God – for wisdom, for strength, for supply. With that certainty he could face any adventure and this, though he would not have analysed it, was the spring of his courage. He could not help having faith, for faith was merely the trust of a child in an all-wise, all-loving, all-powerful Father. At heart, Hudson was a child who needed looking after, who would be lost without the daily care of his Father and the consciousness of the Spirit of Christ just as, on the human plain, he was lost without Maria.

And thus Hudson Taylor reached greatness. To the world he was a feeble creature – of weedy physique, without powerful friends, almost a pauper. But he had thrown himself on God, had become an instrument of the Most High. His intelligence, his will-power and sticking power, his charm, his capacity to inspire and foster affection and loyalty, had all been touched by the Divine; he had become greater than the sum of his parts.

He had no idea, in the last days of June 1865, how God planned to give him the men or means to evangelise inland China. But Hudson had not the slightest doubt that He would.

'Who is that little man?' asked the Dowager Lady Radstock. She invited him to breakfast next morning at her fine house in Portland Place.

Hudson was staying with Amelia in Bayswater on Sunday, July 1st. He felt disinclined to attend Bayswater Chapel but prayed he should be directed where to worship. Passing Paddington Station and the fashionable squares backed by slums beyond the Edgware Road, he had turned down Welbeck Street towards Oxford Street when he remembered that a little group of 'Open Brethren' met in a hall just ahead. He joined their service and stayed to their prayer-meeting, requesting intercession for China and for those about to go there. It was, however, the unselfishness and simplicity of his own petition for a sick stranger whose case someone mentioned but none had remembered, which struck Lady Radstock.

She was the widow of an Admiral, a strong evangelical. Her son, the third Lord Radstock, a year younger than Taylor, became noted in the eighteen-seventies as 'Milord Apostel' who led a no-table religious revival among the nobility of Tsarist Russia. He brought his young wife round from their home in wealthy Bryanston Square to his mother's breakfast. His married sister, Lady

Beauchamp, up from Norfolk, listened equally intently to Hudson
Taylor, who in the next few weeks accepted three further invitations to Portland Place or Bryanston Square for introductions to
likely sympathisers in an exalted, somewhat alarming circle he had
never expected to enter. Lord Radstock became Taylor's warm
friend, marvelling at the audacity of this small Yorkshireman without influence or riches. He pressed for information as to the probable size of the China Inland Mission. Taylor wrote in reply, 'If
the Lord sends money to send out three or four, three or four are
to be sent; but if 17, 17 are to be sent out.' Less than a month
after Brighton he could tell his mother, 'Each week brings new
applications.'

Lady Beauchamp invited Taylor to Langley Park in Norfolk to
speak of China to the neighbouring gentry. Her little boy, Montagu,
remembered the drawing-room meeting because Taylor put on
Chinese dress and pigtail, showed chopsticks, Buddhist idols, and
other exciting curios. According to Taylor's custom money received
no mention. The last guest gone, Sir Thomas Beauchamp in some
distress said he was anxious to give but had nothing spare. Liabilities
were heavy. Taylor's surprise next morning, at being handed £15
was equalled only by his interest twenty-one years later, tramping
in China with young Montagu Beauchamp who had recently joined
the CIM as one of the Cambridge Seven, to hear how the money
came: 'My parents decided that night to give you the sum due for
the insurance on their greenhouses, a large number, and to trust
the Lord to protect the glass. Shortly afterwards there occurred
one of the most violent thunder storms. Thousands of pounds
worth of damage was done for miles and miles around, but just
immediately around our home there was scarcely anything spoiled
with the exception of a very small pane of glass. There was nothing
else to account for it but answered prayer. I have heard my mother
speak of this as an illustration of faith.'

At the end of August Taylor visited Scotland to settle affairs
for George Stott, a one-legged candidate from Aberdeenshire soon
sailing, and to interview other Scots who had applied to the Mission.

He left London by the night express of August 28th, squeezed on one-third of a seat in a crowded compartment. His plans were not precise; he would wait on events. During a day at Edinburgh a Mr Reed offered introductions to the Convenors of an important religious Conference shortly to be held in Perth. Taylor travelled onward that night round the Firth of Forth (the Forth Bridge not then existing) and reached Aberdeen at 3.45 am.

'I sat in the guard's room by the fire till 5 am and then went out. I had a very pleasant walk on the beautiful sands while the sun was rising and then walked about the city till 7 am.' He got a cup of coffee and a bun before taking a slow train up beside the Don to Whitehouse and Bridge of Bence, where his hosts, farmers called Milne, 'prepared me a second breakfast and what with the fresh air and walking I had done I was quite ready to do it justice. I need not say that the egg was fresh, the butter exquisite and the oatcake something *worth* eating.' In the afternoon he called on an applicant, James Lamond, and was dourly rebuffed. The man was harvesting and busy and had changed his mind about China: 'If you were not a stranger I would give my reasons. You are a perfect stranger, man, I do not intend to do so.' After this dose of Scotch Taylor walked to the top of the highest hill.

He returned to Aberdeen for the week-end and went out to Kirktown of Slains on the Monday to call on George Crombie's parents. 'They were both astonished and pleased to see me', more so when a few minutes later 'postie' delivered a letter announcing Crombie's and Barchet's safe arrival in Shanghai.

Taylor doubled back through Aberdeen for Perth. He needed all that stock of courage which he believed so much smaller than it was, to face the august Perth Conference with nothing but letters of introduction. He needed courage to face it without Maria. His love for her invaded all of him, they were 'one flesh' indeed, each mystically a part of the other's thought, action and Christian service. Away from her he felt raw and aching; he missed her smile of encouragement, her laugh, her instinctive understanding of his feelings. In the 6 am train he scribbled to her in pencil, 'It is not pleasant to me to go to strange places and push myself forward, but the Lord helps me... Bless you,' he ended, 'and our precious little treasures. How I seem to miss their little voices, dear little loving pets. Kiss them for me.'

He left his carpet bags at Perth Station and attended the morning session of the Conference, which was graced by leading evangelicals from Scotland and England; no man footed that platform whose credentials were not impeccable, backed by years of grave public speaking. Tremblingly, at the close, Taylor approached the minister to whom he had introductions. The minister passed the letters to the Convenor, Macdowall Grant of Arndilly. 'What?' muttered Grant, 'wants to speak about China... Has founded a new mission... very much in earnest... *missionary* appeal? My dear sir!' he exclaimed to Taylor, 'surely you mistake the character of the Conference. These meetings are for *spiritual edification*!'

'They agreed eventually to give me an opportunity of speaking of China tomorrow; and of prayer [this] evening.'

The evening meeting drew to its close. The Convenor arose, scanned his notes to get the name right, and announced that 'Mr. Hudson Taylor of Ningpo, China, will engage in prayer.' Taylor mounted the platform, gripped the rail to stop his hand shaking, closed his eyes on the largest audience he had ever stood before, and opened his lips. A contemporary has recorded: 'I was deeply impressed with the simplicity and fervour of his prayer, and felt that he was speaking to a familiar Friend in whom he had perfect confidence and from whom real blessing was confidently expected. Hearts opened to this unknown young man who unconsciously lifted the level of the Conference by a prayer. A General invited him to stay. Many pressed round to question. The following afternoon, nervous as before, he had the great audience in the hollow of his hand.'

He told them about a newly married young Chinese who had fallen overboard from a coastal junk into shallow water and deep mud. Taylor had rushed on deck at the splash and cry, found the crew looking helplessly at the spot where the man had disappeared. 'I leapt overboard and waded about in the hope of finding him.

Unsuccessful, I looked around in agonising suspense, and saw close to me a fishing boat with a peculiar drag-net furnished with hooks, which I knew would bring him up.

"'Come and drag over this spot directly; a man is drowning just here!"

"'It is not convenient."

"'Don't talk of *convenience*! A man is drowning, I tell you!"

"'We are busy fishing, and cannot come."

"'Never mind your fishing," I said, "I will give you more money than many a day's fishing will bring; only come – come at once!"

"'How much money will you give us?"

"'We cannot stay to discuss that now! Come, or it will be too late. I will give you five dollars" (then worth about thirty shillings in English money).

"'We won't do it for that," replied the men. "Give us twenty dollars, and we will drag."

' "I do not possess so much; do come quickly, and I will give you all I have!"

"'How much may that be?"

"'I don't know exactly, about fourteen dollars."

'At last, but even then slowly enough, the boat was paddled over and the net let down. Less than a minute sufficed to bring up the body of the missing man. The fishermen were clamorous and indignant because their exorbitant demand was delayed while efforts at resuscitation were being made. But all was in vain. Life was extinct.'

Taylor paused. He could sense hot indignation sweep the Scots at such callous indifference. Quietly he continued, 'Is the body, then, of so much more value than the soul? We condemn those heathen fishermen. We say they were guilty of the man's death – because they could easily have saved him, and did not do it. But what of the millions whom we leave to perish, and that eternally? What of the plain command, "Go ye into all the world and preach the Gospel to every creature?"'

He dilated on the value of a soul, spoke of 'a million a month...' and swiftly arrayed the mass of facts at his finger tips, to murmurs of amazement at this stark unfolding. The beliefs of his audience on heaven and hell, on the uniqueness of Christ as Saviour, on the awfulness of separation from God in this world and in eternity, were his. They knew the terms, the Biblical allusions, accepted the speaker's premises; were genuine in piety but unaware that 'spiritual sanctification' springs from unselfish action.

Taylor passed to the story of an ex-Buddhist merchant, an educated man, who had been baptised after attending the little church in Ningpo. 'He asked me soon afterwards, "How long have you known this Good News in your own country?"

'"Hundreds of years."

'"Hundreds of years! And yet never came to tell us! My father sought the truth, sought it long, and died without finding it. Oh, why did you not come sooner?"'

Taylor began his conclusion. 'Shall we say that the way was not open? At any rate it is open now. Before the next Perth Conference twelve millions more, in China, will have passed forever beyond our reach. What are we doing to bring them the tidings of Redeeming Love? It is no use singing "waft, waft ye winds, the story." The winds will never waft the story. But they may waft *us*...'

In October appeared *China: Its Spiritual Need and Claims; with Brief Notices of Missionary Effort, past and present,* by the Rev J Hudson Taylor, MRCS, etc. (of Ningpo, China). Taylor had adopted the designation and dress of a minister on the advice of Lewis of the *Baptist Times* and Bayswater Chapel.

The pamphlet of one hundred and sixteen pages for sixpence (paper covers) had been printed at Berger's expense, having been mostly dictated by Hudson walking up and down the room hands behind his back, to Maria, who must have transmuted his ungainly sentences into the straightforward, effective English of the pages; Frederick Gough also may have polished.

The book strikes the same urgent timeless note which had stirred the Perth Conference. Taylor opens with an exposition of the Lord's Prayer to emphasise that personal petitions take second place, 'Thy kingdom come, Thy will be done' precedes 'Give us... Forgive us...' Christian Britain reverses the order: 'Instead of honouring Him with the first fruits of our time, strength and substance, are we not content to offer Him the fragments that remain after our own supposed need is supplied?'

He marshals the statistics again, describes past missions in terms of warm commendation and notices that the number of missionaries has dropped from a hundred and fifteen in 1860-61 to ninety-one in March 1865. The time is ripe for a swift expansion of Christianity. The Treaty of 1860 (extensively quoted) has opened the whole Empire; the crushed Taiping Rebellion, by its semi-Christian origins and by its havoc, has shaken 'the confidence of the people in their gods of wood and stone. The Chinese language presents no insuperable difficulty. 'The masses of the people are unable to read or write; consequently persons possessed of a very limited education are competent to act as their teachers too,' although there is 'ample room' for philologists.

Many pages demonstrate from Taylor's own early journals and letters (as edited by the Chinese Evangelisation Society) that it will not, as some might suppose, be 'a hazardous experiment to send twenty-four evangelists to a distant heathen land with only God to look to'. He gives the background of the new CIM and describes his audacious plan, slightly modified from the original: 'our great desire and aim are to plant the standard of the cross in the eleven provinces of China Proper hitherto unoccupied, and in Chinese Tartary. But as it is absolutely necessary to have a baseline from which to ramify,' he does not propose to abandon work in Ningpo.

'Persons of moderate ability and limited attainments are not precluded from engaging in the work, and we shall most gladly enter into correspondence with any such who may feel called to it... Persons desiring to help forward the work with their substance' can send contributions to the CIM's bank or to Berger. 'We value above all things the prayers of the Lord's people.'

The effect of *China's Need and Claims* was electric, especially among those who had responded to the fresh spirit of fervour and dedication percolating through the country since the Revival of

1859 among all classes and churches. The pamphlet was first distributed at the Mildmay Conference in London organised by Pennefather, a prominent clergyman who would have held high office in the Church of England had he lived.

'I have read your pamphlet on my way down here,' wrote Lord Radstock from the Isle of Wight on 27th October, 'and have been greatly stirred by it. I feel very thankful to have received fresh stimulus to work for the Lord in England. I trust I may be called by the Holy Ghost to speak words which shall thrust forth many labourers into the vineyard.'[1] He enclosed £100. Shortly afterwards a slice of London society, coroneted or landed, received an invitation to Bryanston Square 'to meet the Rev J H Taylor of Ningpo, prior to his return to China. He will give information as to the vast spiritual claims of that country, and the means he proposes for spreading the Gospel throughout that land. Tea and coffee 7.30 to 8.15. Conversation 8.15 to 10 pm.'

Pressure increased. Taylor was not released from the Ningpo Revision until January; he must organise a reprint of the pamphlet; rent and furnish the next two houses in Coborn Street as candidate centres, one for each sex; arrange for collecting-boxes for those who asked, set up a printing press in Chinese to take abroad. He lectured all over London and the Home Counties. 'The number of candidates is almost weekly increasing, and many and important questions arise respecting them. The expenses are already great and ever increasing. The correspondence enlarges too... I scarcely know how to get through. So good has the Lord been to us, and so graciously has He enlarged and is enlarging our work.'

Hudson had a bad abscess in the ear in November, and Maria intermittent illness induced by pregnancy, 'so I have had very little help from her. God has sustained me or I would have broken

---

[1]This letter is one of those quoted as verbatim by the official biographers when in fact they have actually changed the sense, for no apparent reason. Part of their version reads (vol ii, p 46) '...I trust *you* may be *enabled* by the Holy Ghost...' (Italics mine) Similarly, Lady Radstock's very natural remark, 'Who is that little man?' is (vol ii, p 35) demurely polished to, 'Who was that?' And in the letter to Radstock, the possible seventeen recruits are tidied to sixteen.

down'. In early December she lay apparently dying for the second time since their marriage, but was saved by a forced premature delivery on December 7th, the baby dying at birth. She did not recover fully before February, and her lungs were permanently affected.

A newly-married couple and a bachelor had sailed for Ningpo early in October, making eight members of the new Mission already in China. (Mrs. Meadows had died.) By January 1st 1866 the Taylors had more than twenty others from whom to select sixteen to make up the initial twenty-four. Taylor's standards were high. He had never forgotten his conclusion in early days at Shanghai that if he had come out as a merchant 'without fixed religious principles' the conduct of missionaries would have sent him home an unbeliever.

The group that converged on Coborn Street for training by Maria and Taylor included a blacksmith, a carpenter and a mason, a governess, a Bible woman and the leisured daughter of a prosperous business-man.

All had been gripped by Taylor's personality. It was not immediately compelling. One of his best recruits admitted: 'I half despised him at first. A sickly looking, hesitating young man, no kicking power in his make up much'. Another was captivated by Taylor's quiet assurance, and said to himself: 'I don't know what missionary life involves of privation and difficulty, but I know I can follow that man, and I can tell the heathen of my Saviour.'

'We were all held by love to Mr. Taylor,' said a third. 'The whole thing was attachment to Mr. Taylor himself... We would rather trust Mr. Taylor than any missionary council in the world. I saw that he was stepping out in faith in God: he dared to trust God. That attracted me to him.'

On February 2nd, at Coborn Street, Berger (who would be Home Director in England), Taylor, and three of the men candidates drew up and agreed upon 'The Principles of the China Inland Mission'. These remained in draft until signed by all the missionaries at Hangchow in May 1867. As the original basis from which developed the direction of a staff of many hundred on un-

precedented lines (a small party only was envisaged in 1866), the
Principles form a breathtaking document revolutionary in the history of Protestant Missions.

'In the first place,' runs Taylor's pencilled memorandum of
the meeting, 'it was stated that I was feeling called of God to do a
work in China, in which I desired helpers.

'That such workers must be satisfied that God had called them
individually to labour in China for the good of the Chinese; must
go forth to China on their own responsibility; and must look to
God for their support and trust to Him to provide it and not to lean
on me. That they must be prepared to labour without any guaranteed support from man, being satisfied that the promise of Him
who has said "Seek ye first the Kingdom", etc.

'That such being the case they promising to work under my
guidance and direction, I would, in the event of my having funds
at my disposal, minister to their need as the Lord might direct *me.* '

His guidance and direction was to be complied with in every
respect, 'where we should go, where and when different individuals should be located, and the positions they should occupy must
be left to me to determine... It was not for the brethren concerned
to decide what they were fit for, or where they were to go.' The
individual could reserve only matters of denominational conscience.

A man who disagreed with a direction must pray to God to
change Taylor's views or his own. Any one 'unable to work longer
under my direction' must resign quietly and had no further claim
on the Mission – he must find his own way home, since 'each one
was going out to China on his own individual responsibility'.

In summary, 'the relation between us was this': they, for their
part, were going out as 'helpers in my work', to the best of their
ability. Taylor for his part, would feel responsible for their welfare
and would do all he could for them, but his word was law, and any
who thought he needed money above that allotted 'must not look
to me but to God to send him more, through such channels as He
might see best'. Taylor warned them not to lean on him. Looking
up at William Rudland, Cambridgeshire blacksmith, the day he
was accepted in the Mission, Taylor's eyes gripped and searched

him. 'Remember this. You are going out to serve the Lord Jesus, not the China Inland Mission. The Mission might fail. Look always off unto Him. He will never fail you.'

Gifts poured in. 'Lord Gainsborough presents his compts to Mr Taylor and begs to enclose a post office order for £3 for the China Mission. Lord G hopes to send the remaining £2 in a day or two.' The noble earl forgot. A Scotsman gave a printing press and valuable medical equipment, a Liverpool shipbuilder £650, ill-paid labourers and servants sent pennies and shillings. One day in March Taylor checked accounts to discover nearly £2,000 received in five weeks, the figure he had reckoned as a maximum requirement for passages and outfits (more was needed eventually).

Taylor kept his own expenses separate, never took money for his own use unless the donor specified. And he made gifts to other enterprises.

'5.45 am. I got to the meeting in time and reached home after midnight. I found a pile of letters which have occupied me ever since. I leave at 6.15 so must soon pack...'

Taylor went north that morning, February 7th, having left Maria, to whom he wrote nearly ever day, at East Grinstead with two of the children. The other two were at Barnsley, where he stayed before meetings at Liverpool and Manchester. In Liverpool a noted Irish Bible teacher, Grattan Guinness, heard him and promptly arranged for a speaking tour in Ireland. Taylor's days swirled into a cyclone of engagements: 'I reached London from Manchester on the 15th just in time to give a lecture, and got home after midnight. Left on Friday at 5 am for East Grinstead, just to spend an hour or two with Maria and stayed till dinner time, then returned to London for meetings on Friday and Saturday. On Monday I reached Ireland and held a meeting in Dublin; Tuesday held one in Limerick, Wednesday had one in Cork; Thursday another in Dublin, and came to Belfast on Friday...'

At Dublin Grattan Guinness introduced his Bible class of young men from professional families. Tom Barnardo, small of body and large of head, whispered to his neighbour when the door opened to disclose the speaker dwarfed by the height and broad shoulders of Guinness: 'Where's the great man? There's a chance for me!' Four of these Irish youths offered themselves to the CIM. Barnardo at Taylor's suggestion postponed China to qualify as a doctor; he went to Coborn Street and the London Hospital. In the East End, among destitute boys, Dr Barnardo discovered his vocation and founded his Homes.

John McCarthy spent over forty years in China. In old age he described Taylor in Dublin: 'so quiet, so very unassuming in manner and address, but so full of the power of God! I knew that night that I had not only received the answer from the Lord as to my sphere of service but had found the God-given leader also... And the little talk in his room after the meeting, and the simple prayer to God for guidance, are among the most treasured memories of my life.'

At Belfast Taylor had no Guinness to make arrangements. He felt frightened 'lest I might not get on well among strangers, and rather stiff presbyterians', and longed for Maria. He preached four times and addressed a public meeting with the Lord Mayor presiding.

March passed mostly in London. Hudson had set his sights on mid-May as the sailing date; Maria doubted 'whether we can possibly manage all by that time'. They had decided not to take their party by a regular P&O steamship run, whether through the Mediterranean, overland and beside the half-dug Suez Canal and down the Red Sea, or by the old route round the Cape, but to charter all passenger accommodation on a windjammer. The slow sea voyage would weld the Mission and lengthen training.

Early in April, with Maria for part of the route, Taylor undertook a three-week tour through Worcestershire, Shropshire and down to the West Country. 'Dear Mother, it grieves me to write so seldom and so hurriedly, but I cannot help it. Lecturing and travelling, and being in strange places fill all my time and require all my strength. Besides which I have an *immense* correspondence.' 'It is very fatiguing work,' added Maria, 'for he generally has to rise early and travel early, and does not get much rest except in bed. I hope the change of air will do him good; but the constant fatigue is very trying.'

'A Lecture on "China and the Chinese"' runs the bill posted on walls and lamp-posts of Malvern, Wellington, Hereford, Bath, Exeter and towns of Devonshire, 'with special reference to missionary work, will be given by J Hudson Taylor, MRCS, FRGS, of Ningpo, China... the lecture will embrace the geography, antiquity and population of the Empire, and the manners, customs, languages and religions of the people, and will be largely ILLUSTRATED BY MAPS, DRAWINGS, IDOLS, ARTICLES OF DRESS, and other objects of interest brought from China. ADMISSION FREE. NO COLLECTION.'

'China, China, China is now ringing in our ears,' said Charles Haddon Spurgeon, 'in that special, peculiar, musical, forcible, unique way in which Mr. Taylor utters it.' He would speak for two hours, a normal span in that patient age; shorter than many political speeches. He was not verbose, had no eloquence other than that generated by mastery of facts and urgency of subject, had a horror of romanticising and an almost exaggerated fidelity to exactness and accuracy; and if his natural fun was allowed an occasional bubble whilst he demonstrated chopsticks or Chinese ink, intense earnestness swept him forward. 'Well do I remember,' wrote a woman present in the Athenaeum at Exeter on 21st April 1866, 'his thrilling words as he pictured the myriads of China passing into eternity, and the children of God sitting at home careless and at ease... I think all the Lord's people thought it a tremendous risk taking out this defenceless little band to such a country.'

Taylor did not rest at describing China's spiritual need and claims. He sought to deepen the spiritual life of the Church 'to such a point as to produce the missionary spirit'. 'What a power the going out of the party was in the Christian world at the time,' recalled a man who followed them next year. 'Many of course said it was madness. Others thought it was a beautiful step of faith.'

May 2nd, after four nights at home, found Taylor in Hertfordshire at Totteridge Park, the home of the Dowager Lady Radstock's brother, Colonel Puget.

At the end of the public lecture Colonel Puget, as Chairman, rose. 'Ladies and gentlemen, at Mr. Taylor's request it was stated on the bills that there would be no collection. But I feel many of us will be distressed and burdened if we do not have the opportunity of contributing to this proposed good work. I trust that as the proposition emanates entirely from myself Mr. Taylor will not object if we pass round -'

'*Please*, Mr. Chairman. Please keep to the condition agreed between us. If you all feel burdened, as the Chairman says, then that is one of the strongest reasons against a collection. I do not want your burden to be relieved by making a contribution here and now under present emotions. Go home burdened with the deep need of China. Ask God what He would have you do. If to give money, give it to any missionary society with agents in China, or you can post it to our London office! But in many cases God may want, not money, but yourself, or giving up a son and daughter to His service, or prayer. A collection often leaves the impression that the object of the meeting has been obtained. But no amount of money can convert a single soul.'

At supper Colonel Puget reproached Taylor. 'The people were interested and we should have had a good collection.' Nothing Taylor said could dissuade him.

Next morning Puget was late for breakfast. Taylor had opportunity to open his letters. One, from Killick, Martin & Co. offered the entire passenger accommodation on the *Lammermuir*, sailing 26th May, for £807 10s. The booking must be made at once; they required a deposit of about half, the balance two days before sailing. Taylor knew that the CIM account did not then stand at £400; some big gift must be coming in today.

The unpunctual Puget remarked that he had not passed a good night. Taylor was suitably sympathetic. After breakfast his host asked him to come to the study, where he passed across a few trifling sums pressed on him the night before. Puget said: 'I thought last night, Mr. Taylor, that you were in the wrong about a collection; I am now convinced you were quite right. As I thought in the night of that stream of souls in China ever passing onward into the dark, I could only cry as you suggested, "Lord, what will Thou have me to do?" I think I have obtained the guidance I sought, and here it is.'

He handed Taylor a cheque, remarking that if there had been a collection he would have given a few pounds. Taylor looked at the cheque: £500.

London Docks on 26th May 1866. Hudson's mother, the Broomhalls, and Aunt Tarn, a host of relatives of the outgoing party. Old James Taylor stayed away. 'I am sorry to grieve you all so much but don't think that I have not suffered also. My coming can do you no good... I am naturally bashful and at my age I can't mix with strangers.'

The Bergers and other friends remained on the ship down river until Gravesend. A last farewell prayer in the saloon. China Inland Mission setting sail – Taylor had prayed for twenty-four 'willing skilful labourers': with eight in China, the fifteen now coming with the Taylors and one to follow shortly made up the tally.

They did not know that a Judas lay among them. Berger, prescient, said to Rudland, 'See that ye fall not out by the way.'

**Part Three**

# THE  INDESTRUCTIBLE

## Chapter 14: ORDEAL BY WATER

The seven men and ten women who sailed for China on 26th May 1866 by the *Lammermuir,* ironbuilt three-masted windjammer of 760 tons (Captain Bell and a crew of thirty-three), formed a variegated, rather improbable assault force.

Lewis Nicol, a swarthy Scottish blacksmith from Angus, and his wife were the only married couple. Also from Arbroath in Angus came James Williamson, a carpenter; George Duncan was a mason from Banffshire. Two were East Anglians: Josiah Jackson, a carpenter, later draper, from Kingsland near March, and William Rudland, that sort of blacksmith known as 'engineer' who serviced harvesters and other newfangled farm machinery, at Eversden outside Cambridge. John Sell, his calling not listed, was of Romford in Essex.

Elizabeth Rose from Barnsley sailed to be the bride of James Meadows; Mary Bell of Epping as the children's nurse, ranking as full missionary. Socially and educationally of better class were Jane Faulding, a Baptist, daughter of a Londoner with a piano-frame business; they lived in the Euston Road; and Emily Blatchley, also a Londoner, who was Taylor's secretary. Of the remaining women, two had been governesses, one of them by birth Swiss, and two Bible women.

Five of the fifteen recruits were Scottish, one Irish. There were Baptists, Methodists, Presbyterians; Mary Bowyer and Jane McLean were Anglicans from Pennefather's parish, St. Jude's, Mildmay. When the party should reach China, together with the eight of Taylor's people already in Ningpo, the China Inland Mission would augment the total of Protestant missionaries by about one quarter.

The four Taylor children, Gracie, Bertie, Freddie, and baby Samuel who was carried for nothing, completed the list, together with Mary Bausum returning under Maria's chaperonage to her mother, now married to an American called Lord. Almost every passenger was sick in the Bay of Biscay.

By June 3rd, a week out from London River, they sailed close under Cape Finisterre in calm weather. 'I should like you to have a peep at us all when we are all gathered together,' Maria, who was not too well, wrote to her mother-in-law, 'to see how happy we all are. God ever keep us so.' Jennie Faulding scribbled in her journal for 6th June, 'Oh I have enjoyed to-day! the sea is so lovely and the air so beautiful. I never thought a voyage would be such a treat. It makes my blood tingle with pleasure.' Another girl wrote: 'I hope I shan't get very fat for I seem to be always laughing.' William Rudland in old age recalled Taylor, whose thirty-fourth birthday had just passed, as 'quite one with the young men of the party. Mrs. Taylor quieter, in some ways perhaps more mature, such rare judgment; calm sweetness about her face always: most restful. She was very thoughtful and gave much time to study of the Bible and prayer. She gave a good deal of time to the children too – used to gather them to the cabin for a little reading.'

They had no stewardess, a steward for table only. Bunks had been arranged on top of their luggage, and the party made improvements and kept their cabins clean. Taylor, a neat hand at carpentry, turned bookshelves for his family and for Miss Faulding, dashed about on odd jobs that could have been left to the younger men, led the singing at the meetings, conducted compulsory Chinese and Bible classes, doctored crew and passengers, and kept a sharp eye out for novel-reading, against which he had an invincible prejudice.

His intention of hardening and disciplining intended pioneers was somewhat hampered. 'Mr. Taylor said before we came on board,' wrote Elizabeth Rose to her father in his little Barnsley cottage, 'it was necessary betwixt the comforts of home and the privations of China to have a sea voyage on purpose to break us in; but really there has seemed to be no breaking in about it. We have not only comforts but luxuries. Every possible kindness is shown to us by Captain and crew.' They were feeding like fighting cocks on food most of them never could have afforded. Dinner on June 10th, a random example, took one and three quarter hours: Hare or chicken soup; preserved mutton, minced hare, or chicken and ham, with potatoes and turnips; plum pudding, apple

or damson pie, blackcurrant or plum tart; biscuits and cheese; and
for dessert, nuts, almonds, raisins and figs.

On June 29th, two days after crossing the equator, Taylor learned
of 'germs of ill feeling and division among our party'. On July 5th,
becalmed in the sultry South Atlantic, the day after the black cat
fell overboard and three home-bound ships had been viewed, he
was asked to go into the stern cabin by Jackson (ex-carpenter),
Nicol (ex-blacksmith) and Duncan (ex-mason). They had a griev-
ance: had their outfits all been issued? Taylor admitted a slight
muddle over stockings, otherwise, yes.

Jackson, spokesman for the others, complained: 'I have seen
the list of articles supplied to Presbyterian missionaries. It is very
different from ours.'

'We do not intend to take the Presbyterians as our pattern,'
Taylor replied. 'They are persons from a different position in society. And they will wear their things in China. We shall wear
native dress.' He assured them he had done what he could.

Duncan said, 'I have a very poor outfit. Very different from
what friends at home expected.' Taylor repeated that if they 'had
special need of anything made or mended' they should tell him.
He went away sad at the implication that these three were going to
China partly to better themselves.

Next day, Friday, Taylor worked hard to remove spreading
discontent. He went round speaking to individuals 'privately and
affectionately', making a particular effort with Lewis Nicol, and
had a special evening meeting of 'confession and prayer for increase of the spirit of love and unity'. At another, on Saturday,
still becalmed, he was horrified to discover by the contrite prayers
that 'the feeling among us appears to have been worse than I
could have formed any conception of. One was jealous because
another had too many new dresses, another because someone
else had more attention. Some were wounded because of unkind
controversial discussions, and so on. Thank God for bringing it
out and removing it.'

The atmosphere improved slowly, helped by the ship escaping

from the doldrums to run before a good wind. Unity was restored, temporarily, and the *Lammermuir* turned the Cape of Good Hope, far out of sight below the starboard horizon, to cross the Indian Ocean.

Officers and crew had been disgusted to hear they would be shipping a boatload of skypilots. The Mate complained it was 'a pretty go. I wish I was out of it. Dreary psalm singing all day it will be!' Captain Bell two years before had been influenced by the Revival movement; his genuine if unobtrusive piety bore no likeness to the spurious religion of the terrible Jones of the *Jubilee*. The ship's company, with an exception or two among the officers, was rough, foul-mouthed and hardened, a crew typical of a windjammer in the 'sixties.

When the passengers had shaken down the seamen noticed first the happiness of these men and women going out to an apparently dismal exile. Laughter. High spirits. Singing all day, but of joyful hymns, some of which evoked memories of mothers' knees. They noticed that everyone wanted to be friendly. Accustomed to passengers who held haughtily aloof, the hands appreciated kindness, courtesy and a readiness to turn skills to the use of the ship. Nicol forged a thing or two, Williamson helped the carpenter. In Hudson Taylor they had that rarity on a merchantman, a qualified ship's doctor. He also found time to give simple lectures on anatomy to watches off duty. His enthusiasm for their interests in a few weeks had made the crew his slaves. 'They are so fond of Mr. Taylor,' Jennie Faulding recorded. And when a pretty girl wanted to hold a Bible class in the fo'c'sle, Mary Bell soon had their eyes more on the Book than on her.

Mary Bell's Bible class began nearly a month out from England, under tropical skies. Mary at once discovered five men 'anxious about their souls'. The next day, June 24th, young Tosh, Second Officer, now close friends with several of the missionaries, said he had become a Christian. On June 25th 'Mary reports one or two of the anxious men to be rejoicing in Jesus.' June 27th: 'Mr. Saunders, one of the midshipmen, has found Jesus. But there is some opposition springing up.' On July 2nd, Taylor, returning early from watching a glorious sunrise, met Mary who said ten of the men before the mast were converted.

Religion became a chief topic of talk, serious or lewd. The most unlikely characters softened under the spell, such as James, 'a regular character, the ruler of everything in the fo'c'sle'. Jennie Faulding wrote to her father, 'outspoken and fiery, scorning anything mean, unable to read, rough, and ready to fight in a moment, with a thoroughly pugilistic countenance, using awful language and keeping the whole crew in awe, though a capital sailor. Miss Barnes noticed him one day and said to me look what a countenance that man has! I'll try and talk to him. So she asked him to come to the meeting, almost expecting to get knocked down, however he promised to come, and soon he was converted and the change in him had great weight with the others and one after another believed and gave up cards and other things, till now the fo'castle is like a different place... I am sure a most entertaining book might be written of sayings and doings on board the *Lammermuir.*'

The dazzling trophy was Brunton the Mate, 'a very violent man,' Rudland recalled, 'at times almost devil possessed. For the sailors he made the ship a hell for days at a time. He was especially violent at night when we were out of sight. Such a bully, all the men feared him, nothing and nobody pleased him.'

On July 8th Brunton asked John Sell to come to his cabin and pray. Excitement among the missionaries seemed scarcely justified, for throughout July Brunton's willingness to talk about religion with any or every passenger was countered by his continuing misery and bad temper, until Thursday, August 2nd, when he 'had a terrible fit of passion and was swearing terribly'. Taylor spoke to him frankly about the state of his soul. 'He seemed almost in despair.' A crescendo of prayer-meetings during the next day, among passengers and converts, rose to the climax of midnight on Friday, when Taylor, instead of going to bed, sought out Brunton as he came off his watch. They talked for two hours. Brunton suddenly cried out, 'I see! I see how blind I have been!'

And Taylor's wondering ears heard prayer to God, of confession, faith, thanksgiving and intercession for each missionary, for Captain Bell, the crew, specially 'all who were unsaved on board, and his own wife and children'.

Taylor ran down, shook Maria awake, and two or three others, for praise and thanksgiving in the small hours. Taylor recorded next day, 'Mr. Brunton feels his burden quite gone and all our party are overjoyed.' 'There was not much done,' wrote Mary Bausum, 'we all seemed as if we couldn't settle to anything. There was such a change in him. His face didn't look the same.' Brunton called out his watch and told them what had happened. One man after another sought out a missionary, male or female, to beg spiritual counsel or to announce new-found faith.

They ran into heavy seas at the end of the week, had a bad accident when the sternsail boom broke and hit a seaman, William Carron. Three more of the crew 'found the Lord Jesus' on following days.

Sailors crowding the nightly meeting in the steward's room now suggested transferring it to the fo'c'sle, where 'card playing had for some time given place to Bible reading, and foolish songs to hymns. But now they and we met as believers.' The swaying ship's lanterns cast their flicker on sailors, missionaries, officers, seated on sea-chests, planks, on chairs from the saloon, or leaning against fittings. A few of the crew, half-shamed, half-attracted, watched from shadows beyond the capstan.

The harmonium played the opening chords of Watts's hymn, *Come let us join our cheerful songs.* After lusty singing the company bowed heads for prayer, led by John Sell, followed by a West Indian seaman. A passage from St John's Gospel was read and talked about. A sailor asked for *0 happy day that fixed my choice,* taken up with nautical gusto deepened by faith. 'Next voyage,' said one of the men, 'we shall all be scattered in different ships and we shall be able to speak for Christ. We must never rest till the whole merchant navy is converted.'

'Mr. Taylor is very tired nowadays,' Mary Bausum wrote to Amelia as the ship sailed through the Sundar Straits between Sumatra and Java, 'I don't think he is well. I am sure he has not enough sleep, and he won't have it. Now he is asleep in the stern cabin because he can't write his letters and it is all because he was up about four this morning. I hope you don't think I am grumbling at him, but I wish he would be more careful.' Hudson's eyes were inflamed. He would be called out of bed if any one fell sick. Maria's health had caused additional anxiety since a bad fall when the vessel gave a lurch.

Because he was run down, Hudson's judgment failed him. At sunset that evening the *Lammermuir* anchored in Anjer Roads. Early next day they all went ashore for the first time in three months, thoroughly enjoying the Javanese market and Chinese shops, the lush tropical vegetation of deep green, blue water, paddy ripening yellow. They laughed as a little brown boy shinned up a tree to cut them coconuts, they bought banyan fruit, bananas and sugar cakes. And that afternoon, in a little stream behind Anjer, Hudson Taylor committed the worst misjudgment of his life.

He had founded an unsectarian mission, announcing unequivocally that in matters of denominational conscience each missionary should be free. During the voyage he had allowed himself to persuade the two Anglicans, Jane McLean and Mary Bowyer, to accept the necessity of Believer's Baptism. This cherished Baptist doctrine, which holds infant baptism invalid and conversion incomplete without total immersion, had become dear to Taylor since he had been rebaptized in Hull in 1851, with the Brethren. To allow his per-sonal convictions to interfere with members of another Church on such a subject flatly contradicted his interdenominational principle.

The shore party held a baptismal service in a little stream be-cause several seamen and midshipmen wished to be baptised. When Taylor not merely permitted but encouraged the Misses McLean and Bowyer, both of whom had been baptised and confirmed in the Church of England, to be immersed at his hands, none real-ised, though Taylor should have foreseen, that this folly might nearly wreck the CIM.

The South China Sea in the typhoon season, after three months' voyage, could be reckoned to bring out a man's worst. Nicol the Scottish blacksmith, a man of some attainments but a rough diamond, showed new disaffection backed by Jackson and Duncan, Brunton the Mate grew tyrannical and moody again, behaving unnecessarily harshly to the sailors, 'several of whom privately threatened to strike him'.

The spirit of mutiny spread. At the Lord's Supper Jackson and Duncan walked out because Brunton intended to receive the sacrament. Their action grieved the rest, who at a special session begged them not to 'set themselves as censors and judges'. Lewis Nicol sat silent. Taylor sought out Nicol and found him 'in a truly deplorable condition. This one and that one had shamefully treated him or his wife.' Taylor brought each who had supposedly wronged Nicol to settle matters face to face, and every instance 'proved to be pure fancies or the most trifling of trivialities. In the afternoon and evening all were explained and through God's goodness ill feelings were removed.' Nicol's propensity to reckless statements did not bode well.

Harmony had been restored, Brunton recovered; in time for the worst storms the oldest hand could recall.

The sunset of Monday, September 10th, showed the imminence of a typhoon. Heavy seas, rain and wind throughout Tuesday strained vessel and crew, who with their passengers were relieved to see a fitful sun on Wednesday, and a sight of Formosa. Hope rose of Shanghai by Saturday. On Thursday a head wind drove *Lammermuir* off course. The gale, the seas and the misery, increased through Friday. 'We were all feeling worn out,' wrote Emily Blatchley, 'with want of rest, with the perpetual tossing, our wet clothes etc.' They were within two days' fast run of Shanghai, but for as much as eight days *Lammermuir* was forced to beat to windward, losing more than she made. The passengers valiantly sang *Rock of Ages, Jesus Lover of my soul, O God our help in ages past,* and other hymns for time of storm, with voices scarcely audible above the roaring, but hearts calm in the belief that their Master rebukes the wind and waves, and must defeat the malevolent hand stretched out to resist the incursion of the CIM upon the kingdom of darkness.

On Friday afternoon all hell loosed upon the shaken *Lammermuir.* 'The decks were swept over by the sea in a manner such as I have never seen before,' Taylor recorded. The gale worsened through the night. In Jennie Faulding's description, 'the vessel was knocked about like a shuttlecock, and rolled and quivered and plunged as you could hardly imagine, the flapping of the torn sails added to the wildness of the scene.' Early on Saturday, with a series of loud intimidating cracks, jibs and stay sails gave way.

Captain Bell, suffering from a painful facial paralysis, with Brunton and a salvage squad had to retire as the vessel dived into the sea. The upper starboard bulwarks on the lee side splintered and were washed away. The jib-boom crashed to the deck, followed by much of the top masts which swung madly on their wire shrouds.

The passengers huddled below saw the door open. Captain Bell staggered in, carrying a revolver. 'The men won't work any more. If they mutiny I shall shoot. Put on your life-belts. She can scarcely hold together two hours. Every volunteer needed.' 'Don't use force,' Taylor said, 'till everything else has been tried.' He went on deck with his men behind him. 'The decks full of water, which poured over both sides as she rolled, were full of floating spars, tubs, buckets, casks, etc. Besides the danger of being washed overboard, there was no small risk of having one's limbs broken by the moving timber. Prayer to God was our only recourse. The probability seemed that our hours if not minutes were numbered.'

He made his way forward to the fo'c'sle where the seamen huddled in despair. He went in quietly, smiled, said God would bring them through but everything depended on their seamanship. 'We will all help. Our lives are in jeopardy as much as yours.' Captain Bell saw the crew file out of hiding.

All morning and afternoon officers, crew, and missionaries hacked and lashed and heaved until danger receded of the side being stove in by swinging wreckage. By nightfall 'the appearance of the wreck was very sad. Rolling fearfully, the masts and yards hanging down were tearing at our only sail... The deck from forecastle to poop was one scarcely broken sea. The roar of the water on the decks, the clang of the chains, the tearing of the dangling masts and yards, the sharp smacking of the torn sails made it almost impossible to hear any orders.' The typhoon's worst had passed. Moonlight filtered through, but at 10 pm the royal and top gallant of the mizzen mast broke off, hanging.

*Lammermuir* was making water heavily next morning. All Sunday exhausted missionaries and crew worked at the pumps, even the ladies tugging at ropes let down into the saloon.

By Monday the seas lessened. Captain Bell, in great facial pain, lapsed into apathy. He refused to believe water in the hold had increased dangerously. Nicol and three other missionaries worked desperately to repair the pumps. Weary seamen grew insubordinate. Taylor's journal states, 'I believe there would have been mutiny and the ship taken out of Captain Bell's hands but for our influence.'

Six days afterwards, on a sunny Sunday morning, 3oth September 1866, a steam tug towed the battered wreck of the *Lammermuir* up Woosung Creek to Shanghai.

## Chapter 15: LAUGHTER IN SHANGHAI

The newcomers to China gaped, more tourists than missionaries, at the dreary amalgam of East and West which was the Shanghai of the 'sixties: odorous mudbanks, timber buildings, narrow streets crowded with sedan chairs, wheelbarrows, coolies carrying their loads on bamboo yokes. 'It seemed like a dream,' wrote Jennie Faulding, 'to be really surrounded by pigtails and little feet.'

Taylor did not waste a moment. Leaving the party on board *the Lammermuir* he hurried to Ningpo by canal, taking Mary Bausum home and Elizabeth Rose to be married, and met most of the eight China Inland missionaries already at work. Within forty hours he was back at Shanghai, his emotions seared by the devastation left by the Taiping rebellion, his mind settled against making his base at Ningpo, overpopulated with missionaries. 'He has decided upon our going to Hangchow,' Maria wrote a week after arrival. 'We intend putting on the Chinese dress as soon as we can and proceeding to Hangchow,' the great sea city on the Bay, between Shanghai and Ningpo. Hangchow was not a treaty port.

In Shanghai William Gamble of the American Presbyterian Press gave hospitality, and his godown for stores. Much had been messed by sea water during the storm. Days passed in unpacking, sorting, washing and re-packing, while Taylor procured passports, now issued for anywhere in the interior. He had Chinese clothes tailored for all.

They paid a final visit to the *Lammermuir.* There was singing, there were sad admissions that rum in port had wrecked the good profession of some, who promised to be better. Sorrow at farewell was unpretended. 'Poor Mr. Brunton says "It is like parting with those that are dearest to me," and it is the same with them all more or less.' After a final service in the forecastle, 'Nearly all the men were in tears, we went into our cabins to take a last look...'

As the missionaries drew for the shore, the crew manned the bulwarks and 'raising their caps gave three hearty cheers... sailors and midshipmen followed on the poop, where they repeated the cheers and stood looking after us till we passed out of sight.'

When the Mission left for the interior Brunton the Mate, former terror of the crew, came a day's journey, spent Sunday at their halt and was baptised by Taylor in the river at sunset. Captain Bell sent after them joints of meat, pots of butter, a barrel of treacle and other delights; the CIM had given him a Bible and travelling rug. Six weeks later Brunton forwarded a considerable subscription got up by the sailors. But in May 1867, Berger received a visit from Brunton, who said that 'the voyage out was the happiest he ever experienced and the voyage home the most wretched'. Drink and the devil had done for most of the converts, in Shanghai or Hong Kong. Captain Bell had turned against Brunton, discouraged his attempts to be chaplain of the ship, and on return to England Captain and Mate were dismissed for brandy-swilling, which 'Mr B denies both for himself and Captain B'. At least Brunton remained a decided and grateful Christian.

Taylor saw that this fizzed-out revival gave a weapon to his detractors. He wished to make a clean breast in the CIM *Occasional Paper,* and would not be comforted by the thought that the crew had none to teach or counsel them further, only the whole gamut of seafarers' temptations.

Two days before going inland Taylor and his men had heads shaved, pigtails woven in, and put on the dress of Chinese teachers. Some of the ladies remarked to Maria, after gazing at Nicol, Rudland or another transmogrified blacksmith or mason in smart new gown, 'The young men look a good deal more respectable in their Chinese clothes than their English. They are dressed like *gentlemen*!' Mrs. Taylor had changed, but the outfits of the other women were delayed a week or more.

The International Settlement erupted in a spate of ridicule, blended with protests at Taylor's 'cruelty' in taking unmarried ladies inland: all China had only fourteen other European single women, and they were in Hong Kong or the treaty ports. Taylor proposed to divorce his ladies from the refinements of western civilisation and to sacrifice their safety and their modesty in the appalling uncertainties of the interior, on the altar of his ridiculous ambition.

Shanghai missionaries, admiring faith and courage, did not conceal conviction that the misguided Taylor's China Inland Mission would have a life solitary, poor, nasty, brutish, and short. The Americans, Rudland says, were more friendly than the English. 'Poor Mr. Gamble had to suffer a good deal' for his sympathy.

The newspapers echoed the opinion of merchants, consular officials, opium traders. 'Mr. Taylor must be either a madman or a knave, and there is no reason to believe him a madman.' Taylor appeared unruffled. As Rudland wrote: 'So characteristic of JHT – nothing said about it! No reference to any unfriendliness. He did pass over things so graciously – let them drop.' One or two of the CIM read the press comments with shocked incredulity; they thought themselves to have gone up in the world by leaving forge or carpenter's bench. Instead, they were laughed at.

More than any other factor, adopting Chinese dress annoyed

the western community as it had ten years previously. A single eccentric might be ignored. Seventeen could not. The best course was to sneer.

Maria admitted, nearly a year later, that 'I had a misgiving before leaving England about ladies wearing the Chinese dress, on this ground: the Chinese despise their own females while they respect foreign ladies; will they treat us with as much respect and shall we have as much weight with them, if we change our dress? But I have found no ground for retaining this misgiving.'[1]

Hudson had no doubts. He recognised that 'merely to put on their dress, and to act regardless of their thoughts and feelings, is to make a burlesque of the whole matter', but to become Chinese to the Chinese was essential. Words written at this time were in advance of contemporary missionary opinion by fifty or sixty years: 'the foreign dress and carriage of missionaries (to a certain extent affected by some of their pupils and converts), the foreign appearance of chapels, and indeed the foreign air imparted to everything connected with their work has seriously hindered the rapid dissemination of the Truth among the Chinese. And why should a foreign aspect be given to Christianity?... it is not the denationalisation but the Christianisation of these people we seek. We wish to see... men and women truly Christian but truly Chinese in every right sense. We wish to see Churches of such believers presided over by pastors and officers of their own countrymen, worshipping God in their own tongue, in edifices of a thoroughly native style.'

Such sentiments appeared dangerous or absurd to Europeans in the mid-eighteen-sixties. And under the Chinese gowns of one or two of the *Lammermuir* party doubts began to rise.

The CIM left Shanghai by canal late in October. Gamble, having said goodbye, was about to get into the sampan to go ashore; 'he turned back, placed a roll of dollars on the nearest seat and was

---

[1] Maria appears not to have adopted Chinese dress at Ningpo after marriage. On the other hand, Amelia Broomhall had a distinct memory of her arrival as a 'Chinese' in Bayswater in 1860. Probably she wore a Chinese outer gown but had not done her hair, etc, in native style.

gone.' It was the payment pressed on him by Taylor for board and lodging.

They proceeded south in three boats. The young men had one. On another the servants lived and cooked, and with them sailed Tsiu, Taylor's evangelist and teacher from Ningpo, whose gentlemanly nails amused the recruits: 'they are quite an inch and a half away from his fingers.' The third was 'a fine large mandarin's boat with three rooms in it' for the Taylors, their children and the women. The leisurely journey, at first 'such a romantic and gypsy-like existence', quickly palled. It was a breaking-in. The men were sore from head-shaving and awkward in unfamiliar clothes, though Jennie Faulding thought them all 'improved by the change except Mr. Taylor'. They did not acquire the correct manners of the *literati* swiftly and Taylor was impatient that after his teaching they showed themselves 'so uninstructed as to Chinese ideas'. Maria, over six months pregnant, valiantly schooled her women. 'The nearer we come to the Chinese in outward appearance,' she would say, 'the more severely will any breach of propriety according to their standards be criticised. I must never be guilty, for example, of taking my husband's arm out of doors! And in fifty or a hundred ways we may, without great watchfulness, shock the Chinese by what would seem to them grossly immodest and unfeminine conduct.' Occasionally the party enjoyed relaxation. 'We all went to the hills for a day,' Jennie wrote early in November, 'and had such a treat. I used to think that when I came to China I should see no more pretty scenery, that everything here was cut and dried and ugly, instead of which I am more and more pleased every day; the canals are like beautiful rivers and if the strawberries have no taste, the wild raspberries are very nice (we have had a pie made of them). The birds sing to one's heart's content and were it not for the temples and the people it would be hard to imagine myself in China.' Berger had given Taylor a shotgun. John Sell astonished his friends and the Chinese by shooting three wild geese with a single charge. Taylor had 'only succeeded in shooting a magpie a sparrow and 5 rooks. I hope however to get some better game soon.'

In crisp late-autumn weather they drew near Hangchow. Duncan and Jackson were inclined to separate themselves from united devotions. The Swiss girl, Louise Desgraz, grew spiteful towards Emily Blatchley and Jennie Faulding, those two close friends and loyal supporters of the Taylors. Emily's scrappy journal contains a cryptic cry: 'Let the unhappiness of this journey, reaching a climax towards the close, go unrecorded. To me, just once or twice, a sudden dash of joy. Yet God did not leave US.'

Taylor had planned to settle the men in some city by themselves with his Chinese evangelist, taking the women to Hangchow. No landlord would receive such a large, gauche miscellany of unChinese male shapes and sizes. Even Taylor tasted dismay at continual rebuffs. He wrote on November 20th, 'Hope deferred makes one feel disheartened at times. Just now our teacher has come in to tell me that once more we are foiled in our attempts, so we must move on to-morrow morning to Hangchow. I will be thankful when we do get settled, for many reasons.' He brought the party entire to Hangchow in the last days of November, chilled, several unwell, the children sickening. One of the three western missionaries in that vast city, an American called Kreyer, offered them a temporary home.

Hangchow stood at the head of the Bay, astride a great river. Long ago it had been the Imperial capital, and traces of past glories remained: the West Lake, its pretty pavilions, the almost incredible extent of walls built across hill and dale enclosing tracts long since reverted to fields. Hangchow was one of China's leading cities, but the Taiping invasion had decimated a population of a million and a half, and thrown large areas into ruins. About two years before the CIM an Englishman of the Church Missionary Society, George Moule, and Kreyer and Green of the American Baptists, had established missions. The inhabitants remained surly and suspicious: if a westerner walked the walls, he spied; if he shot birds he had shot men.

George Moule and his wife were 'exceedingly kind to us'. Moule concealed for the present his profound disquiet at the appearance of a large party, mostly half-trained, masquerading as Chinese, led by a man who had never been to university, and representing varied denominations. Dissenters were tolerable only if sponsored by an official body at home. This mixed multitude had no credentials, and Anglicans who joined dissenters in any enterprise of this nature were sadly astray.

Taylor detected nothing but the warm welcome.

He succeeded within a few days in leasing a place big enough for all his people. The stout old landlord agreed to a reasonable rent because Sunday happened to intervene at a crucial stage of the negotiations, and when Taylor did not reappear to continue bargaining the man feared he was losing good tenants.

It was a rambling, dilapidated jostle of curved roofs and ups and downs, of timber and brick, and paper partitions, of gloomy passages, draughty rooms, and dragons curled round water-butts and cracked porcelain ginger jars; of Chinese faces peeping from unexpected holes; a cold place where braziers scarcely served to keep finger tips warm, and floor boards creaked eerily in the night.

'This seems to be the very place we want,' the ever-cheerful Jennie wrote home. 'It is in the midst of ruins and we can get a short walk in any direction without being much seen, at the same time we can soon be in the heart of the city if we wish. This has been a Mandarin's residence, it is an immense place capable of being made into sixty rooms I should think, at present it is very dirty and out of condition but I expect it will soon suit English notions a little better than it does now.' She added, 'we can get plenty of air and exercise without going away from our own premises.' Taylor said, 'There is a deficiency in the wall of my bedroom 6 foot by 9 foot closed by a sheet, so that ventilation is decidedly *free.*'

The December weather and the atmosphere of decay made one chilled missionary write of the 'sad removal into that desolate house, the work of making it habitable for the bitterly cold weather which was already upon us'. Tempers had been tried by the restrictions of the long journey in canal boats. Now, instead of longed-for freedom, they must behave with the utmost circumspection lest they stir the latent hostility of the Hangchow Chinese. Nor could they relax inside their compound while previous tenants remained in part, as they did for some weeks. 'The people living here come to our Chinese prayers and I think they feel much more at home with us, seeing that we eat rice and dress like themselves.'

Taylor required more than ever a strict obedience, for he alone had experience of what might and might not be done. He allowed relief on Christmas Day. 'No one knows what good things we are not going to have,' Jennie wrote on Christmas eve, 'Mr. Taylor has been giving orders and I am not in the secret.' They had pheasants and haunches of venison, plum pudding and fruit pies and sweets. 'We were barbarians enough to go back to knives and forks for once.' The ladies were allowed English dresses, and someone had sent the *Illustrated London News*.

Christmas was a shaft of light in the shadows. The year 1866 ended under foreboding of disaster. 'Dec. 30, Sunday,' Emily Blatchley inscribed in her journal. 'The smouldering fire showing flame, now. The young men met in Nicol's room – asked for Mr. Taylor – "Mr. T's being changed." Dissatisfaction brooding.'

## Chapter 16: THE BATTLE OF THE CHOPSTICKS

Early in 1867 Hudson Taylor settled several of his team in hinterland cities where missionaries had never lived. To Siao-san, only ten miles from Hanchow, went the Nicols.

Three months in China had convinced Lewis Nicol that he was an efficient, experienced missionary. Instead of a blacksmith hammering in a forge, touching his cap to gentry when they brought in horses, he was a man of consequence. He regretted, however, that wearing Chinese dress imposed a limitation which Taylor emphasised strongly: he must treat with deference, as his superiors, Chinese who were of higher rank than a teacher. He chafed at such a reversal of facts: was not even a mandarin a mere native?

Foreigners were mistrusted by the inhabitants of Siao-san. Gossiping over braziers in the tea-houses and eating-shops and in the crowded market where the villagers brought in their scant winter produce, men sucked at their pipes and argued the case. On balance the red-haired barbarians could be tolerated because the man wore civilised dress and pigtail, and the woman, though her feet were as big as a prostitute's, at least dressed her hair like a decent lady. But coolies who took away the mission's night-soil tubs had seen in the yard suspicious boxes which might be for storing babies which barbarians were known to steal, kill and salt down. Women in neighbouring streets, chatting as they lighted incense sticks outside their houses, decided that if the barbarians were wicked they would soon emerge in their true colours.

People crowded into the downstairs room which Nicol used as a chapel, where the teacher who had come with him from Hangchow helped his faltering colloquial. They treated him as one of themselves, allowing him that nuance of respect given to teachers – more than to a craftsman, far less than to the lowest mandarin. Nicol disliked it. He wanted them to treat him with the deference shown to George Moule. He banished the reflection that Moule was a distinguished scholar in written and colloquial Chinese, and in origin highly educated and cultured. Nicol decided that the difference lay in dress. Moule wore whiskers. Moule ate with knife and fork. Nicol's whiskers might take time to grow again. There need be no delay in other matters.

Chinese dress and chopsticks were stuffed away in trunks. The Nicols walked the streets in western dress. A shudder ran through the markets and eating-houses – Siao-san's fears were realised. The foreigners must mean mischief.

John Williamson, pigtailed and robed, and Tsiu came over from Hangchow for a Sunday. The weekend passed normally and they were to leave on Tuesday morning.

On Monday evening, 28th January, the Nicols and Williamson sat writing upstairs. Tsiu and the servant, downstairs, heard a commotion outside. The front door burst open. Tsiu saw the street full of lanterns, and a mandarin's sedan chair. He ran for the foreigners, who hurried down to find the chapel-room crowded with retainers, and the magistrate standing at the foot of the stairs.

Nicol bowed. The magistrate seized him by the shoulders and turned him round. Nicol indignantly turned back and faced him. The magistrate became a little more polite.

He sat down. Nicol sat also and called for tea. 'I do not want it,' said the magistrate. 'Do you think I would drink foreign tea? How many foreigners are here?'

He refused to look at their passports, which bade all Imperial officials provide unhindered passage and every aid throughout the Empire. He waved them away contemptuously. He demanded Mrs Nicol, and when she came in her English dress he stared at such outlandish costume and made coarse remarks. He insisted on inspecting the house; his unsteady movements, his boisterousness alternating with courtesy showing him slightly tipsy.

Downstairs again, the magistrate asked bluntly what they did here. Tsiu told him. The magistrate who had not even asked Tsiu's name or city, looked at him as a man looks at a louse.

'The Christian religion,' he said, 'is a depraved and prohibited religion... On your knees!' Tsiu knelt in kow-tow, forehead on the ground.

The magistrate flicked a finger.

Before Mrs Nicol's horrified eyes, Tsiu was stripped of his nether garments and beaten upon the thighs and buttocks with stout bamboos. A hundred, two hundred, three hundred strokes – Mrs Nicol closed her eyes against raw and bleeding flesh, her ears against piteous screams. Four hundred, five hundred, the minutes of agony wore on. After six hundred blows, the retainers seized Tsiu's pigtail, pulled him roughly on to his back and lashed his face one hundred times with a leather thong.

'Stop!' commanded the magistrate. 'Before the punishment continues, let the foreigners say if they will depart at once.' They agreed instantly. Tsiu was released. As the magistrate departed he threatened that any of them who remained after the following morning would be summarily beheaded.

While the missionaries were tending Tsiu's stripes a rough knocking and shouting again frightened them. Runners had returned with orders to drag Tsiu instantly to the *yamen*. Nicol decided to accompany him. The magistrate thereupon did not appear, but sent orders that they were to leave Siao-san that very moment. Nicol refused. He promised to depart first thing in the morning, and took Tsiu away. At midnight another messenger knocked them up to repeat the mandarin's order. Tsiu left at once. The Nicols and Williamson packed hastily and at sunrise went to the river. Publicly disgraced, they were unable to get a passage except at exorbitant rates.

Tsiu limped into Mission headquarters. On hearing the full story later from Williamson and a highly incensed Nicol, Taylor reported to the British Consul, R J Forrest. In due course the British Representative at Peking, Sir Rutherford Alcock, lodged a protest at their expulsion in violation of the treaty.

Taylor had received Nicol with sympathy despite the flagrant disobedience which had caused the calamity, and allowed three days for recovery before raising the question of dress. Maria was present at their talk, forty-eight hours before her confinement for the birth of Maria Hudson Taylor.

Taylor asked Nicol gently: 'Will you change back into Chinese clothes ?'

'No, I won't,' replied Nicol. 'You want me to make a fool of myself. What would people think of me changing and changing back. I will not be bound neck and heel to any man.'

Taylor's gorge rose. He mastered it. Maria could see 'how tried my dear Husband was, and I was struck with the meekness and patience which were given him from above, and with the quiet way in which he spoke'.

'Your course,' said Taylor, 'is injurious and possibly dangerous.'

'Then I suppose I had better make my way at once to one of the free ports.'

'I am not sure that may not prove to be the best course. Don't do anything rashly, brother. Pray about it. I urge you to pray.' Nicol did not go to a treaty port, nor pray. He went at once to George Moule and told him that Taylor had refused to speak to Mrs Nicol unless they both promised 'all sorts of unreasonable things'.

The Reverend George Evans Moule, a few years senior in age to Hudson Taylor and afterwards bishop in succession to Russell, was an older brother of Handley Moule, the saintly evangelical leader who was Bishop of Durham in the early twentieth century. Handley 'felt him to be one of the nearest I have ever known to the ideal of the Christian'. Handley Moule did not know that George had 'the misfortune to wish to set everybody else right', as a member of the CIM wrote. One of his own colleagues admitted that 'the only person beyond Mr M's criticism is Mr Russell, and even he is not perfect'.

Moule had decided that the infant interdenominational mission was a monstrous mistake that must be strangled before it could grow. He was, however, a man of charity and courtesy. He did not wish to wound feelings. He was always affable to members of the CIM: 'when he was seeming friendly and we knew nothing about it, he had been writing we know not what, when of course we could not defend ourselves.'

Moule had been offended that Jane McLean and Mary Bowyer, Anglicans, had not carried letters of introduction to him from their clergyman in England. He told them they should consider him and his wife their protectors. Jane McLean took him at his word. Inevitably he soon extracted the awful truth that Hudson Taylor had re-baptised them on the voyage out.

Moule accepted Nicol's story instantly. He did not seek Taylor's version, but fanned the flames of disloyalty. Jane McLean put on her western dress and did her hair again in the fashionable Paris net. John Sell, her fiancé, snipped off pigtail, stopped having his head or whiskers shaved, and wore jacket and trousers. They had to use chopsticks and china spoons at the CIM, but whenever they could hurried across to the Moules to eat with knife and fork. They and the Nicols tried to persuade others to join them. Just when Taylor's methods appeared to be succeeding, when services were crowded with friendly Chinese so relaxed that one careful listener might be mending a shoe, another nursing a dog, another combing her child's hair, and Jennie Faulding's constant cheerful visits to homes were giving her the local name of 'Miss Happiness', just then the CIM's unity was threatened by this battle of West and East – fork against chopstick, whisker against pigtail.

Nor did Moule hesitate to stoop to personalities. He wrote England that Taylor was a dictator of the worst kind: pastor, doctor, paymaster and confessor, who even opened everyone's incoming letters and insisted on being told every action, thought and feeling; the CIM were miserable and had spent the outward voyage quarrelling.

Maria was recovering from her daughter's birth when she received 'a great shock and grief'. Moule had written to say that Mr Taylor's practice of kissing the unmarried ladies was most objectionable and should cease. He insinuated what he wrote openly to England: 'Mr Taylor is a hypocrite and his faith and work a sham and a delusion.'

Taylor and Williamson called on Moule, wishing to explain that the rumour must have arisen because Jennie Faulding and Emily Blatchley, treated practically as members of the Taylor family, received good-night kisses on the forehead from Maria and Hudson. Moule, with the utmost courtesy, smiling his charming smile, declined to hear any explanation unless Taylor undertook to disband the household and put the unmarried ladies elsewhere. He greatly regretted they had come, and did not believe an unmarried female could do the slightest good in China. Hudson stopped his good-night kisses.

Accusations mounted. Reports on Moule's libels percolated back from England. Berger urged the Taylors not to be distressed. 'My hair would almost stand on end if I thought you capable of doing such a thing,' he wrote at the charge of opening private letters. 'Poor Mr Moule,' thought Maria, 'I believe he thinks he is "doing God service", but the amount of mischief that he has done is difficult to estimate.'

In April 1867 the George Moules sailed for furlough in England, where they continued to campaign against Hudson Taylor.

They left in Hangchow a China Inland Mission split, in acute danger of collapse.

The young men, as they tramped the lanes with Chinese helpers, argued with priests in the shade of gloomy Buddhas, or listened to Taylor describing his schemes for inland stations, could not forget Moule's advice that they resign. The Nicols refused to join Chinese services, but with Sell and Jane McLean had daily prayers in English. Nicol sent Berger 'sweeping and severe' assertions. Jennie Faulding wrote, 'He has been a great trouble to Mr Taylor and done much to injure the mission, still Mr T thinks he may be useful among the Chinese. My own opinion of him is, that he is a Christian, but of a self-sufficient, jealous disposition... Mrs Nicol is an earnest good woman but wholly led by him.'

Jane McLean's sister Margaret arrived from England with the McCarthys. 'Poor Margaret McLean!' wrote Maria, 'we were very sorry for her, she was drawn into the party we believe without knowing it, and we could not get at her. She and her sister almost invariably asked to be excused from the table before meals were over, never set to work or write in the common sittingroom, but were generally with Mr Sell or the Nicols or all together. We longed to show her kindly feeling and to screen her from the influence of party feeling... but we could get no *formal* opportunity of quiet conversation with her.'

The Nicols, still in western dress, returned to Siao-san, where the Chinese authorities were slowly summoning humility to apologise. (They never did so, but sent Nicol presents: silk, and a fan, an umbrella, coffee cups, a teapot, fruit and cigars.) In May, shortly before his wedding day, John Sell caught smallpox and died. The bereaved Jane turned on the Taylors.

The Mission cracked wider. Even Jennie Faulding and Emily Blatchley cooled towards each other.

The crisis had been reached. The split must be healed or the Mission collapse. These months of spring and summer, 1867, brought full maturity to Maria and Hudson. 'I have known him under all circumstances,' Jennie told her father, 'and if you could see him daily you would indeed admire his self abnegation, his humility and quiet never flagging earnestness. Very few in his place would have shown the forbearing loving spirit that he has done.

No one knows how much he has felt these troubles nor how much he has suffered from depression. If he were not in the habit of casting his burdens upon the Lord, I quite believe that what he has passed through he would have sunk under. Grace, not natural temperament, supported him.'

Hudson Taylor was no plaster saint. Maria wrote: 'I am more intimately acquainted than anyone else can be with his trials, his temptations, his conflicts, his failures and failings, and his *conquests.*' Reproach, unfairness, inefficiency, all that most annoyed him was his constant lot; only to Maria, and occasionally to Jennie, did he betray his feelings. Maria knew, and none else, how Nicol hurt him. Hudson wanted his people to regard 'me not only as the head of the Mission but as a friend and helper. It is very painful to feel, and humiliating to have to acknowledge, that the reverse is the case with some.'

He was driving his feeble frame to the limit. 'I get along much as usual – that is, much more to do than I can possibly get through ... overwhelmingly pressed with work.' In addition to administration he had a hundred out-patients daily, a few inpatients, and the chief burden of preaching to nearly two hundred each day, his command of the colloquial enabling him to preach extempore.

He was never self-important. 'He is so anxious to make us comfortable and by inexpensive ways in all his multitude of work, he is always contriving something or other that will be to our advantage.' In later life, when he was internationally respected, his assistants often had to stop him doing lesser men's chores, and what Griffith John, a veteran of the LMS, wrote at the time of Taylor's death was true in 1867: 'He was the *servant* of all, though the head of the Mission. He never asked any man to do what he was not prepared to do himself, or to endure what he was not prepared to endure.' Griffith John ascribed much of Taylor's influence over men to this, and to 'his kindliness of heart, his self-abnegation and self-denial'.

Taylor's colleagues told how in these early days 'He would work until he was too weary to work any more, and then lie down and sleep whether it was night or day. He was gifted with that happy power of commanding sleep whenever needed. To insure a quiet time for uninterrupted prayer, he always rose very early in the morning before daylight and, if nature demanded it, would continue his sleep after his season of prayer.' He once admitted to a friend that 'the sun has never risen upon China without finding me at prayer'.

His single relaxation was shooting. 'I think it has done him such a great deal of good and me too,' Maria wrote after a short holiday in the hills. 'He went out every day with his gun and spent almost the whole time out of doors. I so enjoyed climbing the hills with him or going among the fields to carry any game he might happen to shoot.'

In facing the crisis Taylor knew that he must cling to essentials. He had readily admitted his folly in re-baptising Anglicans and never again swerved from a true inter-denominational position.[1]

He would not be moved from his conviction that the wearing of Chinese dress was vital if missionaries were to evangelise the interior. Neither spiteful press articles (one of May 1867 assured its readers the Mission had exploded because of the trouble over dress), nor friendly admonitions from Consul Forrest, nor the courteous libels of Moule could deflect him. He knew that more than the shape of garments was at stake. Behind the choice of trousers or gown, whiskers or pigtail, fork or chopsticks lay the whole question whether Christianity should spread in China as a universal or a western religion. And behind a missionary's adoption of the dress must lie a willingness to forswear the company and approval of westerners in order to gain the friendship and confidence of the Chinese; the Pauline principle of becoming 'all things to all men'.

He wrote to Berger: 'It will never do for persons to come out here so untrained in this principle as to fall the easy victims to the first missionary, *in* or *out* of our number, who may meet them with "what tyranny not to let you wear your hair in a net!" Or "to

---

[1]In course of years he built a strong Anglican section. Three CIM missionaries became bishops since 1895 when Cassels of the Cambridge Seven was consecrated.

want you to sacrifice your beautiful beard and whiskers!" Or "to confine you to chopsticks!" I would put the question to any unprejudiced person – why is it that in every part of every province in China, R C missionaries are both able and willing to live, while away from the ports scarcely one Protestant missionary is to be found? ...Without any doubt foreign tailors and foreign cooks, foreign houses and foreign furniture lie at the root of the matter. *Our mission will prove a failure* so far as any extensive evangelisation of the interior is concerned unless this principle is taken up by its members as a body. Give me a score of men such as Williamson and Duncan and McCarthy and with God's blessing in less than four years time there will not be a province without its missionary. But let me have a few more persons who oppose this principle at every turn, and if we are not broken up altogether it will be of God's own special interposition.'

## Chapter 17: THE CRISIS BREAKS

At the height of the crisis, when the Mission rocked on its foundations, Taylor's sight was focused on the untouched inland. In the heat of June he took Duncan and McCarthy, Tsiu and two local Christians westwards to explore possible stations.

They travelled upriver in a flat-bottomed boat, tight-packed under its bamboo awning with passengers who cooked and ate, smoked opium, gossiped or slept. For one stage McCarthy lay pressed against a chained murderer. Hudson scribbled to Maria on June 20th, 'My darling one, I can now only in imagination hold your loved form in my arms. Perhaps dearie the Lord will account that *we* do make some little sacrifice for His name and work's sake. I wish you could be with me. How you would enjoy this magnificent scenery! For my sake and for the Lord's sake take great care of your health... O if I could but give you one kiss, instead of writing that, I remain with a husband's fond love your own Hudson.'

Maria had been left in charge at Hangchow. She had every right to be. Despite her 'fragile body and sweet expressive face' she was no insipid, faded, Victorian mamma. Indeed, some members thought 'she was the backbone of the Mission at that time. Hudson Taylor had so learned to value her judgment and prayerfulness that he never took a step without consulting her.' But she did not obtrude. She was remembered by Emily Blatchley as 'humble, retiring, almost to shyness'.

At thirty years of age Maria had reached her prime. She was worn with privation and recurrent illness; she had been tubercular since 1865. Thinness accentuated her height, and suffering would have left her pale had her complexion not been naturally rather dark.

The younger missionaries were slightly in awe of her. She was so obviously a lady, and she had sharp intellect and powers of concentration. They admired her skill in the language, literary and colloquial, and the way she got close to the Chinese. They admired her strength of will, 'a woman of indomitable perseverance and courage, through troubles of every kind'.

This awe was tempered by affection. 'Ever since we left England she cared for me and treated me as one of her own family,' said James Williamson. 'Such a mother to us who were young in years and young in grace,' recalled one of the recruits of 1868. Like Hudson, 'she always sympathised with everyone and everybody. It showed often in little things.'

She was bright and animated in manner and conversation but never impatient or ruffled, always serene whatever might stir without – or within her. When Nicol first disobeyed by reverting to western dress, Maria 'felt as if I *could not* take my seat at the table'. But she sat there without displaying a trace of coldness towards the man who was betraying her husband. A comment to Mrs Berger reveals her human feelings: 'I hardly dare to trust myself to speak of Mr Nicol's letter for the downright falsehood.' She did not resent opposition. 'We have come to fight Satan and he will not let us alone.'

Hudson could lean hard on her, drawing vigour from her spiritual maturity, her tranquillity and faith, her unwavering affection. Ten years after their engagement they were still passionately in love with each other. She gave him and their work all she had, every ounce of strength, every thought that crossed her intelligent mind, all the force of her love. She allowed him to drain her, and if sometimes his demands were unconsciously selfish, she was no more aware of it than he was.

Hudson and Maria were devoted to their children. And therefore both suffered agonies at the calamity which broke the crisis in the Mission and ensured its survival.

During Hudson's absence on tour the family cow fell ill and Maria feared for the baby's health. Their servant, Djun-keng, pointed out that Chinese do not drink cow's milk and that as it was a Chinese cow it should not be treated as if English.

'Very well,' said Maria, 'when Djun-keng is unwell he must not come to Mr Taylor for English medicine!'

Fortunately Rudland remembered Cambridgeshire cattle-lore, it recovered, and baby Maria thrived.

On July 12th Hudson returned unexpectedly with a heavy cold. Before he went away again to Ningpo to ordain Lae-djun, their companion of London days, as pastor, Bertie, now six, was bitten on the cheek by an infuriated dog, but mercifully did not develop hydrophobia.

Of the five children, Gracie, the eldest, aged eight, was the apple of the Taylors' eyes. She was the one link with their former life in China. She was bright and happy, she was able to understand more than her brothers what their parents were doing and why. Like most missionary children she was a passport to the hearts of the natives, she could prattle about religion in a way that might seem precious to a less sentimental generation, but which was sincere.

They went to the hills early in August 1867 because the heat at Hangchow was 103°, Maria was ill and Hudson recovering from inflamed eyes. The Taylors stayed in the compound of a half-ruined temple called Pun-san. A few days later Gracie was un-well. Hudson could not diagnose the complaint and the Taylors were anxious. He had to go to Hangchow for a day on Mission business and hoped to find her better on his return, but in Hangchow

he received an urgent message that Jane McLean at another station was critically ill. Yearning to be back beside Gracie he naturally went to Jane, found she was not in danger at all, and carried
her back to Pun-san. Gracie was unconscious. Too late Hudson
diagnosed water on the brain. She died at 8.50 on the night of
August 23rd.

In the Taylor papers is an agonised pencilled note in Maria's
hand, dated six weeks afterwards and presumably the draft of a
reply, probably never sent, to a complaint from the ungrateful
Jane McLean that she had been neglected. Maria reminds her of
the circumstances of Gracie's death and asks if the thought has
not come to her 'which has occurred again and again – O how
painfully at times – to one of the grief-stricken parents – had the
husband, the father returned at the expected time to the anxious
mother and his stricken first born instead of giving the preference
to the claims of a member of his Mission whose life he feared was
in danger, might the early detection of the true nature of his child's
disease have resulted in *her* recovery? In other words, was the life
of the child sacrificed to the life of the missionary? Perhaps not.'
The death of Gracie released a wave of sympathy and love
throughout the Mission. Jennie and Emily came together again.
The split no longer widened; it began, slowly, to heal, until only
the two McLeans, Nicol and his weak-willed wife were left in
contumacy. Gracie had saved the CIM.

The Taylors were loth to abandon hope of Nicol, who continued to campaign against the principles of the Mission, seeking
especially to deflect the loyalty of new recruits fresh from England.
In December Maria wrote to Mrs Berger, 'I fear Mr Nicol is setting
himself to undermine my dear husband's influence where he can.
What is to be done I do not know, and where it will end I do not
know. I feel as if the personal ingratitude I could bear as a personal wrong, to end with ourselves; but it is hard to see those who
might be so useful *poisoned,* in their turn perhaps to poison others.'

At length, but not until the autumn of 1868, Taylor made up
his mind. 'I shall have to put away one of the *Lammermuir* party
– Nicol – from the Mission,' he told his mother. 'He has done us

much harm; and unless restrained by the Lord, if the most unscrupulous lying can do us any harm, he will still cause us much injury.' The letter of dismissal 'for continued and persistent misrepresentation and untruthfulness' was sent on September 17th, 1868, and most of the CIM thought it should have gone months before.

Of Nicol's subsequent history nothing is known except that Taylor kept in touch and did many kindnesses. According to an unpublished note of Howard Taylor's, Nicol never forgave.

The McLeans resigned and worked on in China with missions which did not require Chinese dress or chopsticks. The decks had been cleared. The Mission was single-hearted.

By then, the Taylors were in the interior, were fighting another crisis, and had nearly lost their lives.[1]

## Chapter 18: RIOT

Yangchow was a city off the Grand Canal a dozen miles north of its junction with the Yangtze River. It was populous, wealthy and proud. Marco Polo had been its governor in the thirteenth century. Its turreted walls enclosed innumerable curved-roofed temples, storied pagodas, great houses round cool courtyards secured from the noisy streets. Here mandarins, scholars, and rich merchants retired to end their days in congenial company and to be buried in ornate tombs beyond the walls, satisfied that Yangchow would never neglect its duties to ancestors.

Although the neighbouring city of Chinkiang on the southern bank of the Yangtze, opposite the junction of river and canal, was a free port where steamers called on the route to Hankow, and American and British vice-consuls resided, Yangchow was totally free of foreign influence. It was symbolic of the China which the CIM had come to conquer. If lodgement could be secured there it could be secured anywhere deeper inland. The Mission had not been destroyed by storm, by ridicule or by internal explosion. Would it be destroyed by the Chinese?

---

[1] Mary Barnes also resigned. Stephen Barchet had never adopted Chinese dress. He now preferred to continue 'as a friend but not a member' of the CIM. He remained on excellent terms with the Taylors.

Hudson and Maria arrived at Yangchow on June 1st, 1868, with their four children, a new nurse called Mrs Bohanan,[1] Emily Blatchley, and six Chinese evangelists or servants. They had been living in boats nearly two months since leaving distant Hangchow, where Pastor Lae-djun, John McCarthy and his wife, and Jennie Faulding had been left to develop the Mission; it had prospered despite dissensions and external difficulties, despite Hudson Taylor's frequent and necessary absences to his other centres, and two serious illnesses.

For a week, in heavy rains, the missionaries who had reached Yangchow stayed in their leaky boats while house after house was denied them because officials and gentlemen exerted hidden persuasion on possible landlords. They moved on June 8th to the comparative comfort of an inn; twenty or thirty more houses slipped their grasp. The common people crowded to the inn, for curiosity, for medical help, for the preaching. Maria was glad to be there. 'The fact that my dear husband had his wife and children with him stamped him in the eyes of respectable people as a respectable man; not one likely to swindle them and be off without sign or trace.'

Not until July 20th, in oppressive weather, could Taylor take possession of the premises soon to cause an international storm.

Maria, this last part of July, was in Shanghai, having taken the baby for vaccination, nursed it through a dangerous attack of measles and whooping cough, and awaited a new recruit. At Shanghai on July 26th she received a pencilled letter from Hudson. It was not the words but the wobbly handwriting that convinced her he was desperately ill and in need of her. July 26th was a Sunday. The river steamer left that day for its twenty-four-hour journey to Chinkiang. Nothing would induce Maria to travel on a Sunday; she had taught the Chinese that it was a day of rest and worship, not even medical emergency should deflect her. She left before dawn on Monday up the canals in a hired foot-boat, a light express craft which was propelled by one man using his foot for the oar, one hand on the tiller, the other to hold his pipe; no mast or

---

[1] She was sister of the former nurse, Mary Bell, who was now married to William Rudland after a passing affair with Tosh, second mate of the *Lammermuir*.

sail. Two days and two nights she urged him on, and when he needed rest she took the oar herself.

It was symbolic of her life. Maria loved Hudson fiercely, protectively, with instinctive awareness of his need. She did not fear for him now. Her mind was in perfect peace because in perfect accord with her Saviour, her closest Companion, the source of her courage and wholeheartedness and her astounding ability to ignore physical weakness and fatigue.

Hudson was better but the local situation bad. Handbills had appeared, to warn honest folk.

Rumours common to China at this time were being spread assiduously in Yangchow: foreigners forcibly took eyes out to make medicines; they salted down children; they gave enquirers pills which would make the eyes of the sincere gleam brightly but could cause death to the insincere: several respectable citizens had had narrow escapes. Buddhists and Taoist priests fed the wild surmises of the illiterate by proclaiming to all Yangchow the filthy truth about that spurious deity whom Christians worshipped.

Deeper than common ignorance and priestly hostility lay the gentry's fear of the West. 'You know very well and I know very well,' a mandarin once said to Hudson Taylor, 'what the policy of England is with regard to China. You found China too strong for you to absorb as you were absorbing India. And you determined by opium to impoverish the country, and by missionaries to deceive the hearts of the people and to win yourselves a party in the country, and then to seize the whole land for yourselves. We know perfectly well what your designs are.'

And to make the situation explosive, the foreigners offered exceptional prospect of loot. Taylor had intended to set up the Mission printing press in Chinkiang, but a promised house was withheld. William Rudland and his wife, with Louise Desgraz, brought the press on to Yangchow with the Taylors' household goods. Five boat-loads were carried, box by box, to the Mission house. All Yangchow stirred. It was too hot to work. A riot would relieve tempers.

In the second week of August Taylor received anonymous warning of impending attack. Visitors, hitherto friendly, turned truculent. Stones crashed through the windows of the house. Taylor informed the chief mandarin (the *fu* or prefect) and received an evasive reply. On Saturday August 15th a second and more explicit warning made Taylor wish to send the women and children to safety. Maria writes: 'With one consent we begged him not to do so. For us to have gone away at that juncture would probably have been to increase to those that remained any danger that there might be.' That evening George Duncan arrived from Nanking.

A battering on the Mission house door, early on Sunday morning. The young men, Duncan, Rudland and a newcomer, Reid, barricaded it. The noise increased. Suggesting they go out to pacify the people, Reid unbolted the door and walked into the toughs crowding the narrow passage which led to the street. The three missionaries edged the intruders outwards, and blocked the passage with chairs. As they reached the street the crowd let out an angry roar.

Reid was astonished at its size: 'There were now facing us some hundred and fifty to two hundred of the roughest of Yangchow. Some with distorted features, others with one eye blind – here one with a diseased scalp – here one with some four or five plasters on his almost naked body; but all more or less appearing to have forgotten the use of water.' The worst were not the dirty but those primed with liquor. Yet it was not a dangerous crowd, having been too obviously hired for the occasion.

Taylor recognised this. He was only convalescent but summoned all his strength and all his love. Reid 'never felt more the power and value of speaking gently than on that day. Dear Mr Taylor spoke often to those assembled, in a very kind manner; and while we watched, those inside the house prayed, and God graciously brought us through that day, and more confirmed in our hearts that promise, "Lo, I am with you always".'

They remained in a state of semi-siege. 'Today (Monday) the people have been much more quiet, but fresh bills have been posted, more vile than the first.' The house should be burned down on

Tuesday. The missionaries had sealed every entrance except the front passage. 'Once or twice the mob has seemed inclined to break in by force,' Emily Blatchley scribbled that Tuesday afternoon to Mrs Berger (letter-writing steadied nerves). 'Having done all that *we* can do to fortify ourselves we know that whatever happens will be by God's permission... As I write He is sending thunder and the threatening of rain, which will do more for us, Mr Taylor says, than an army of soldiers. The Chinese shun the rain.'

On Wednesday Taylor wrote to the prefect and received a courteous reply. The crowd of loiterers thinned. Danger receded rapidly and on Saturday morning no toughs were seen.

In the early afternoon the American vice-consul, Captain Sands, and a Mr Drew came to satisfy themselves that the Europeans were safe, and returned to Chinkiang relieved. They had naturally worn foreign clothes. A rumour at once swept the tea-houses and exercise-grounds and along the streets: 'Twenty-four children are missing!... The foreigners ate twenty-four children!'

At about four pm a mob converged on the Mission house, a mob out for blood. Urgent messages for assistance were ignored; the prefect hoped the missionaries would be frightened into flight. He probably did not intend deaths.

As the hot summer night descended thousands of rioters surged on all sides by the light of flaming torches, yelling 'Foreign Devils', throwing bricks at the shuttered windows, struggling to break down doors and barricades.

Taylor knew how feeble were their defences, knew the unmistakable tone of blood-lust. No soft words would turn away that wrath. He looked at the women, and his children. Maria stood radiantly serene. She had even put the children to bed and soothed them asleep. 'She was as calm as when in the parlour in London, and I am quite certain that if she could have altered any of the circumstances she would not have done it, for she was satisfied that God's ordering was wisest.'

Time passed. Taylor saw that their one hope was the arrival of soldiers from the prefect. He had sent Chinese messengers and they had not returned. He must himself run the mile or more to the *yamen*. 'Duncan, you come too. The crowd is so large and violent that we may never get there.'

'We committed ourselves to the care of our Heavenly Father,' writes Duncan, 'and set out, not knowing if ever we would again see our dear friends.' After the brief prayer and a kiss for Maria, they slipped into the neighbour's house and out into the night. They had not run far before they heard the cry, 'The foreign devils are fleeing!'

'Quick!' called Taylor, 'I know a path by the fields.' This gave them deeper darkness, and misled most of their pursuers, who thought they fled for the open country, and took a short cut hoping to head them off at the east gate. 'But when we turned into the main street we were assaulted with stones and a mob gathered behind us, increasing at every step. Our rapid strides still kept a clear space between us and them, but we were nearly exhausted and our legs so hurt with the stones and bricks thrown at us that we were almost fainting.'

As they summoned their last energies and the yelling rose to a crescendo of hate, Taylor saw, to his horror, the gates of the *yamen* closing. If the guards had time to drop the bolts, the gates would not be reopened, the furious mob would catch them up and he and Duncan be torn in pieces.

They ran at the gates. 'We pushed with all our might and the door burst open, letting us fall flat on our faces.'

At the Mission house Rudland and Reid and the servants kept the doors and windows, hoping to slow the attack and only retire, point by point, as they were forced.

The mob broke down a wall which had been hastily built across a side entrance. They were in the compound and the front door became untenable. At the back an undefended wall had been breached, to which Rudland hurried, and found the weight of attack shifting there, with stones and bricks splintering the shutters and making the whole side dangerous. The mob had realised that the richest loot was at the back. The front of the house quietened. Reid left servants in charge and joined Rudland.

Upstairs in dim candlelight the women, European and Chinese, took the children to Mrs Taylor's room, which was safer from the showers of stones, 'and gathered there ourselves,' writes Emily Blatchley, 'to plead with God to protect and save us, and especially to take care of our brothers who were in the forefront of the danger. Sometimes a fresh outburst among the rioters made our hearts chill for a moment, but we preserved our calmness and sustained our courage by wrestling in prayer. Presently Mr Rudland came up so exhausted that he could hardly stand, and with his clothes all stained with mud.'

He told them the mob would be up any moment. But should they close the trapdoor at the head of the stairs and weight it with boxes, they would cut off Reid. What to do? 'Any little mistake might sacrifice all our lives in a moment.' Yet Taylor had been absent an hour and a half. Rescue must be coming.

Maria was magnificent. Her mind pulsated with anxieties: would Mrs Rudland have her baby prematurely then and there? Would she herself have a miscarriage? (she was expecting her sixth child in November). What about baby Maria's dysentery? – they had not been able to give her medicine that night; miraculously the trouble seemed checked. Above all, 'Where was my precious husband? How was it he and Mr Duncan had not returned? Had they fallen a prey to the violence of the mob outside?' Not a tremor crossed her face. The others had only to look at her to renew their courage.

The rioters in the house grew louder, nearer. 'We were expecting every moment to see them come up the stairs, when Mr Reid called out from the court below, in a hollow, hoarse voice as if utterly exhausted. "Mrs Taylor! Come down if you can. They are setting the house on fire, and I can't help you."'

They knotted sheets and blankets from the bed. Rudland climbed out on the roof which projected under the window. He let down Mrs Rudland, the Chinese printer's young wife and Bertie, and Reid hurried them to concealment in the well house.

Just then, a tall, strong man, naked to the waist, entered the room.

When Taylor and Duncan found themselves on the floor inside the gates of the *yamen* they recovered at once and rushed into the judgment hall shouting *'Kiu-ming!'* ('Save life!'), the cry that a mandarin was bound to attend to at any hour of day or night.

They were taken to the room of the secretary and kept three-quarters of an hour; from time to time the wind blew the yells of the mob who, for all they knew, were killing or torturing.

At last the prefect received them. 'Ah, Mr Taylor,' said the prefect affably, 'tell me, what did you *really* do with those babies?'

It was almost more than Taylor could bear, to answer composedly the mandarin's questions on the cause of the riot. After a little he said roundly that the cause lay in His Excellency's neglect of firm measures the previous week, and that he must request him to act instantly to save the lives of any survivors, or answer for the consequences.

'Very true, very true,' replied His Excellency with utmost calmness. 'First quiet the rioters and then make enquiry. Sit still and I will see what can be done. All depends on your keeping out of sight. Twenty thousand rioters are out!'

Two hours of suspense passed before the prefect returned with the military commander. 'All is quiet. The mob is dispersed. I will send you back in chairs, under escort.'

They swayed through strangely quietened streets. One of the escort put his face to the window and grinned. 'All the foreigners have been killed.'

Smoke hung over the Mission house, but it stood. They dismounted and walked in. The torches lit up a scene of frightful debris – broken furniture, smashed surgical instruments, charred books and papers, dressing-cases and toys. And an eerie silence. Nothing to indicate the whereabouts of Maria and the rest except a horrible stench which the two shocked men believed to be burning human flesh.

At the entrance of the man naked to the waist Maria had accosted him.

'What do you want? We are only women and children here. Are you not ashamed to molest us?'

'Do not fear. I come from the prefecture. What money will you give me to protect you?'

Maria asked to see his card, pretending to believe him to gain time. He parleyed a few moments and then stepped up, put his hands on her bosom and felt for money that might be hidden beneath the thin cotton clothes. His eye caught the purse at Emily's waist. He seized it and found the seven dollars she carried in case of sudden evacuation by boat, and roared for more. 'I will cut off your head!' he screamed. She noticed he had no knife. He tore Louise Desgraz's pocket away, snatched an ornament out of her hair, and turned to ransack the room.

Other looters passed in and out. The children's nurse, carrying the baby, courageously stepped behind one of them who had a large box in his arms, disappeared down the stairs and through the fire, shielded from stones and brickbats by her unwitting escort's box, and ran for the safety of the well house.

Rudland calmly continued to let down Freddie, Samuel, and the little Chinese girl Louise Desgraz had adopted. Maria screened him from the half-naked looter, who suddenly saw her wedding ring which he pulled from her finger.

'Mr Reid was again calling us to hasten, and the smoke was by this time becoming oppressive; while the noise of falling walls, and the almost fiendish yelling of the mob, warned us that no time must be lost. Miss Desgraz was just safely down when the men below cast a heap of burning materials immediately under the window and cut off escape from us who remained.'

Before Maria and Emily could decide what to do, the half naked man spotted Rudland on the gable. He seized his pigtail and dragged him backwards to the tiles, felt him and found his watch. Rudland struggled and threw the watch into the night, hoping the man would go down after it. Instead he lost his temper and tried to force Rudland off the tiles. The women tugged hard at the man and pulled him into the room. He picked up a loose brick to crush Rudland's skull. The women caught his arm. He did not turn on them; Emily believed he would have killed them had not Maria's pure Chinese made him regard her as a mandarin's lady.

Rudland had scrambled into the room and on to his feet, 'in a position for fair play; the man, like a true Chinaman, preferring not to face his opponent under these circumstances', disappeared to bring up reinforcements.

Escape was impossible until Reid, under an increasing hail of stones, dragged away the fire below.

'Jump!' he cried. 'Jump, and I will catch you.'

It was twelve to fifteen feet. Maria jumped. He only half caught her and she fell on her side. Emily jumped. At that instant a brick-bat struck Reid full on the eye, blinding and concussing him. Emily fell on her back. She did not lose consciousness. The instinct to escape drove her to her feet. She saw Rudland who had jumped by himself and had warded off a murderous attack from a club, helping a shaken, bruised Mrs Taylor. Reid was semi-conscious, in great pain, crying that someone should lead him away. Showers of stones rang upon the cobbles and thudded into the timber buildings around.

Rudland got the injured into the shelter of a wall, collected the children and others from the well house, and at last, they scarcely remembered how, all escaped into their neighbour's, who hid them in an inner room.

There they lay, Reid groaning from his serious wound, Emily marvelling she was still alive, Maria, faint from loss of blood, comforting the children. 'I was anxious not to let anyone know how much I was hurt, as I felt it would alarm them, and it seemed most important that all should keep calm.' None dared express the deepest fear – for Hudson and Duncan. 'But God was our stay. This confidence He gave me, that He would surely work good for China out of our deep distress.'

At last Hudson found them, and brought them back to the now guarded Mission house.

On the Sunday morning Taylor sent one of his Chinese with a verbal message to the British vice-consul, Allen, in Chinkiang.

The guard withdrew soon after light. Looters returned. Taylor strode through the mob. 'I mounted a broken chair and addressed them in a tone of indignant remonstrance.'

Thieves in other parts of the compound continued to carry off boxes, furniture, equipment, but those in earshot of Taylor stopped ashamed, silent under the lash of his eloquence. 'We were a party of strangers,' they heard him say, 'we came from a distance to seek your good. Had we meant evil, should we have come unarmed? Or in such small numbers? Or with our women and children? Without provocation you have broken open our dwelling, plundered our property, wounded our persons and tried to burn down our premises. And now you are back in your greed of plunder to do us more mischief.

'Would we not have been justified last night in defending ourselves by attacking you in return? But we did not raise a stick against you, or throw one stone. Are you not ashamed in the face of Heaven at such outrages? And now we are defenceless. We cannot withstand you. If we could, we would not. We are here for good, not for evil. If you kill us we die with a good conscience that *we* have not hurt any man's eye or injured any man's limbs. There are sick and wounded here, and women and children! If you abuse us or kill us we will not retaliate. But high Heaven will avenge. Our God, in whom we trust, is able to protect us and punish you, if you offend against Him.'

He got down and walked swiftly to the prefecture. Once more, interminable delay. The prefect had not risen... had not taken his bath... or his breakfast.

Taylor was told after a third or fourth message that the military commander would accompany him back. The man did not come for an hour, but said then he had dispersed the crowd, and added, 'Write a letter to the prefect. Be careful to call last night's proceedings a disturbance, not a riot. Ask for a proclamation to quieten the people, and punishment for the offenders. We may restore peace by to-night and you will not need to leave the city.' The letter Taylor wrote on returning to the Mission house was, he thought, mild but truthful. It was returned by the commander as unacceptable. Once again Taylor went to the prefecture. He told the commander that facts could not be altered.

The commander replied: 'If you persist in sending that letter, I will have nothing more to do with the affair. You may protect yourself as best you can. I warn you, the lives of your party will probably be sacrificed.'

Taylor yielded. He wrote, almost at dictation, a letter that could be passed to Peking without risk of the prefect incurring Imperial displeasure. The commander took it. He said, 'My subordinates cannot keep down the people. I will send you under escort by boats to Chinkiang. When we have repaired the house, we will invite you to return.'

A few miles after leaving Yangchow the battered party met vice-consuls Allen and Sands and a merchant called Carney coming to their rescue. They were overwhelmed with kindness and sympathy, Sands and Carney turning back to accompany them to Chinkiang and make them comfortable.

Young Consul Allen proceeded grimly to Yangchow.

## Chapter 19: THE BRINK OF WAR

A few evenings after the riot Maria, who could not walk unaided and ached in every bone, sat at dinner in Carney's home in Chinkiang. A young English merchant asked her what punishment she would inflict on the rioters if the matter was in her hands. He knew what *he* would do to the rascals.

'Punishment?' answered Maria, 'I really have not considered the question as it is nothing to do with me. The *revenge* I desire is the wider opening up of the country to our work.'

When the attitude of Hudson and Maria had become a burning political and international issue she amplified her views, in a letter to Mrs Berger: *'In the riot* we asked the protection of the Chinese mandarin; my dear husband did not see it right to neglect this means of possibly saving our lives. But after our lives were safe and we were in shelter, we asked no restitution, we desired no revenge.'

It was ironic that Hudson Taylor, who told his missionaries 'Go not to officials! Claim nothing, earn love,' should become almost a *causus belli* between China and England, and be accused of wanting to evangelise China by gunboat.

A westerner resident in Chinkiang who had a nodding acquaintance with the Taylors wrote, without their knowledge, a stirring account of the Yangchow riot for the Shanghai newspapers. Public opinion forgot its ridicule of the CIM and ran strongly in their sympathy, demanding prompt and decisive action by the British. 'It was looked upon,' Maria thought, 'as a climax to a series of provocations which the English had received from the Chinese.' Britain seized the opportunity to settle off several old scores.

The Consul-General, Walter Medhurst, reached Chinkiang on August 30th, 1868. He called at once for a full account from Taylor, who said he did not want redress. Medhurst said he was going to press for redress, most decidedly. Medhurst was not a fire-eater, was sensitive to Chinese feelings; and he disapproved of westerners wearing Chinese dress. But he told the British Minister at Peking, Sir Rutherford Alcock, that he could not recall an outrage 'more unprovoked on the part of the sufferers, and in which the evidence of neglect and culpability on the part of the local authorities has been more marked'. To Taylor he said his simple desire was to secure for them and for all missionaries 'freedom to pursue their avocation without molestation or restraint, so long as they keep within the bounds of reason and discretion'.

He paid a formal call of protest on the Tao-tai at Chinkiang, immediate superior of the prefect of Yangchow. The sequel showed the Chinese thoroughly unrepentant: the local minor magistrate in Chinkiang posted an anti-foreign proclamation, and a gang of toughs beat up a man willing to rent Taylor a house. On September 2nd angry crowds attacked the Tao-tai's *yamen* and threatened the British Consulate.

Even Emily Blatchley waxed bellicose. She wrote to Jennie Faulding, 'the Chinese authorities here are behaving shamefully. Medhurst the Consul is very indignant; sees with us in all the points, and seems determined to carry the matter through. A war frigate will be up to-day or to-morrow; pray that the matter may be brought through without loss of life and bloodshed, if it be His will. It is a very serious case, everyone feels that; and may involve war with China. Anyhow, may it be the *opening* of China to the Gospel.'

HMS *Rinaldo* (Commander Bush, RN) anchored off Chinkiang on September 4th. Medhurst took a guard of marines to visit the Manchu general, who promptly pacified the city. The Viceroy at Nanking refused to send a high official to Yangchow with the Consul-General, who thereupon took seventy marines to Yangchow, inspected the scene of the riot and formally demanded redress and the punishment of the retired gentlemen who had been instigators. The prefect said he could not punish them; they were his seniors in rank.

On September 10th Medhurst sailed in *Rinaldo* for Nanking. Neither the prefect of Yangchow nor a special representative of the Viceroy kept his promise to come. At Nanking satisfactory terms were nearly concluded when Commander Bush fell ill and withdrew HMS *Rinaldo* to Shanghai, thereby leaving Medhurst in a 'humiliating and helpless position'. The Viceroy, no longer looking down the guns of the British Navy, repudiated all concessions. Bush said 'it never entered my head that the presence simply of a small man-of-war could have the effect of influencing the Viceroy'.

Alcock in Peking ordered the Admiral commanding the China Station, Sir Harry Keppel, 'to repair the mischief by sending such naval force to the mouth of the Grand Canal as shall enable him, if necessary, to apply effective pressure both on the local authorities and populace at Yangchow and on the Viceroy at Nanking'.

The Royal Navy sailed up the Yangtze deep into Chinese territory: HMS *Rodney,* flagship of the station, reinforced later by *Rinaldo, Stanley, Icarus* and *Zebra,* a powerful force ready to bombard, burn and kill because Hudson Taylor wanted to evangelise the Chinese.

At first, as Maria looked out at *Rodney* anchored in the Yangtze, she thought that good might come. Though the CIM had not asked for redress and did not desire to be a cause of war, 'I shall count our physical sufferings light,' she wrote on 7th October, 'and our mental anxieties, severe though they were, well repaid if they may work out the further opening up of the country to us for the spread of our Master's kingdom. And if it please God to use, as means to this end, measures adopted by our government authorities, I believe the facts that English *women* were rudely handled, and that their blood was spilt in a precipitate escape from a wooden house where large fires were already kindled below stairs, and robbers and one would-be murderer at least were upstairs, are calculated to strengthen their hands, to say the least.'

Her sentiment was thoroughly nineteenth-century, as was the whole episode: warships dictating terms within the territory of a sovereign state, the British demanding at gun-point that treaty obligations be met, bluejackets swelling with indignation that Chinks had dared molest British women and children.

It formed the worst background for the expansion of Christianity in China, and was the first of those incidents in which politics and religion appeared to join hands, bequeathing a legacy of mistrust and at least some excuse for Communist vilification of all missionary endeavour as a cloak for western imperialism. Certain Roman Catholic missionaries openly encouraged political arid military pressure to gain their religious objects: before the end of the century the Imperial government had been compelled to grant Roman bishops the rights of the highest rank of mandarins. Other priests, faithful, courageous and humble, were the unwitting tools of foreign powers. And so, in the Yangchow Incident, was Hudson Taylor; he deplored that his activities, born of love for China, should conjure up gunboats, that the wrongs he was content to forgive and forget, provided he might be free to bring the Gospel to inland China, should be redressed by threat of force. He was the pawn of statesmen. Worse, in a few months, he became an unwilling shuttlecock in British politics.

The fault may have lain partly with the economic and political ambitions of western nations. But very much of the blame lies on the shoulders of the Imperial government and of the formidable

Empress Dowager. Had China behaved as a normal power, honouring treaties, allowing natural intercourse for trade or the exchange of ideas, and giving foreigners justice, gunboats would not have sailed, the shame of extra-territorial concessions would not have been forced upon her.

'Foreigners travelling in the interior have a perfect and legal right to claim legitimate local protection,' the British Consul in Hangchow had assured Hudson Taylor in 1867. The Tao-tai gave renewed assurance to the Consul after the settlement of the outrage against the Nicols at Siao-san: 'When your countrymen go in the interior whether for the object of teaching their religion, for pleasure or for trade, they will in all cases be secured peace and quiet, and be free from all molestation and hindrance.' But it was calculated delay by the Chinese authorities which provoked the Yangchow riot. The attitude of the Viceroy afterwards was exasperatingly out of accord with the treaty of 1858, which had been ratified in 1860. Not until the Convention of Chefoo in 1876, signed literally under the guns of the British fleet, did China at last open the country in fact as well as theory.

The Navy did not bombard Nanking. Prince Kung at Peking, the realist of the Imperial government, conceded sufficient of Sir Rutherford Alcock's demands to provide a reopening of negotiations. These dragged on, at northern and southern capitals, until November. The Chinese made full apology. The prefect and one of the magistrates of Yangchow were dismissed.

On November 18th 1868, Hudson and Maria re-entered Yangchow ten days before the birth of Charles Edward Taylor. 'This day,' wrote Hudson, 'we have been reinstated in our house here by Mr Medhurst, the Tao-tai from Shanghai as the Viceroy's deputy, and the two district magistrates of the city. The result of this case will probably be greatly to facilitate missionary work in the interior; and I know not how to express our indebtedness to Mr Medhurst, whose kindness and courtesy have only been equalled by the ability with which he has conducted the whole investigation.'

Europeans in Shanghai now thought the world of the CIM,

which by its blood had helped to open China to the West. 'Sort of popularity,' runs a note in the Taylor papers, '– top of the wave business – *success* – all this unfolding of the flag about them.'

The news of the Yangchow riot reached England slowly. On November 20th the British Foreign Secretary, Lord Stanley, instructed Alcock 'to press the case upon the Chinese Government', and commended Medhurst warmly. *The Times* said 'Our political prestige has been injured and must be recovered.'

Lord Stanley was a Tory. A general election was in process and Disraeli's ministry tottering. He resigned on December 2nd and the Queen sent for Gladstone; it was the famous occasion when the royal message found him at Hawarden cutting down a tree.

The Earl of Clarendon took office as Liberal Foreign Secretary and at once executed a *volte-face* over China. The Liberals had disliked Disraeli's forward policy and wanted an excuse for an attack on his agents, Alcock and Medhurst. Moreover, the American minister at the court of Peking, Anson Burlinghame, had been touring Europe and the United States on behalf of the Chinese, a peculiar arrangement whereby he constituted China's first foreign embassy. He denounced Britain's 'tyrannic, dagger-at-throat policy', and condemned the Yangchow affair as 'high handed action'. Lord Clarendon believed him.

*The Times* of December 3rd, announcing with glee the fall of Disraeli, now published a leading article roundly condemning 'a company of missionaries assuming the title of China Inland Mission...' *The Times* said: 'The Gospel of Peace ought not to be made an occasion of war... The Apostles and early missionaries certainly did not propagate their faith under the protection of fleets and armies. They did not bring war in their train... When we read that imposing displays of force are made, heavy guns pointed against quiet inland cities, all on behalf of men whose mission is to preach and pray, we may be excused if we feel rather shocked.'

Its readers were rather shocked too. The unknown Hudson Taylor was catapulted into notoriety as the fire-eating fanatic who outraged innocent Chinese by violent denunciation of ancestor-worship, and then loudly demanded redress and gunboats. 'It is very hard that the British people are to be forced into a quarrel, as disgraceful as it may prove costly, because persons never heard of before are hoping to convert the Chinese.' Former opponents of the CIM, George Moule delicately and sorrowfully at their head, renewed their energies for its extinction. A few friends rallied to the CIM; many supporters deplored that Taylor had, as they supposed, demanded redress. Donations fell off, intending candidates doubted their vocation, and at the moment when in China the settlement of the Yangchow Incident had widened the avenue of advance, the means to make it appeared withheld.

Public agitation in Britain mounted to the crescendo of the House of Lords debate of 9th March, 1869.

The Duke of Somerset, a former Liberal First Lord of the Admiralty, an elderly man whose wife was a noted beauty, granddaughter of the playwright Sheridan, wanted to know 'what chance we have of reducing these missions or, at least, of not allowing them to go still further up country. They have already got as far as Yangchow, and I am afraid they will go further into the country unless they are stopped, and,' he added with peculiar logic, 'the farther they go the more it will be prejudicial to the interests of Christianity.'

The noble Duke had read the correspondence so carelessly that he thought the offenders belonged to the London Missionary Society, who had 'much better send its missions to some other part of the world and leave China unconverted than pursue their present course. Will the Government not adopt some more efficient and stringent mode of dealing with these missionaries, either by sending them out of the country, or by telling them that they should go no farther and imperil our friendly relations with China by their proceedings?'

The Foreign Secretary, Clarendon, supported Somerset. 'We are always on the brink of war, not on account of the violation of any British rights, of any insult to the English government or flag, or of any injury done to commerce, but on account of the protection of good but impudent men.'

Duke and Earl were roundly opposed by the newly enthroned Bishop of Peterborough, the staunch evangelical Conor Magee, afterwards Archbishop of York. He pilloried the Duke's advice 'to leave some parts of the world unconverted, or flee from attempts to convert them because, forsooth, these attempts might prejudice British trade'. The youngest and the least zealous missionary, the Bishop declared, would reply that there was something in his eyes 'more sacred even than that sacred opium trade for which Great Britain once thought it worthwhile to wage war – namely, obedience to the command of his Master to go forth and seek to convey the Gospel to every living soul'.

'It was surely unworthy of a Christian nation,' he continued, 'to say that its subjects engaged in any trade, however demoralising, should be protected from the least infraction of their rights or from the least insult, by all the might of Great Britain; but that if missionaries happened to displease the Chinese they should be left to their fate or saved from the mob by a forcible expatriation.'

Next morning *The Times* sneered at the Taylors as practically ignorant of the Chinese language and totally without understanding of 'the religion they seek to displant'. The whole breed of missionaries were 'very commonplace persons, not very educated, not quite gentlemen, very much given to long stories', whose annual reports 'are apt to be received with unbelief and contempt by those who give the tone to political discussions'. Berger wrote to Taylor on March 11th, 'you can scarcely imagine what an effect the matter has produced in the country... the all-absorbing subject'. He was getting twenty or thirty letters a day, 'such an enormous increase that I am in danger of breaking down entirely'.

*The Times* had the fairness to invite Berger to write a reply to criticisms. He was hampered by the Taylors' desire to shield Alcock and especially Medhurst, whose great kindness and energy on their behalf had been rewarded by a black mark from his new Liberal chiefs at the Foreign Office. Berger was asked not to state specifically that Consul and Minister 'took up the matter without any application from us'.

Taylor wrote, 'I must say I have been astonished at the wilful falsehoods circulated by the newspapers and political men to suit their own ends.' Maria said the best plan was to go on with their work 'and leave God to vindicate our cause'. Hudson agreed, but inwardly he was desperately hurt, not so much by newspapers and politicians as by friends and supporters who had believed the accusations against him.

## Chapter 20: MIDNIGHT

The CIM were back at Yangchow. Borne there on bayonets of marines, they were determined that love and trust should erase from local memory both riot and gunboat. Maria's refusal to await Charley's birth in the safety of Chinkiang made a strong impression, especially as the new baby was a boy. Immemorial custom brought all neighbours to congratulate; they were at once attracted by these foreigners whom they had looted and injured; each had recovered, each seemed glad to be back.

The innkeeper and his wife were the first baptised. During 1869 the missionaries could reflect that blood had indeed proved the seed of a church. 'The converts here,' Emily wrote at the end of the year, 'are different from any others we have known in China. There is such life, warmth, *earnestness* about them.'

Hudson Taylor had been reconnoitring forward even before their return to Yangchow, and had placed several of his older missionaries farther inland. In the spring of 1869 he toured these new stations. 'The country through which I have just passed,' he wrote to Maria, 'is most beautiful-mountain passes, foaming torrents, hills terraced and covered with wheat now about a foot high, sweet perfume from the flowers of the bean and mustard, lovely valleys, orchards of fruit trees in flower of various hues.' His boat floated through town after town, village after village; he saw temples and shrines and graves, watched priests burn paper furniture and hell money at funerals; met on every side people in their tens and their hundreds, industrious and amiable. Their spiritual destitution weighed him down.

Darkness of spirit deepened as he looked ahead. 'I incline to think that we are on the eve of no slight persecution in China,' he wrote to his mother on 13th March 1869. He believed that 'The *power* of the Gospel has been little felt heretofore. The *foreign* element has been the great stumbling block.' The far interior would meet Christianity in native dress; the devil would be attacked with unblunted weapons. There would be no compromise. And the resulting conflict must be grievous.

Other disquiets vexed him. 'I am inclined to think that we need to pray specially that the Gov. may not compel us to put off the native dress, or otherwise interfere with our freedom of action.' When Taylor understood the attitude of the new Liberal administration in England he dreaded a peremptory order for the recall of all missionaries from the interior, with the Chinese authorities told that any who remained would receive no support if attacked by rioters or punished by mandarins.

He was not alarmed by the decline in funds. He had survived too many such crises. His faith and experience would have made him expect what, unknown to him, was already happening: George Müller, within a few days of the Yangchow riot, had begun to widen his support of CIM missionaries. At the news of the riot, before the political storm broke, Müller enlarged his gifts. He did not believe the libels about Taylor, and he did not know that funds would drop. Eventually it was reckoned that money received in 1868-70 through George Müller equalled almost exactly the loss from other sources.

More worrying to Taylor was the calibre of some of the new recruits. He had accepted that he must not again take 'a large number of untried persons', or expect raw material to mature quickly. 'Some persons seem really clever in doing the right thing in the worst possible way, or at the most unfortunate moment,' he told Berger. 'Really dull or rude persons will seldom be out of hot water in China, and though earnest and clever and pious will not effect much. In nothing do we fail more, as a Mission, than in lack of tact and politeness.'

Taylor had often to write at this period a letter such as this, to a newcomer who had complained of his senior: 'I know he has sometimes a trying way; perhaps however your ways may be as trying to him as his are to you... and you especially will be wise to bear in mind your great inexperience, your ignorance of the language, habits and feelings of the people, which must lead you very very frequently to erroneous opinions and incorrect judgements.'

Taylor's skies darkened during this spring and early summer of 1869. 'Envied by some, despised by many, hated perhaps by others; often blamed for things I never heard of, or had nothing to do with; an innovator on what have become established rules of missionary practice; an opponent of a strong system of heathen error and superstition; working without precedent in many respects, and with few experienced helpers; often sick in body as well as perplexed in mind and embarrassed by circumstances; had not the Lord been specially gracious to me, had not my mind been sustained by the conviction that the work was the Lord's, and that He was with me in the thick of the conflict, I must have fainted and broken down.'

A young recruit in Yangchow, called Judd, saw Taylor as a 'toiling, burdened' Christian. Taylor knew it. He confessed to his mother, 'I cannot tell you how I am buffeted sometimes by temptation. I never knew how bad a heart I had.'

Ephemeral popularity in the International Settlement had been dispersed by the chill winds from Westminster and Printing House Square. When Taylor took the family for a ten-day holiday in May 1869 on the sandy beaches of Pu Tu Island near Ningpo, the Shanghai papers reported that he had gone to make mischief and had been recalled by the Consul after Chinese complaints. They castigated Taylor's 'pestilent folly' and 'impudence'. 'It is not to be borne that an individual who has already by his stupidity produced serious political complications should be permitted to roam about the country preparing ill feeling and ill treatment for every foreigner who may be unfortunate enough to follow his route.' One editor devoutly hoped Taylor would be admitted to the hospital for incurable idiots. The *Shanghai Evening Courier* said 'this restless apostle is as difficult to lay hold of as a flea in a blanket'.

The Consul publicly denied the Pu Tu story. The *Evening Courier* had the courtesy to apologise, rather feebly and indirectly. But the articles had frayed Taylor's nerves. China was opening but he wilted at the immensity of his task. He sank towards black despair, 'the awful temptation', as an unpublished note in the Taylor papers runs, 'even to end his own life'.

Maria stood between Hudson and suicide. The one human factor still stable in his disintegrating world was their love: 'It hasn't worn off or worn out.'

The letters they wrote in 1869 when separated reveal the mutual passion that nearly twelve years had not sated. Hudson 'dreamed last night that I was once more by your side and while conversing with you a noise awoke me and – you were far far away. I was *so* disappointed darling. When shall *I really* see you and once more fold you in my arms?' Maria wished 'I could lie down in your arms to-night, or pillow my head in your dear bosom, instead of writing a letter that I do not know when it will reach you.' 'My own fonderly loved,' she wrote when sending him supplies, 'my priceless treasure... I should like to put myself among the things that are coming.'

One thought Hudson could not bear: that Maria should fall prey to one of the multitudinous ills which could snuff out life in a few hours, that their gallant, impossible adventure together should end, and he be left alone. 'I do thank God, darling, for having given you to me, and for so long sparing you to me. May he long do so! But O! may he ever give us both to love him *best,* most constantly and with unfailing constancy. Then we shall not love one another *too much...* and now, a *long warm fond embrace* from your own absent but loving husband.'

'I hated myself; I hated my sin; and yet I gained no strength against it.'
   The summer months intensified Hudson Taylor's inward conflict. He prayed, agonised, fasted, made resolutions, read the Bible more, without effect. 'Every day, almost every hour, the consciousness of failure and sin oppressed me.' He knew that in Christ lay the answer. 'I began the day with prayer, determined not to take my eye from Him for a moment; but pressure of duties,

sometimes very trying, constant interruptions, sometimes so wearing, often caused me to forget Him. Then one's nerves get so fretted in this climate that temptations to irritability, hard thoughts, and sometimes unkind words are the harder to withstand.'

The more he struggled for holiness, for inward vitality that gave outward serenity, 'the more it eluded my grasp, till hope itself almost died out'. He never doubted that '*in* Christ was all I needed, but the practical question was how to get it *out*... I prayed for faith but it came not. What *was* I to do?'

As Taylor travelled his Mission stations or worked in the city between hills and river, Chinkiang, where the printing press and his home were now located, he talked much about 'the need of more life, power in our souls'. Others felt as he. His colleagues thirsted for spiritual satisfaction, for serenity. 'As for Mrs Taylor,' wrote one of them, 'she wondered what we were all groping after!'

In August Hudson was down at Hangchow where John McCarthy, the young Irishman, was in charge. McCarthy had an Irish temper, was by nature harsh, rude and censorious. When Taylor talked of his own compelling desire for 'oneness with Jesus', for a sense of His presence and the evidence of His power, McCarthy said little, but it was 'the subject of all others which occupied my thoughts'. McCarthy was afflicted by 'a consciousness of failure. A constant falling short of that which in my own mind and thought should be aimed at. An unrest – a perpetual striving to *find* some way I might continuously enjoy that communion, that fellowship which sometimes felt so real, but more often – how much oftener – so visionary, so far off!'

Hudson did not fathom McCarthy's thought. He left him, to return north still worrying 'how to get it *out*. Christ is rich, but I poor; He is strong, but I weak.' Hudson stopped at each Mission station on the way homewards to Chinkiang, and at each must settle problems, give advice, lead prayer, preach, examine catechumens, call on awkward mandarins, resolve mild tiffs between missionaries, strengthen the discouraged; and all the time battle with himself.

He reached the tiny, crowded house at Chinkiang on Saturday

September 4th. After hugs for Maria and the children and a quick exchange of views with missionaries and Chinese teachers, he hurried to his room to start catching up on correspondence.

He opened and skimmed through letter after letter from the stations, from home, from Shanghai.

He came upon one from John McCarthy, written a day or two after Hudson had left. It was a long letter. He read on and on, attention riveted. 'I seem,' McCarthy wrote, 'as if the first glimmer of the dawn of a glorious day has risen upon me... I seem to have sipped only of that which can fully satisfy.' McCarthy had found the secret they sought. Hudson looked at the letter again. 'To *let* my loving Saviour work in me *His will...* Abiding, not striving or struggling ...'

Hudson came to the last paragraph. 'Not a striving to have faith, or to increase our faith but a looking at the faithful one seems all we need. A resting in the loved one entirely, for time, for eternity. It does not appear to me as anything new, only formerly misunderstood.'

Hudson was amazed at his own blindness. His eyes opened wide. As in Barnsley twenty years before, as at Brighton four years before, a long inward struggle resolved in a split second. 'As I read I saw it all. "If we believe *not, He* abideth faithful." And I looked to Jesus and saw (and when I saw, oh, how joy flowed) that He had said, "I will *never* leave you".' In shorter time than it took to describe afterwards, Hudson grasped that he must not struggle to have strength or peace but rest in the strength and peace of Christ. 'I have striven in vain to abide in Him. I'll strive no more. For has not He promised to abide with me – never to leave me, never to fail me ?' The effort to 'get it out' was a mistake.

'I am *one* with Christ,' he cried as he explained the glorious discovery to the whole Chinkiang household, hastily gathering them together and reading McCarthy's letter. 'It was all a mistake to try and get the fullness *out* of Him, I am *part* of Him. Each of us is a limb of His body, a branch of the vine. Oh, think what a wonderful thing it is to be really one with a risen Saviour.' And in some such words as he wrote a few weeks later to his sister Amelia in England, he expounded the truth he had missed so long: 'Think what it involves! Can Christ be rich and I poor? Can your right hand be rich and your left poor? or your head well fed while your body starves?'

A few evenings later Hudson went up the canal to Yangchow. Judd came in to the sitting-room to welcome him, and was astonished: 'He was so full of joy that he scarcely knew how to speak to me. He did not even say, "How do you do," but walking up and down the room with his hands behind him, exclaimed: "Oh, Mr Judd, God has made me a new man! God has made me a new man!"'

Judd, and every man and woman who came in close contact with Taylor noticed the difference. A magnetism of love and happiness radiated from him. The years rolled away, and instead of premature middle age he was again a man in his late thirties. 'He was very kind to me,' recalled a new, youthful missionary, C T Fishe. 'He appeared quite a young and lively man. He was fond of music and singing, and used to play the harmonium for the Chinese on Sunday evenings for an hour at a time, and have them sing hymns.'

'As to work,' Hudson wrote to Amelia in October, 'mine was never so plentiful or responsible or difficult but the weight and strain of it is *gone*. The last month or more has been perhaps the happiest of my life.'

In November, on tour, he received an urgent letter from Maria, 'to tell you the serious news we have just heard. A Roman Catholic missionary has come down from Anking and says that our premises there have been pulled down, and that theirs have been plundered. The local authorities seem to have done all in their power to help the missionaries...' Anking was the furthest outpost. For a time it was believed that Meadows and his wife had been murdered. Taylor did not lose his new confidence. 'Mine is to obey, *His* to direct. Hence I am not only able to bear up against this new trial at Anking but to be *fully* satisfied... "Even so, Father, for so it seemed good in *Thy* sight."' And when the rumours cleared, the situation was better than it had been painted.

Physically, Hudson's reserves continued slight. 'My dear husband is pretty well,' Maria told Mrs Berger at the end of 1869, 'but such a little thing knocks him up and renders him unfit for work; and, as you know, he keeps on long after most people would give up.' 'The pressure on us this year has been very great,' Hudson wrote to Barnsley, 'I am always on the run, and correspondence about business is almost more than I can get through. But I am more happy in the Lord, than ever I have been... Things may not be, in many respects, as I would wish them; but if *God* permits them so to be, or so orders them, I may well be content.'

This bold statement was about to be put to an utmost test.

## Chapter 21: GLORIOUS MORNING

An American magazine for April 1870 carried an article by a Baptist missionary who had visited most of the CIM's dozen stations scattered over three provinces, meeting many of the thirty-three men and women.

'They have an excellent spirit,' he wrote, 'self-denying, with singleness of aim; devotional, with a spirit of faith, of love, of humility. They are willing to live upon less than half of what the missionaries of the older societies receive, and are willing to do about twice as much work as some of them do.' They were in close contact with the Chinese, could rough it, and they had success. They were not generally educated men but from 'the humble labouring classes', with zeal and skill in labouring for souls. 'Hence they will not,' he concluded with a slightly unfair shaft at men of George Moule's sort, 'be likely to fritter away foolishly their time in reading dusty old Chinese tomes, and in making books and tracts that nobody will read.'

As this commendation was being read in America, China slid towards the violent crisis in her international affairs which culminated in the notorious Tientsin massacre of ten French nuns, two priests and the French Consul, who alone deserved his fate. 'A time of great trial,' Hudson Taylor said later, 'a time of the greatest difficulty I have ever known in China. From Peking to Canton the people were agitated. We did not know from day to day what would take place in our inland stations. But I had unspeakable rest in my soul...' 'We need your prayers,' runs one letter from Chinkiang to Jennie Faulding at Hangchow, 'things look very dark. One difficulty follows another very fast-but *God* reigns, not *chance*. At Nanking the excitement has been frightful but appears to be subsiding. Our people have met with no insult, even in the street, but had the [Roman Mission] been sacked, they would scarcely have escaped scot free... Here are rumours, I hope passing away, but at Yangchow they are very bad... My *heart* is calm, but my head is sorely tried by the constant succession of one difficulty after and upon another.'

This was the backcloth to the final drama of Hudson and Maria.

Early in 1870 the Taylors realised that Bertie, nearly nine, and Freddie, aged seven, should return to England before another hot season. Five-year-old Samuel was exceptionally delicate; he must go too, with little Maria as playmate, leaving only baby Charley in China. Emily Blatchley volunteered to take them home and stay as foster-mother.

Fear of the parting was too much for Sammy. He died on the Yangtze on February 4th and was buried at Chinkiang in the rough cemetery at the foot of the hills, a mile from the river bank, the first of a little corner of Taylor graves. Six weeks later on March 22nd, at Shanghai, Hudson and Maria wept their farewell to the children.

They sailed back up the Yangtze by slow junk to save the expense of steamer tickets. At one of the river ports they heard that at Chinkiang Mrs Judd lay dangerously ill, and Hudson dared not leave a patient he was bringing from Shanghai. Maria therefore pressed on alone, enduring the bumps and bruises of a fast, springless wheelbarrow all the way home. Arriving in the middle of the night, she insisted on Judd's going to bed. 'Nothing would induce her to rest. "No," she said. "You have quite enough to bear, without sitting up any more at night. Go to bed, for I shall stay with your wife whether you do or not."'

The summer of 1870 in the Yangtze valley became one of the hottest in memory, a contributory cause of popular agitation.

The June weather badly affected Maria's lungs, reduced as they were by tuberculosis. She was pregnant again too, expecting another baby in mid-July. Maria refused to abate work. She carried on classes, literary projects, much correspondence. 'She felt better, seemed stronger, was more cheerful than for a long time back,' wrote Hudson, 'and I had a strong conviction that she would be preserved to see her Chinese-English vocabulary through the press, and see the dear children once more in England.' He knew now that she could not live to old age, but certain signs made him believe the disease checked, 'though often my heart ached when I saw her thin wasted frame'.

On June 29th William and Mary Rudland came to Chinkiang. They had recently lost their child. The couple's arrival taxed the hot little house to its limits, and Hudson and Maria separated so that Louise Desgraz could sleep in Maria's room while Hudson, and Reid also, put up beds in the main passage. The two men had to retire late and get up early because of comings and goings. A fatal curtain was rigged in Maria's bedroom, 'so both she and Miss D. were private and alone. This was the more needful as Maria had generally more or less a tendency to diarrhoea.'

Maria managed to endure the summer heat by taking frequent cool baths during the night. On July 5th Hudson said goodnight and went to sleep in the passage. Maria had a bath in the alcove of her room. Coming out she threw herself on the bed unclothed to rest a few moments, and fell asleep. Had the curtain been down, Louise might have seen Maria's danger, for the temperature suddenly changed. 'It became very cold and windy, and my darling awoke conscious that she had taken a chill.'

A sharp attack of cholera supervened. She said afterwards, 'the pains of labour would be a relief compared with what I suffered then.' She did not rouse Hudson, or Louise, who would have fetched him.

In the morning Hudson was shocked at the change.

'My darling, how *could* you be so thoughtless, so unkind, as to let me sleep when you were suffering so?'

'Don't say so. I couldn't bear to diminish, even by an hour, your little chance of sleep.'

Maria lay weak, unable to keep down food, in constant pain and discomfort, 'and withal, within a fortnight of her confinement'. The medicine Hudson gave seemed effective, and he held to his confidence of her recovery 'on the simple ground that it seemed as if her staying were more needful for the Mission, and her work not done'.

She was somewhat better the next day, 7th July, but that afternoon Williamson was leaving up-river for Anking, taking little Sammy Meadows to his parents. The effort of giving directions about Sammy's clothes prostrated her.

At about a quarter to five Hudson came in to say he thought he would see Williamson to the quay, and buy her a little brandy on the way back.

'Don't stay long, love,' answered Maria, 'for I may possibly need you to-night, and you will have to make all preparations for me this time.' She nodded towards the pile of baby linen.

Hudson asked if her time was on her, nearly a fortnight early. She thought it might come that night, not immediately; she had merely wanted him to come straight home if Williamson was delayed.

This conversation made the two men look for brandy on the way down to the quay. As soon as it was bought Hudson bid Williamson goodbye in the street, and went home. Rudland greeted him with the astonishing news that the baby had just arrived after the shortest and easiest of Maria's eight confinements. 'A fine, fat boy he is too.'

Hudson hurried in. 'She was delighted to have got it so well over. I had my misgivings for I did not like the feel of her pulse.' He mixed brandy and water in case of need, and attended to the baby. At dusk Maria dozed and on waking said she felt refreshed. 'At this moment Mrs Rudland brought in a candle. I saw the colour leave her lips, and she turn deadly pale. I instantly put my hand on the womb, under the bandage.' An internal haemorrhage.

Hudson was convinced that had he been out of the room that moment, or no brandy had been in the house, she would never have come round.

During the following week the cramped room was like a furnace. Outside in the city the tension rose with the thermometer. Maria rallied slowly. She was able to take so little nourishment that weakness increased, yet she insisted she was better and must recover.

They called the baby Noel, except Charley, who called him Di-Di. Noel was 'such a dear little chubby fellow, with soft silky hair nearly the colour of dear Mamma's, and had soft little eyes and long silky eyelashes; and a dear little mouth just like Gracie's used to be'.

They bottle-fed him for a week. Then his throat developed thrush and his little inside went wrong. They searched for a wetnurse. The anti-foreign feeling was too strong and none offered until Wednesday July 20th. She was too late. He died that afternoon, aged thirteen days. As Hudson wrote to his parents: 'All this told on his dear mamma. It brought out the *matured grace*, but told on the enfeebled *nature.*' She chose two hymns for the funeral on Friday evening. On his way home Hudson called on a merchant named White to accept his invitation to remove Maria there, for 'it was evident that a change *might* afford a chance of recovery; remaining, none'.

It was nearly eight o'clock when he got back to Maria, who seemed much the same. He asked her if she would be moved to White's.

'Could I have my bath there as often as I liked?'

Hudson assured her, and she was delighted at the plan. 'Travelling always suits me!'

He was very tired, lay down beside her and fell asleep. She motioned Louise Desgraz to cover him with a blanket. He woke after about an hour and asked if there was anything she needed.

'No,' she replied. 'You must go and get some tea. Mrs Rudland has some waiting for you.'

Hudson went next door. He was drinking the tea and eating his rice, chatting to Mary Rudland, when Louise, between the two rooms, heard a faint, 'Hudson!'

He 'rushed in and found Maria up and very faint, unable to speak or get into bed'. He lifted her in, put pillows and bolsters under her hips and legs, forced sips of brandy between her lips, rubbed her extremities. Apparently she had wanted the commode, did not wish to disturb Hudson at his meal and convinced herself she was strong enough to walk unaided. At a few steps she had collapsed.

As Hudson worked on her he said to Rudland, 'Please pray for me. I had no idea how far Mrs Taylor's illness had gone. It is consumption of the bowels and I fear there is no hope. Please pray for me that I be kept calm through it all. Her lungs have been affected for some time, they were better, the cough had not been serious.'

Rudland saw that Taylor was 'very much crushed – so sudden, he had no apprehension before'.

As Maria came round her breathing grew excessively laboured, but his treatment succeeded, the breathing settled down, and she seemed better.

'My *head* is so hot!' she said.

'Oh, I will thin it out for you, shall I?' Hudson knew she did not like her hair cut short because it could not be done nicely in the Chinese way.

Her hair was matted and tangled by sweat. He began to cut it all off except for an inch-long fuzz.

'Would you like a lock sent to each of the three children? What message shall I send with it?'

'Yes, and tell them to be sure to be kind to dear Miss Blatchley... and... and... and to love Jesus.'

When he stopped cutting she put a hand to her head.

'That's what you call thinning out?' she smiled. 'Well, I shall have all the comfort and *you* have all the responsibility as to looks. I never do care what anyone *else* thinks as to my appearance. You know, my darling, I am altogether yours,' she said. 'And she threw her loving arms, so thin, around me, and kissed me in her own loving way for it.'

Louise brought cold wet towels and they applied them. Maria felt relief, and dozed. Immediate danger had passed. Leaving Louise to change the towels Hudson suggested to the Rudlands and Reid that they should go into a room where they could not be over-heard by Maria, and pray. All four prayed, 'but I noticed that no one was led to pray unreservedly for her recovery'.

At midnight he gave her medicine and a little liquid food. She dozed off and he sent the Rudlands and Reid to bed.

At 4 am on this Saturday July 23rd 1870, he found Maria sleeping. He crept into the next room to prepare her food. She awoke and was sick. 'This alarmed me. I found the head very hot again, and with the cold well-water affused it. I soon stayed the sickness so that by 4.30 am she was able to take part of her food.

'By this time it was dawn, and the sunlight revealed what the candle had hidden, the death-like hue of her countenance. Even my love could not deny, not her danger, but that she was actually dying. As soon as I felt sufficiently composed I said to her, "My darling, are you conscious that you are dying?"

'She replied with evident surprise. "Dying? Do you think so? What makes you think so?"

'"I can see it, darling."

'"What is making me die?"

'"Your strength is giving way."

'"Can it be so? I feel no pain, only weariness."

'"Yes, you are going Home. You will soon be with Jesus."

'"I am so sorry."

'"You are not sorry to go to be with Jesus ?"

'"Oh, no!" (I shall never forget the look she gave me, as look-ing right into my eyes, she said:) "It's not that. You know, darling, that for ten years past there has not been a cloud between me and my Saviour." (I know that what she said was perfectly true.) "I cannot be sorry to go to Him," she whispered. "But it does grieve me to leave you alone at such a time. Yet... He will be with you and meet all your need."'

She gave him many kisses, and more for the children. She remembered that Freddie had no Bible and told Hudson to get him one as her last present. The household silently gathered. They brought little Charley and she kissed him.

She got weaker. Hudson asked her if she had any pain, and she said, 'No'.

At about 7.30 she sank into unconsciousness. A short spasm shook her at 7.45 and she lay still again, breathing gently. In the unforgettable words of Hudson's daughter-in-law long after: 'The summer sun rose higher and higher over the city, the hills, and the river. The busy hum of life came up around them from many a court and street. But within one Chinese dwelling, in an upper room from which the blue of God's own Heaven could be seen, there was the hush of a wonderful peace.'

Soon after nine the breathing sank lower. Hudson knelt down. With full heart, one of the watchers wrote, he 'committed her to the Lord; thanking Him for having given her, and for the twelve and a half years of happiness they had had together; thanking Him, too, for taking her to His own blessed Presence, and solemnly dedicating himself anew to His service'.

The breathing stopped at 9.20. 'When she was really gone,' wrote Rudland, 'he just went out into another room – some time before he returned. It seemed that as though the victory had been won – alone with God. He seemed calmer then until the end.'

The great heat compelled that she should be buried that evening. Hudson went himself to buy the coffin. As they coffined her he spoke the words, 'The Lord gave, and the Lord hath taken away. Blessed be the name of the Lord.'

Rudland was beside him. 'At the very last when she was in her coffin he stood taking the last long look. He had to rush away again upstairs to be alone for a time.'

His baby. His wife. 'My heart *wells up* with joy and gratitude for their unutterable bliss, though nigh to breaking. "Our Jesus hath done all things well."'

## Author's Note

Those who would like to read about the remaining thirty-five years of Hudson Taylor's life – the great advances of the CIM; his second, very happy marriage to Jennie Faulding; his journeyings in many parts of the world, unselfishly promoting all China Missions, and deepening spiritual life; the further times of opposition, criticism, peril and pain; his reflections and meditations – are warmly recommended to study the late A. J. Broomhall's magisterial seven volume life, *Hudson Taylor and China's Open Century* (Hodder and Stoughton/Overseas Missionary Fellowship, 1981-90) which includes full use of the Hudson Taylor Papers. Those are now deposited in the archives of the School of Oriental and African Studies, London University, and may be consulted on prior application to Overseas Missionary Fellowship, Station Approach, Borough Green, Sevenoaks, Kent, TN15 8BG.

Hudson Taylor died suddenly at Changsha in the heart of China on June 3rd, 1905, at the age of seventy-three.

## LIST OF SOURCES

### Manuscript Sources

*The Hudson Taylor Papers.* (Letters, journals, etc, of Hudson and Maria Taylor, Jennie Faulding, Emily Blatchley, William Berger, and others in the Archives of the China Inland Mission.

*Letters of Mary Ann Aldersey to London Missionary Society.* (Typescript in LMS archives, where the originals are also.)

### Pamphlets by Hudson Taylor

*China: Its Spiritual Need and Claims* (1865).
*A Brief Account of the Progress of the China Inland Mission* (1868).
*After Thirty Years, 1865-95* (Not dated).
*A Retrospect* (1891).

### Periodicals of the CIM

*Occasional Papers* (London: 1866-75).
*Monthly Gleaner* (Yangchow: 1870-71).
*China's Millions* (London: 1875- ).
(Now *The Millions,* London, Philadelphia and Melbourne.)

### The Official Biography

Dr and Mrs Howard Taylor: *Hudson Taylor in Early Years* (1911).
*Hudson Taylor and the China Inland Mission* (1918).
(The shorter Lives by M Broomhall, Mrs Howard Taylor, etc, are directly derived from the above.)

### Other Printed Sources

Anderson, Flavia, *The Rebel Emperor* (1958).
Burns, Islay, *Memoir of Rev W C Burns* (1873).
Chinese Evangelization Society, *The Gleaner* (1851-58).
Davies, Evan, *Memoir of Rev Samuel Dyer* (1846).
Edkins, Joseph, *The Religious Condition of the Chinese* (1859).
Keppel, Sir Harry, *A Sailor's Life* (1899).
Latourette, K S, *History of the Expansion of Christianity,* Vol. VI (1947).
*These Sought a Country* (1950).
Martin, W A P, *A Cycle of Cathay* (1896).
Meadows, Thomas, *The Chinese and their Rebellions* (1856).
Medhurst, Sir Walter, *The Foreigner in Far Cathay* (1872).
Mitchie, A, *The Englishman in China* (The Life of Sir Rutherford Alcock) (1900).
Moule, A E, *The Story of the Chekiang Mission* (4th Edition 1891).
Reason, J, *The Witch of Ningpo.*
Scarth, John, *Twelve Years in China* (1860).
Stott, Gracie, *Twenty-six Years of Missionary Work in China* (1897).
Thompson, R W, *Griffith John* (1906).

# Sue Grafton and Kinsey Millhone

**A is for Alibi**
Grafton has created a woman we feel we know
. . . Smart, well paced and very funny'
*Newsweek*

**B is for Burglar**
woman to identify with . . . a gripping read'
*Punch*

**C is for Corpse**
C is for classy, multiplex plotting, strong
aracterization and a tough-cookie heroine'
*Time Out*

**D is for Deadbeat**
'D is for deft and diverting'
*Guardian*

**E is for Evidence**
'E is for Excellent, Ms Grafton'
*Sunday Times*

**F is for Fugitive**
'Of the private investigators, Sue Grafton's Kinsey
Millhone is one of the most convincing in operation'
*Independent*

**G is for Gumshoe**
'G is for Grafton, Gumshoe and Good'
*Sunday Telegraph*

**H is for Homicide**
'S is for Super Sleuth in a scorching story'
*Daily Mail*

**I is for Innocent**
'I could also stand for incomparable . . . Riveting
throughout, cracking finale'
*Observer*

**J is for Judgment**
'Kinsey Millhone is up there with the giants
of the private eye genre, as magnetic as Marlowe,
as insouciant as Spenser. It's all exhilarating stuff'
*Times Literary Supplement*

**K is for Killer**
'Another excellent novel from the
excellent Sue Grafton'
*Daily Mirror*